THE ROYAL TRAINS

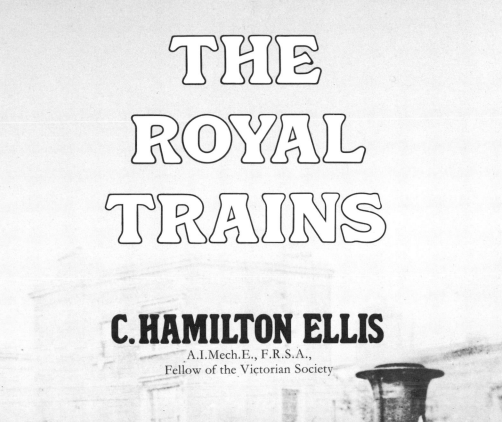

THE
ROYAL
TRAINS

C. HAMILTON ELLIS
A.I.Mech.E., F.R.S.A.,
Fellow of the Victorian Society

Routledge & Kegan Paul
London

First published in 1975
by Routledge & Kegan Paul Ltd
Broadway House, 68–74 Carter Lane,
London EC4V 5EL
Set in 11/13pt Monophoto Garamond
and printed in Great Britain by
BAS Printers Limited, Wallop, Hampshire
© C. Hamilton Ellis 1975
ISBN 0 7100 8293 2

CONTENTS

PREFACE AND ACKNOWLEDGMENTS

What, at a time of world-ranging aircraft, and of swarming motors, is so important about the subject of royal trains? Surely it is that they set new and unprecedented goals in the provision of travelling comfort and convenience. Sooner or later, what had started as a criterion became a standard. Then a new goal would appear over the skyline of future history, and a new advance would be made. A new sumptuosity, tried out on the Monarch who usually (though not always) approved, would later benefit the public through first-class, then second-, and ultimately even third-class passengers. So, paradoxically, royal usage produced revolutionary effects.

When, after much persuasion by Prince Albert, Queen Victoria travelled in 1842 from Slough to Paddington by the Great Western Railway in a large and luxurious carriage behind a puissant broad-gauge locomotive driven by a man whom she was later to create a baronet, she was making English history. She was demonstrating that the train was *respectable*; also – in the face of a militant anti-railway lobby in Parliament – that it was *safe*; further, that at its best it was a very agreeable sort of conveyance, fast, smooth-running and free from the dust of ancient roads. From being a timid, though exalted, candidate, she became an inveterate railway traveller. (The unkind sea troubled her sorely.) It is quaint that her first really long journey, from north-eastern Scotland to the South, was made because fog bound the royal yacht at Aberdeen.

The process continued, as the following account will show, though the ageing Queen in later years was actually to stultify progress in her own arrangements by her increasing dislike of change. By the 1890s, the British royal trains had become decidedly old-fashioned compared with ordinary expresses running up and down the country. Imitation had outpaced example. Not until Edward VII succeeded came new and wondrous improvement. It was King Edward, in his turn, who was to make the motor-car respectable, as his mother had done for the train, while two beautiful trains built specially for him were to last in service for many years, with some of their vehicles, now anciently elegant, surviving to this day.

C.H.E.

Acknowledgments

Plates 49, 51, 54, 55, 60, 61, 62, 64, 88, 89, 91, 92, 93, 94 and 95 are reproduced by gracious permission of Her Majesty the Queen.

Colour plates nos I–IV and plate 18 are reproduced from oil paintings by Hamilton Ellis.

Other plates are reproduced by kind permission of the following: Berlin State Library, 53, 56, 57, 58; British Railways Board: Eastern Region, 76, 77, 78, London Midland Region, 7, 8, 71, 72, 75, Scottish Region, 16, Southern Region, 3, 45, Western Region, 10, 17; H. C. Casserley, 99; F. C. Coleman, 1; R. W. T. Collins, 69; Maurice W. Earley, 63; FIAT, Turin, 82, 83, 84; Foto FS, 33, 38; Italian State Railways, 34, 35, 37; Museon di Rodo, 31, 32, 36; Museum of British Transport, York, 2, 4, 5, 6, 9, 12, 13, 14, 15, 19, 20, 21, 46, 65, 66, 67, 68, 73, 74, 98; Netherlands Railway Museum, Utrecht, 79, 80, 81, 86, 87; New South Wales Government Railways, 96; Konrad Pfeiffer, 29; Portsmouth City Library, 50, 70; Portuguese Railways, 39; Pullman Standard, 44; *Rand Daily Mail*, 103; South African Railways, 100, 101, 102, 104, 105; Dr Fritz Stöckl, 26, 27, 28, 43; Swedish State Railways, 40, 41; H. A. Venton, 85; Victoria and Albert Museum, London, 42; Victorian Government Railways, 97; Vienna Railway Museum, 23, 24, 25, 59.

1

THE QUEEN TAKES A TRAIN

Who knows when royal journeys began?

Nobody, even though known history goes back a long, long way, to Egyptian and Chinese records of days when the rest of people were normally savages! Whether savage or organised, their Monarch was indeed Ruler, or else his time was short. In remote times, nomad kings rode, and carried their ladies, on animals of one sort or another, the former housing the latter, very carefully, in tents. Equally remote river kings may have carried their queens in papyrus canoes, or in dugouts. But, coming to civilised rulers in the Levant, Pharaoh – whether king or queen, whether Rameses III or Hatshepsut, or some other – used a royal barge up and down the Nile, with a kitchen tender keeping its nidor decently to leeward. On land, kings rode their horses; queens, when absolutely necessary, rode in various sorts of litter.

In the Middle Ages – and certainly in England – there were some quite frightful travelling wagons for exalted or distinguished ladies, each decently covered by a gaudily painted canvas tilt on hoops. Each had four massive wheels on two fixed axles, thus needing to be manhandled round bends, to the distress of the occupants. The old English name for them was *Whirlicotes*, which may have had a coarse punning significance, for while the old litters made the poor ladies dreadfully sick as they rocked and pitched and swayed between horses or mules, these ponderous vehicles could throw them all over the place. A poor consolation for being what later English society was to call 'carriage people'!

Centuries before these frights, Imperial Rome had a sort of sedan-chair for city use, and quite admirable fast gigs for taking important personages, couriers and mails over long distances on her splendid roads. Philip the Deacon had a rewarding ride in one as guest of Queen Candace's Treasurer, on the Gaza road (Acts VIII, 26–39). But progress was not to be constant; far from it!

Only with the late sixteenth century did the *coach* become both practical and important, thanks to the swinging axle, and springing, both unknown before. Through the seventeenth and eighteenth centuries it was refined, latterly helped by great improvements in road construction as of John Macadam and Thomas Telford, while railways were as yet a form of industrial machinery. Richard Trevithick produced a practical steam carriage for roads in 1802, and a railway locomotive in 1804, but a quarter-century later, the steam railway passenger train still had not quite arrived. It was to do so in 1830, between Liverpool and Manchester, though of course passengers had ridden thus ere then, on occasion. Twelve more years were to elapse before Britannic Majesty did so. Victoria was ten years old when the Stephenson's engine *Rocket* was awarded the £500 prize in the Rainhill contest. The Realm was still just under George IV. Even William IV was never to ride in a train, though his widow, the Dowager Queen Adelaide, was to be awarded a sort of sleeping car as early as 1842. Her once rather comely self had suffered somewhat in looks with the years, and by that time she liked, if possible, to travel with her feet up. Victoria succeeded on 20 June 1837, a stripling girl with prominent blue eyes, in her night-gown, facing her Prime Minister and her Archbishop of Canterbury in Kensington Palace, at a somewhat uncomfortable hour in the early morning. On 10 February 1840, she married her cousin, Prince Albert of Saxe-Coburg-Gotha, and he it was, more than two years later, who induced her to travel by train. He had already sampled the process himself, and so had the King of Prussia, Frederick William IV. It was then twelve years since the first real main-line railway, with steam traction, up and down roads, proper stations and even signals of a sort, had started to function in her Realm. A train was still regarded in much the same way as was a passenger aircraft in 1923 or so–much. *Was it safe?* In the opinion of many people, it was *not*.

Now, this is the importance of these early royal journeys. A great invention had emerged, through toil and disappointments, to visible achievement, just as motors and aeroplanes were to do some time later. Royal patronage gave it the accolade. It suddenly became *respectable*, through being found *safe*, even unto the safety of the Sovereign. Responsible persons in all the world were watching. But, as suggested, there were dissidents. Further, royal patronage was to set a criterion in passenger transport, which was to be followed – tardily indeed in some instances – but still followed. There were some curiosities, indeed. The young Queen Victoria was the first in her Realm to enjoy the convenience of a lavatory *en route*, but to her dying day she never consumed a meal cooked on the train, although the dining car arrived in the 1860s, in North America, and in Great Britain before the 1870s were out. She is reported to have required that she never should be carried at a speed exceeding 40 miles an hour, though records show that this was frequently the case. If the carriage ran smoothly and quietly, as a railway carriage ought, she noticed no excesses. On the other hand, she was liable to notice excuses, crossly.

But she showed, as a queen ought, part of a way of life that was at once new. (More than a century later, there would be a Queen's Flight!) For a long time to come, there were to be the Royal Trains, and here they are still, even though nowadays the Queen often drives to Slough (where indeed Victoria began such things) to take one, while a glum little diesel shuttles back and forth on what is now a single track thence to what used to be the Great Western Station at Windsor. Sometimes indeed, a start is made from the Southern Station. At Windsor, the heirs of the South Western have won, just as in the far west of England and Cornwall they have lost to Paddington. But that was to be a long way on from 1842, and with that year we begin!

By 1840, all the then existing main-line railways were expecting, and hoping for, royal patronage. They ran from London to the Midlands and the North; they ran from London to Southampton; they ran nearly from London to Bristol, save for an awkward gap caused by the Wiltshire oolite ridge, successfully tunnelled in the following year. (Yes, the South Western *did* get in first between capital and sea-city. Not that Southampton was much of a city, compared with Bristol, at that time!) There were many other railways, and several other inter-city railways already, since the Liverpool and Manchester of 1830, and including such prodigies as that from Amsterdam to Haarlem (for the Dutch knew business when they winded it). At home there was the Birmingham and Gloucester Railway, complete with its Lickey Incline over the great ridge between Bromsgrove and Blackwell, between the basins of Severn and Trent.

Railway companies which could be possibly concerned with royal travel were quickly involved, and foremost were the Great Western, the South Western, and what was to become, by amalgamation, the North Western, owning the three great main routes out of London.

Windsor Castle was prominently visible from the line of the Great Western Railway where it passed through Slough, and it was scarcely to be expected that the company would regard it merely as an interesting item in the scenery. They saw in it a lucrative, as well as exalted, source of business, and their bait was quickly taken; as early as 1839 when the Princes Ernest and Albert of Saxe-Coburg-Gotha came to visit the young Queen at Windsor. As is well known, the brothers were co-suitors, and the Queen was to accept Albert, and to marry him in the following year.

One can imagine – no more – Albert saying to Ernest: 'I say! Shall we try these new railroads? There's one to a village near Windsor.' Prince Albert had, throughout his relatively short life, a keen appreciation of applied science and what is now called technology. The train was to delight him. So on 14 November 1839, having made their visit to the Royal Girl at Windsor by what were then conventional means, the Princes drove to Slough and took train to Paddington in the then Far West End of London. They may have ridden in an ordinary first-class carriage, of which the Great Western sort was extremely good, even at that early time. It is equally possible, even probable, that they rode in what on the Great Western was called a 'posting carriage', which was a rather short four-wheeled saloon carriage, waisted like a very large omnibus between its broad-gauge wheels, with central doors each side, fine leather sofas and tables between, and a clerestory roof. Such were among the Great Western company's earliest passenger rolling stock. Though showy and elegant, they rode less easily than the ordinary carriages on six wheels.

So Albert married Victoria, and having sampled the Great Western already, he used it several times, the special trains laid on for him in the autumn of 1840. On 21 September the engine *Sun* covered the $18\frac{1}{4}$ miles between Slough and Paddington in $22\frac{1}{2}$ minutes, making an average speed just short of 49 miles an hour; quite a prodigy, over so short a distance, from start to stop, in 1840! On one of these journeys, the Prince made that much-reported remark, which seems to go best – as it probably did – in a gentle German accent: 'Not quite so fast, next time, Mr Conductor, please!' If indeed H.R.H. rode in one of those short – if visibly luxurious – posting carriages, the motion may have been indeed somewhat rough. The *Sun* was a 2-2-2 engine with 6 ft driving wheels, designed by the young Daniel Gooch, very much on Stephenson 'Patentee' lines but considerably bigger. Built by R. and W. Hawthorn of Newcastle upon Tyne in April 1840, the *Sun* was rebuilt in 1863 and lasted ten years longer.

Two years were to elapse before he persuaded the Queen to venture on such jaunts, which quite soon thereafter were to become part of her routine. The Great Western Railway, of course, had been watching for this. In that same year of 1840, to quote E. T. MacDermot's *History of the Great Western Railway*, quoting again a newspaper description of the time:

> The Great Western Railway Company, anticipating the Patronage of the Queen and her illustrious Consort, Prince Albert, and of the Members of the Royal Family, have just had built a splendid railway carriage for their accommodation. It is a very handsome vehicle 21 feet in length and divided into three compartments, the two end ones being four feet

six inches long and nine feet wide, while the centre forms a noble saloon, twelve feet long, nine feet wide, and six feet six inches high. The exterior is painted in the same brown colour as the others of the Company's carriages, and at each end is a large window affording a view of the whole of the line. [One is to presume, from that description, that there were no carriages marshalled before or after this one; which is absurd. 'The whole' was a favourite item in contemporary journalese, which regrettably became an apparent fixture in commercial English, not least in the correspondence of railway companies.] The interior has been most magnificently fitted up by Mr. Webb, upholsterer, Old Bond Street. The saloon is handsomely arranged with hanging sofas of carved wood in the rich style of Louis XIV, and the walls are panelled out in the same elegant manner, and fitted up with rich crimson and white silk and exquisitely executed paintings representing the Four Elements by Parris. [How engaging can be one's speculations about the allegorical portraiture of Earth, Air, Fire and Water! Female, no doubt!] The end compartments are also fitted up in the same style, each apartment having in the centre a useful and ornamental rosewood table; and the floors of the whole are covered with chequered India matting.

Ernest Leopold Ahrons, who attended to the mechanical records in the first volume of MacDermot's *History*, recorded that the coachbuilder was David Davies, of London, and that an old woodcut suggested that it was of the same type as the posting carriages, i.e. with a waisted body and a clerestory roof. That would account for the 'hanging sofas' which, suspended from pillars, would have been the only type possible in a vehicle whose width, at waistline, declined from 9 ft to less than 7 ft.

This carriage began as a four-wheeler, and with a length of 21 ft must have been little better than a posting carriage (18 ft 6 in. long) when it came to steady running.

So it seems to have been, anyway! Both Prince Albert and poor Queen Adelaide sampled it as a four-wheeler, and when, in January of 1842, it was likely to be required by the King of Prussia (Frederick William IV, 1840–57; died insane, 1861), a Great Western Minute of its General Traffic Committee recorded on 19 January 1842 that it 'needed improvement', being less safe on its four wheels than were the ordinary first-class carriages which, 24 ft long, 9 ft wide and 6 ft high inside, were six-wheelers, and very good vehicles of their time. The great, but probably anxious, engineer, Isambard Kingdom Brunel, recommended eight wheels for what was to become, some years later, the 'Old Royal'. So, doubtless with the practical assistance of Daniel Gooch, it was altered before the Queen used it. Just how the conversion was made is doubtful. Your author long ago unearthed at Swindon drawings of an extraordinary eight-wheel carriage on enormous C-springs, but the design of the body does not tally with the description just quoted. However it may have been done, the rebuilding produced one of the first eight-wheel railway vehicles in the world and certainly the first in Great Britain. The King of Prussia, already mentioned, essayed the carriage on 24 January 1842, he having come over for the christening of Albert Edward, Prince of Wales, who, long years after and somewhat ironically, was to dislike the German Emperor William II quite cordially. Frederick William IV was the first reigning monarch to ride in a train.

On Saturday afternoon, 11 June 1842, intimation came from Windsor Castle that the Queen, Prince Albert, and family, would need a train to take them from Slough up to

London at mid-day on Monday.

Charles Saunders, the Great Western Secretary, with I. K. Brunel as Engineer and Daniel Gooch as the company's still very youthful Superintendent of Locomotives, not to mention many other people on the G.W.R., doubtless had a laborious week-end. The moment for which they had been waiting for two years had come on them with a sudden bump.

Complex arrangements had to be made; further, a train had to be assembled from the best resources of motive power, and the best suitable rolling stock, in less than 48 hours. As to the former, the engine *Phlegethon*, of Gooch's design on the enlarged Stephenson model, with 7 ft driving wheels, had been delivered by Fenton, Murray and Jackson in May, and must have been just run-in. That she was named for a fiery river in the Underworld was immaterial. The train must have adequate braking, so the next vehicle was one of the Great Western's extremely Spartan second-class carriages, with open sides above the waist, wherein the brakesman normally sat with his vertical-screw hand-brake column amid the usual second-class passengers. After this came a posting carriage, previously described, for part of the Royal Suite, and next the Royal Saloon. Fourth came another posting carriage, and then three carriage-trucks for such vehicles as the Party might be taking with them. (Doubtless fresh horses were awaiting these at Paddington.) Really, it made quite a creditable train at short notice! The Great Western company had become used, already, to the provision of *specials*. On 5 June 1838 two had been put on for the Eton *Montem* (and that school had been most hostile to the advent and availability of the railway a little while before).

So to this momentous first journey by Queen Victoria, and one quotes gratefully from E. T. MacDermot's official *History*. He in his turn quoted freely and properly from many earlier sources, as in this instance:

> At Slough the Royal party, on their arrival at the station a few minutes before 12 o'clock in six carriages, were received by Mr. C. Russell the Chairman, Mr. E. P. Barlow one of the Directors, and Mr. C. Saunders the Secretary of the Company, and conducted to the splendid apartments at the station designed for the reception of Royalty. Her Majesty, however, during the delay necessarily occasioned by the placing of the carriages of the attendants on the trucks, proceeded to examine the line and the Royal Saloon, enquiring very minutely into the whole of the arrangements. Precisely at 12 o'clock the train left Slough for Paddington, Mr. Gooch, the Superintendent of the Locomotive Department, accompanied by Mr. Brunel, the Engineer, driving the Engine.

MacDermot's footnote to this passage is worth quoting:

> It is as well to state here, in view of legends to the contrary, that Brunel told the Parliamentary Committee on Railways in 1841: 'I never dare drive an engine, although I always go upon the engine; because if I go upon a bit of line without anything to attract my attention, I begin thinking of something else.'

From Windsor Castle to Slough, the Royal Party had travelled in three carriages, escorted by a detachment of the Royal Horse Guards. No word has been found of a

Guard of Honour at the station, where Charles Russell, Chairman of the Great Western company, received the party, which included the Queen's uncle, Count von Mensdorff and his four sons. Queen Victoria's children had been dispatched to London by road with Lady Lyttelton, accompanied by Prince Albert's equerry, General Sir Edward Bowater of the 3rd Foot Guards. In my picture (Colour Plate I) Colonel C. G. J. Arbuthnot of the Grenadier Guards is supposed standing at the end of the platform-ramp, between Daniel Gooch (on the engine) and I. K. Brunel (standing easy as usual), the Colonel having just expressed the Queen's desire thoroughly to inspect all the railway arrangements before entraining. One can imagine Brunel saying, as he consults his watch: 'By the way, Colonel Arbuthnot; pray don't step backwards too sharply!'

The other Queen's Equerry at the time was Lieut-General W. Wemyss, and Prince Albert's, apart from Sir Edward Bowater, was Colonel E. W. Bouverie of the 15th Hussars. Like many other things on the present occasion, this information has been gratefully received from the Archivist and the Librarian to H.M. Queen Elizabeth II at Windsor Castle. There is a contemporary account of the departure in the *Windsor and Eton Express* of 18 June 1842.

There was no hitch:

> At Paddington by 11 o'clock the centre of the wide space apportioned for the arrival of trains was parted off and carpeted with a crimson carpet, which reached from one platform to the other. [A custom which has survived, within limitations, for more than a century. The German Emperor even had Persian carpets put out!] The whole of the arrangements for the reception of the Royal party were under the superintendence of Mr. Seymour Clarke, the Superintendent of the line, assisted by Supt. Collard of the Company's Police. Capt. Hay, Assistant Commissioner of Metropolitan Police, and Supt. Lincoln and a large body of D. Division were also present. [Seymour Clarke was to be General Manager of the Great Northern Railway from 1850 to 1870, to which he had gone straight from the Great Western, his previous title having been, at Paddington, London Traffic Manager.]
>
> Before 12 o'clock large numbers of elegantly dressed ladies consisting of the friends and families of the Directors and Officers of the Company were arranged on each side of the part apportioned for the arrival of the Royal train, and at five minutes before 12 o'clock Her Majesty's Carriage drawn by four horses arrived from the Royal Mews at Pimlico, and a few minutes afterwards a detachment of the 8th. Royal Irish Hussars under Captain Sir G. Brown arrived from the Barracks at Kensington for the purpose of acting as escort to Her Majesty.
>
> Precisely at 25 minutes past 12 o'clock the Royal Special train entered the terminus having performed the distance in 25 minutes, and on Her Majesty alighting she was received with the most deafening demonstrations of loyalty and affection we ever experienced. H.R.H. Prince Albert alighted first. Her Majesty, on being handed out of the Saloon, in a most condescending manner returned the gratulations of the assembly present. [That adjective *condescending* was later to fall on evil days; even to become a pejorative. At the time, it really meant *gracious*, or decently friendly, on the part of an exalted personage. What it came to mean later was the lofty patronising of a newly-rich woman visiting the less-unsavoury slums to distribute cheap dress-lengths to the mothers and pennies to the children of the respectable artisans.]

The cheers were re-echoed by the numerous persons who crowded the Bridge over the Terminus leading to Paddington Green and lined the avenue towards the Junction Road, along which the Royal cavalcade passed. Her Majesty reached Buckingham Palace shortly before one o'clock, round which a large assembly of respectable persons was awaiting her arrival, by whom she was loudly cheered.

This bridge across Paddington was a viaduct of short arched spans which not only supported the road, but contained some of the station offices, and formed their façade. The original station was quite inferior to the magnificent ones at Bristol and Bath. The new and splendid Paddington which, fortunately, we still know, was to replace it in 1854.

Not everybody was pleased. Led by Colonel Sibthorp, Hon. Member for Lincoln, there was a potent anti-railway lobby in Parliament, and it attempted to have a successful field-day, being supported by influential parties of the landed aristocracy, just as, a century later, it was to be supported by powers of the motor industry. There was a Question in the House, by Sibthorp, about the Royal Person being exposed to *such peril*! A long-forgotten newspaper called *Atlas* darkly suggested the awful possibilities of a long Regency (supposing the Queen to have been killed in one of *those Royal railway excursions* . . .). Whether the Queen had been already annoyed by her Hon. Member for Lincoln – and certainly she could be very gravely annoyed by some people – your author does not know, but she surely made a suitable, if tacit, retort to the Proprietors and Editor of *Atlas*. On 23 July she returned to Windsor, using the Great Western Railway in the reverse direction from Paddington to Slough, behind a locomotive appropriately named *Mentor*. Albert Edward, Prince of Wales, was then eight months old. Victoria and Albert took the future Edward VII with them on the outrageous conveyance, to the fury of Colonel Sibthorp and many other people. Thereafter she was to use the Great Western line between London and Windsor for the rest of her days, even unto the conveyance of her funeral long years on, in 1901.

Now, the anti-railroad lobby *had* a case. People *had* been killed in accidents to trains. Even a Great Western train had run into an earth-fall near Reading with unhappy results for such as were riding as cheaply as possible by night goods train. For that matter, people – not least children – were being trampled and crushed by horses and vehicles in city streets every day, and at that time, whether your house burned down or was saved by brave men with manual fire engines depended on whether you had insured it with the right company owning the appropriate engine. But in the 1840s the train was still on probation, with many enemies. Further, just over a month before the Queen's first trip, there had been the world's first awful railway disaster, by which one means a thing on major shipwreck scale. That was in France, near Versailles, on 8 May 1842, when France was once again, though temporarily, a kingdom.

There had been a royal function at Versailles, at the end of which many guests were returning to Paris by train with two engines. The leading one broke an axle and turned over. The second engine bucked on her predecessor, scattering her blazing coals over the wreckage of the following wooden carriages, which in those days were very flimsy. Furthermore, the passengers were locked into these, with some unfortunate regard for security (the country had experienced horrors of proletarian mob-anger in the past) and

57 deaths, chiefly by burning, were recorded. There may have been more. The Reverend Sidney Smith, then at perihelion as a witty commentator, suggested that things would go on like this until a railway burned a bishop. ('Even Sodor and Man will be better than nothing!') Smith, though a Canon of St Paul's in London, might have been contented with a dead Admiral! Admiral d'Urville was among the many victims.

This accident did not terrify Victoria and Albert in advance. It *did* frighten the French Government, however. Travel by railway was voted and decided to be too dangerous for Royal Majesty, at any rate in such a state of recent history as that of France. The King had wanted to go by train to Rouen. He was advised (pretty peremptorily) to do nothing of the kind. What followed will be noted in the next few pages.

Of her first experience on the Great Western Railway in England, Queen Victoria wrote to her Uncle Leopold, King of the Belgians, that she was 'quite charmed'. Comparing it with the usual, and very unattractive, route down the flats of the lower Thames Valley which now contain so much of London Airport (Heathrow) she was pleased at the absence of noise and dust. There is no doubt about her pleased surprise that she had made what might be called the business part of the journey in 25 minutes instead of taking up much of the afternoon.

Victoria's Aunt Adelaide, the Queen Dowager, had already essayed the rail, as noted, and in that same year of 1842 the London and Birmingham Railway, later to be a constituent of the mighty London and North Western company, built for her a sort of sleeping car, or at any rate a reclining coach wherein she could be comfortably prone. The design was not new. It had begun as the 'bed-carriage', available for hire some four years before as a railway equivalent to the patrician *Mail* on the roads.

Queen Adelaide's carriage – 'saloon' is not the right expression, though frequently, even officially, employed in the past – was a four-wheeled vehicle whose coachwork was essentially that of existing road practice while mounted on a railway underframe and wheels with their appropriate sort of suspension. It has been often described and illustrated, and still exists. Its upper structure contains two compartments and one 'chariot' or *coupé*. The end compartment was coachwise similar to the middle one. An inter-partitional distance of 5 ft 6 in., as in the 'bed-carriages', was not long enough for even a modest Dowager to stretch out comfortably fore-and-aft without stubbing her toes; hence the boot, into which those toes could be extended by the raising of a hinged flap (suitably upholstered on what might be called its obverse side to form the back of its daytime seat). Between those seats there could be a stretcher, bearing an ordinary stiff square cushion for the support of the passenger's loins, or an upholstered stool exactly fitting the same foot-space in what was then an ordinary first-class railway carriage. The Royal Old Lady could then lie prone on her back, or even on one side, in comparative ease, stretching her poor feet and, to the last, fearing murderous mobs. As noted, her carriage was treasured after her death by the London and North Western Railway and still can be inspected. As a piece of post-Regency coachwork, it is superb; most beautifully painted and armed. As a convenient travelling carriage it must have had its limitations, for it was only 5 ft 6 in. wide at the waistline, the body being thus considerably narrower than the frame on which it rested. That, however, permitted the servants to move to and fro at their royal mistress's behest without having to descend to the ballast or the platform. One doubts that they were required to do so while the train was in motion. Maximum inside height to camber of roof is 6 ft, height to cantrail each side being 5 ft 6 in. Length between end-pillars at waistline is 16 ft 6 in., and extreme width over the lower footboards, 8 ft 6½ in. Lighting after dark and through the tunnels by day was provided by pot-lamps burning rape-oil, which still survive in the preserved vehicle. Sanitary provision (which does not) was doubtless by ordinary pots under the seats, long used before railways came in private road carriages, as were red-hot bricks in sand-filled trays for heating. The builders were the famous firm of Hooper, London, which was known and respected in the pre-railway era and which was to continue making bodies for Rolls-Royce cars long into the motor era.

Queen Adelaide, daughter of George, Duke of Saxe-Coburg-Meiningen, had married the Duke of Clarence, afterwards William IV of England, in 1818. Her only children died in infancy, hence Victoria's succession. She died in 1849. The Continental revolutions of 1848 had terrified her, but she felt safe in a train.

Thus old Adelaide (to be sure, she died before she was sixty) enjoyed quite reasonable comfort on the rail about as soon as did her Exalted Niece, in this carriage, and earlier on the Great Western.

Victoria, having tried the train twice, was very pleased with it. Thereafter she used the Great Western between Slough and London whenever she could, and she was quick to use other trains in other directions. The London and Birmingham was of course an early candidate, and so was the London and South Western between London and Gosport, which last town served Portsmouth for a while and continued to do so for certain royal journeys unto the Queen's very last. Both companies, as had the Great Western before them, moved quickly to have special rolling stock in advance.

On 28 November 1843, the Queen paid a visit to Sir Robert Peel, her Prime Minister since the defeat of her old friend Lord Melbourne in 1841. Peel represented Tamworth from 1832 to his death in 1850. Very properly, he lived in his constituency, and there he was the Queen's host. The Queen did not – as was soon to be the custom – take train up to Paddington and down from Euston. She and her suite travelled by road from Windsor to Watford by way of Harefield; that was 22 miles. At Watford, the London and Birmingham company's station – very different from the rather bleak Watford Junction many Londoners know at the time of writing – was 'in deep cutting' and 'situate close to the bridge on the high road leading to St. Albans'.

There the Queen was received by George Carr Glyn, Chairman of the company, afterwards Lord Wolverton, and first Chairman of the Railway Clearing House, and two of his officers, Creed the Secretary and Philip Hardwick who had furnished the railway with some of its already distinguished architecture.

The Royal Party was escorted to special waiting rooms, which were most elegantly appointed and were to set a precedent in such accommodation at railway stations, whether improvised as in this case, or sumptuously permanent as they were at certain termini, and at stations closely adjacent to the royal residences. There, at Watford, there was a welcome pause of 20 minutes while the royal equipages were mounted on carriage-trucks

1 Queen Adelaide's carriage, London and Birmingham Railway, 1842. Observe (left) the boot extension for the Queen Dowager's feet.

2 London and Birmingham Railway, 1842: Queen Adelaide's 'couch'.

3 South Eastern Railway: royal saloon
built in 1850 by Richard Mansell.

4 South Eastern Railway royal saloon,
1850: the 'Guardian Angels' picture.

5 London and North Western Railway: Queen Victoria's twin saloons of 1869, with bellows communication and Webb's radial axles each end.

6 London and North Western Railway twin saloons, as rebuilt in 1897.

7 Day-saloon of Queen Victoria's carriages, 1869, as running in 1897.

8 *opposite above* London and North Western Railway Queen's saloon, 1869: Queen Victoria's bed on the right, Princess Beatrice's on the left.
9 *opposite below* Dresser's compartment. Note the large electric bell about two o'clock from vanishing point!

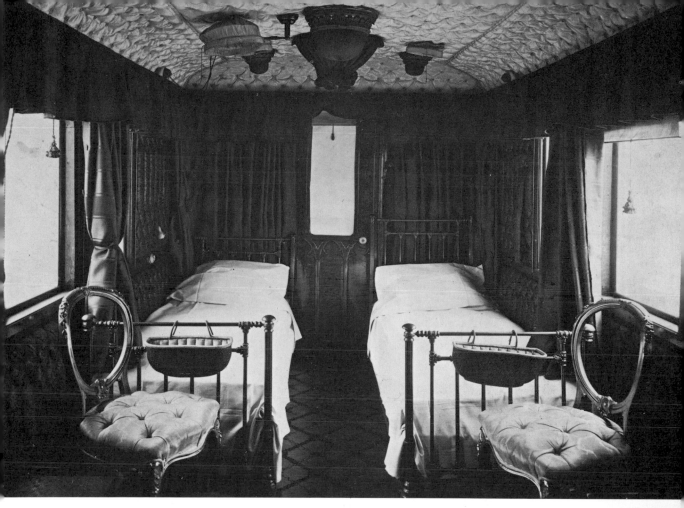

11 Great Western Railway: royal saloon taken from the Jubilee Train, 1897, and here beflowered for the wedding of Princess Mary to Viscount Lascelles, 28 February 1922.

10 Great Western Railway: Queen's carriage of 1874, as first rebuilt on bogies; body unaltered.

12 *left* Preserved portion of the Great Western Railway's Queen's carriage of 1874. The table survives in Windsor Castle and was borrowed for the photograph.

13 *right* The Great Western Railway's royal waiting room at Windsor.

14 London and South Western Railway Queen's saloon, 1897; rebuilt from double family saloon of 1885.

15 London, Brighton and South Coast Railway: royal saloon by William Stroudley, 1882. It survived into the 1920s as a saloon for hire.

16 Great Northern Railway: royal
saloon of 1889 as running in Scottish
departmental service as late as 1947.
Little change, apart from electric
lamps at deckrail.

17 Great Western Railway locomotive
Lord of the Isles, 24 June 1873. The
engine, designed by Sir Daniel Gooch,
ran on the broad gauge 1851-84 and
was preserved until 1906. She here
bears the Royal Arms and the Royal
Standard, the colours of Great
Britain, Italy, Turkey, France and
apparently (front) of Denmark.

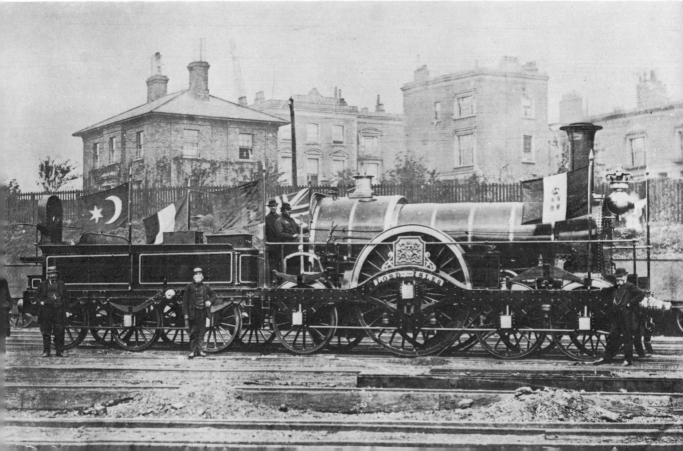

18 North British Railway: Crampton patent locomotive No. 55, by E. B. Wilson's Leeds Railway Foundry, painted in Royal Stewart tartan, 1850. The engine, though rebuilt to the point of reincarnation, lasted until 1907.

below left to right
19 London and North Western Railway Queen's saloon of 1869: door details, including the insignia of the Order of St Patrick.
20 Gilded lion's head on headstock.
21 Great Western Railway royal train: Queen Victoria's lavatory basin.

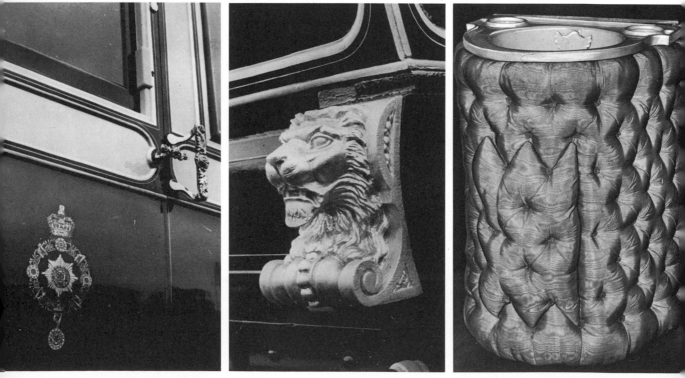

22 Queen Victoria traverses the Tay Bridge and ascertains that the train is not truly at sea, 1879. The bridge, for which she knighted the designer, Thomas Bouch, fell with the mail train on 28 December of the same year. (From the *Illustrated London News*, 5 July 1879.)

for the railway portion of the journey. There were three of these, together with four coaches and a saloon carriage. The train proceeded leisurely over the London and Birmingham Railway, via Wolverton, where a stop was made for refreshments, and Rugby to Hampton-in-Arden, where the Midland Counties Railway took it over. The Queen was to visit Tamworth and Lichfield; later going on to Derby and Chesterfield. A visit was paid to Chatsworth. The same route was followed on the return.

In November of next year, Euston Station in London was the place of departure for a visit to the Marquess of Exeter at Burghley House. Leaving at 9.20 a.m., the train reached Tring, $31\frac{3}{4}$ miles, in 53 minutes. That made an average speed of nearly 36 m.p.h., a remarkable performance for the London and Birmingham company at that time, especially in view of the slow start from Euston up the Camden Bank. Great Western men already would have laughed at it, but they had the advantage of broad gauge and of an almost level line, at least from Paddington to Swindon. It is recorded that on this journey the royal saloon had been 'richly embellished' and considerably improved; probably as a result of previous comments. It was a four-wheel carriage with a main saloon – arranged something like an audience chamber – and two very small end-compartments, looking like the vestibules of later years, but in fact having no internal communication with the saloon, which had its own side doors, one each side. Reputed dimensions were 'about' 13 ft long by 7 ft wide and 8 ft high inside. The last sounds improbable for that time. The box-like end compartments – which had no seats – were probably for hardy soldiers, or footmen, detailed to open and close the Queen's doors at stations.

In the middle of the saloon roof there was quite sophisticated ventilating apparatus, covered outside by a very large and ornate crown. The inside of the carriage was quilted to deaden the racket, to which end, also, there were wooden wheels with iron tyres. There was as yet no water-closet; indeed it is recorded that even in the Royal Palaces, the progressive Prince Albert had had some difficulty in persuading the Queen that such apparatus really *worked* without unmentionable accidents. Wonder of wonders, however, there was real heating apparatus; first travelling advance on the hot brick or hot-water bottle. It was an invention of Jacob Perkins, who had made a steam gun to confound and terrify the Queen's possible enemies. (It did not, however, although it was a very clever secret weapon to invent.) Perkin's carriage heater was under the floor and comprised a little oil-fired flash boiler and a cistern, feeding a closed-circuit pipe set inside the double flooring and warming the carriage through a grating.

The iron-tyred wooden wheels were an invention of Joseph Beattie, then Resident Engineer and Carriage Superintendent of the London and South Western Railway. They were used also on a Great Western Queen's Carriage which was to be built at this time. Beattie's Chief was then John V. Gooch, he being at once Locomotive Superintendent of the South Western company and brother of the more famous Daniel Gooch who was the same for, and ultimately Chairman of, the Great Western Railway. Beattie was one of the Grand Patentees who were beginning to flourish with the advance of mechanical engineering and, later succeeding John Gooch with the locomotives of the South Western, was able to make his company build and use his appliances with considerable royalties to himself. He became rather rich.

At the moment, however, he was engaged with the passive carriage on his patent wooden wheels, and one such next concerns us. In, or possibly before, 1843, he schemed a fine royal saloon for the South Western.

Its appearance is to this day familiar, for in its original form it is well portrayed in a well known set of French prints. It was still in existence a century later on the Shropshire and Montgomeryshire Railway, which was being used for transport training by the Army in the 1940s, and it was latterly used as a sleeping-van for soldiers. It followed the primeval three-body railway version of the single-body road coach, but the middle 'body' was made into a saloon with a single long window each side, while the outer ones were ante-rooms with chariot ends, though with the same longitudinal dimensions.

Inside, it was most splendidly furnished by Herring, the London upholsterer in Fleet Street, and it was at first most ornately decorated outside too. It was on four wheels, but was to be a six-wheeler by 1852, to revert to the original form later.

This carriage is important, not only on account of its longevity but because the French King – forbidden by his own Government – made his first railway ride in it; at least officially. For, in the autumn of 1844, Louis Philippe made a State Visit to England, and landed at Portsmouth on 6 October. The Queen, accompanied by the Duke of Wellington, had already sampled the South Western in 1843, and therefore knew that, by proper standards, it was *a nice line*. All the same, it had not yet reached *Pompey Proper*, so the King of the French had to be entrained at Gosport, across the water, whither the company had a branch through Fareham from its main line at Eastleigh, then called Bishopstoke. At Portsmouth Prince Albert and the Duke of Wellington met him and took him across to the train at Gosport.

They took him to Farnborough where the train arrived at 2.0 p.m., and thence they drove to Windsor. The visit was finished just within a week, and on 12 October the King was driven back to Farnborough and put on the London and South Western royal train for Gosport via Bishopstoke, as before. As so often in October there was a menacing south-westerly gale blowing up the Channel, and French Majesty scarcely fancied it, feeling that the Short Sea Route might make his and others' sufferings less prolonged. So the South Western train was re-engined at the other end, and set off, eastwards once more, to Nine Elms, Vauxhall, in London. (Waterloo was not to exist for four years yet.) At Nine Elms, which was long to maintain a royal private station, royal carriages were waiting to take the French King across to the South Eastern Railway at what was later to become the London, Brighton and South Coast company's station at New Cross. It was then the property of the London and Croydon Railway, which was party to a locomotive pool with the London and Brighton, and the South Eastern companies.

That very same evening it had a major misfortune. Its extensive locomotive and carriage depot at New Cross caught fire. This was about nine o'clock at night. The French King reached Nine Elms just an hour and a half later and took coach with *entourage* for New Cross. Ahead of them, as they bowled down through Camberwell and Peckham, there was a vast glare in the south-eastern sky. As they drew nearer, people in the streets, scarcely aware of Foreign Royalty, were crying: 'It's Noo Crawss! It's the engine-'ouse!'

The great Octagon – what America would have called the Roundhouse, with the turntable ('radiator') in the middle of it – collapsed with an awful burst of fire to the night sky. The King may have thought back to a thing or two. But nobody was being burnt alive as at Meudon near Versailles; only several locomotives (which could be repaired) and several railway carriages (which could not, for they were mostly burnt to fine white wood-ash).

Royalty, Nobility and Gentry had for long been trained to display no emotion, no distress, at such misfortunes. A lady might drop her new silk mantle in the muck and just say: 'Oh, it's messed a bit; never mind!' Admiral Lord Nelson may have said: 'My God! They've cut my bloody arm off!' And so it was at New Cross. The South Eastern officers, who had been hoping soon to go to bed, politely received and escorted the French King, who was heard by someone to make a testy remark about having to step over leaky fire-hoses, to the best train they could manage at such short notice.

At any rate, the lighting was uncommonly good!

The King was got off about 11.15 for Dover, but owing to the fire and the shortage of rolling stock, some of his suite and most of the royal baggage had to follow him later. So ended the first State Visit to England to involve the railway. The French prints of that visit, already mentioned, gave excellent representations of the South Western saloon, inside and out, and a spirited one of the departure from New Cross by firelight, though in that last case the representation of the engine was a thing *pour rire*, showing as it did something like a coffee-pot on a cart, wheel arrangement, including tender, being 0-2-0; also, it showed the burning engine-house on the wrong side of the abbreviated train (one coach and one carriage-truck), probably through drawing directly on the stone or plate.

So His Majesty of the French got home, while, in those days of primitive telegraphs, Victoria and Albert had doubtless gone to bed without knowing much about the adventures of their important guest. Meanwhile, Ernest Augustus, King of Hanover, had been busy. He had ordered a replica of Queen Adelaide's carriage for his personal use in Germany. He, too, was a pragmatical man. When railways converged on his capital city, which already had furnished Great Britain with the Four Georges and William IV, he is said to have required that no trains should connect there, so that the passengers would have plenty of time to go shopping and thus to enrich his subjects. Ever thereafter, German railways were planned on lines of commercial, as well as of military, viability. Both points were good ones.

The steam railways had received Royal Recognition, which was a great thing for them. Many nations were watching.

The London and South Western company was to build two more saloon carriages very much on the same lines as the first, which ended its days on the Shropshire and Montgomeryshire Railway, over a century later. One was shown at the Great Exhibition of 1851, and this was the vehicle reputed to have been the Queen's favourite. The present writer had a ride in it as recently as the early 1930s and found it excellent, even on the very moderate permanent way of the Kent and East Sussex Railway to which it had gravitated by way of the Plymouth, Devonport and South Western Junction. The three went through several metamorphoses, such as conversion from four- to six-wheel arrangement and back again. The original vehicle had its roof raised and its external decorations sobered. By appearance, the same sort of thing must have happened to the others, unless such improvement in design had been made already. All three belonged to the South Western company's royal train exclusively, at least until 1877, when something more advanced was furnished by Joseph Beattie's son, William George, who had succeeded his late father.

Meanwhile, and a long way back at that, Queen Victoria had made the first of many royal railway journeys between Scotland and England; (the first was southbound). George P. Neele, latterly Superintendent of the Line, London and North Western Railway, recorded many valuable and curious items regarding the Queen's railway journeys in his *Railway Reminiscences*, including this one from Scotland, and from such the present author will quote without qualms in one place or another. In respect of his own line, Neele is very trustworthy. Sometimes he allows himself a sniff at other parties, or even a lapse from exactitude with people's names. But then, the London and North Western Railway, as it became by amalgamation in 1846, had a certain *hauteur* towards other railway companies. It, and the Great Western, were mutually hostile, though long royal journeys periodically compelled them to partnership, as with the South Western, which the Great Western detested. (Feeling was reciprocated!)

To quote Neele:

> Her Majesty's marine residence in the Isle of Wight, and her fondness for sea-voyaging, caused most of her autumn excursions to have their start from Osborne. Her published diaries [the famous *Leaves, 1848–1861*, Smith Elder, London, 1868] will shew to what an extent the royal yachts came into requisition, but occasionally a railway journey was associated with the arrangements.

The Queen loved to visit places; hence the alleged 'fondness' in days when the steamship was the most reliable means of transport in the waters of a seagirt kingdom. But she was prone to seasickness, and on that account she was later to be enthusiastic about the Channel Tunnel. The Duke of Cambridge seems to have dissuaded her, on strategic grounds.

On the morning of Friday 29 September 1848, it had been arranged for the Queen and Prince Albert to travel south by the Royal Yacht from Aberdeen. There was, however, dense fog, not only off the harbour but extending far down the East Coast. At that time the new Aberdeen Railway had penetrated as far north as Montrose, whence there was direct railway communication with London, though it was still rather unfinished, even thus far. Half an hour after noon, the Aberdeen company's engineer, Mr Errington, who was in Aberdeen at the time, received an urgent courier from Balmoral. A train was to be provided at the Montrose railhead, for departure as soon as possible after the arrival of the royal party. Errington sent his assistant Ker posting to Montrose immediately. Only half an hour after Mr Ker's arrival, the Queen and her party arrived, also, presumably, having had relays of post-horses. By now, a wet, foggy evening was setting in, while the Aberdeen Railway had at this short notice assembled a train of its best available rolling stock headed by its most reliable locomotive. The vehicle furnished for the Queen was an ordinary first-class of the period, i.e. having three compartments, each seating six persons under normal conditions. Doubtless some modest extra comforts were moved into it, and so they should have been, for Victoria was to travel in it until the day after tomorrow.

She had night-breaks, however. The distances from Montrose to Perth was just over 50 miles. The line was barely finished, still with single track between Forfar and Glamis, whereon there was 'a very narrow escape of trouble through a blunder' which must have made some people's hair stand on end. Apparently a goods wagon was shunted across, in the path of the royal train, and in view of what happened to certain express trains under similar circumstances in later years, it was a narrow escape indeed. All was well, however. Nobody told the Queen about the hazard. The train covered the distance in less than 2 hours, and at Perth the Queen was dined, bedded and breakfasted, to go forward quite comfortably at 10.30 next forenoon. On such railway journeys, Perth was to refresh her to the end of her days. The great event was breakfast (which everybody needed) after the long night rumble from the South.

Certainly the Aberdeen Railway, barely finished, and the Scottish Midland Junction Railway from Forfar to Perth, had made some very creditable running with little warning, and everything therefore improvised. The alarm on the former's line had been serious, but Stationmaster Boyle of Aberdeen Joint in later years remarked: 'There were no newspaper reporters in those days.' He was wrong, of course, but they were not then in positions to watch the Royal Progress from first to last. The Queen, having become used to it, trusted the train far more than some other hazards. That year of 1848 was revolutionary over many parts of Europe, and saw the overthrow of that fat and fussy Louis Philippe of Orleans who had been allowed to ride on the South Western and South Eastern lines in England. In the same year Marx and Engels issued the *Communist Manifesto*. But Queen Victoria was to be more bothered by the people then calling themselves Fenians (the I.R.A. of the period).

Now she sank back on the cloth-covered horsehair of the Aberdeen Railway's first-class carriage, heading south, and as last night, expected the best that could be managed. During the night, urgent messages had been sent to Carlisle for all proper preparations. The Scottish Central Railway took her to Greenhill near Larbert (45 miles), and the Caledonian Railway took her on. The distance of 150 miles was covered with four stops in $4\frac{1}{4}$ hours. Even at Carlisle, only 15 bare minutes were allowed. ('The Queen rested.') Now the Lancaster and Carlisle Railway took over, for the next 90 miles, over mountain as had been the Caledonian stretch; and at Lancaster there was quite a long stop, for the Queen had to receive a ponderous Mayoral Address on behalf of her County Palatine. At length the London and North Western Railway took over the train, and by 7.0 p.m. got it to Crewe, where for the second time on that journey, the Queen was lodged. She left that strange new town, entirely railway-created, at 7.0 a.m. and on to Euston in her Capital, 209 miles from Lancaster, to arrive 'about 11.0 a.m.', quitting the Aberdeen company's modest first-class carriage at last for what one expects was a good luncheon.

Thereafter she may have put up her feet awhile – the early carriages were somewhat upright – but she was a game young lady, eleven years a Queen and still not yet thirty. Before we leave these, her early travels under steam, we should notice one of 1849, if only because it involved one of her scarce visits to Ireland. She first set foot in her Third Kingdom at the Cove of Cork, which she well-meaningly renamed Queenstown. Long years after her death it was officially to revert to the good Erse Cobh. At that time there were indeed railways in those parts; nevertheless the Royal Party set off for Dublin by sea again, round the uneasy waters to the south-east. Before rounding the Tuscar Rock, 'I and the poor children were very sea-sick', but, still quoting her *Journal*, as to her arrival at Kingstown (Dun Laoghaire):

> An Immense multitude had assembled, who cheered most enthusiastically . . . it was really very striking. The space we had to walk along to the railroad was covered in; and lined with ladies and gentlemen strewing flowers. We entered the railway-carriages with the children, the Clarendons, and the three ladies, and in a quarter of an hour reached the Dublin station.

That station, terminus of the original Dublin and Kingstown Railway, was the fore-runner of the partly terminal and partly through-running station known to many genera-tions of Irishmen and their visitors as Westland Row, and now named Pearse. The Dublin and Kingstown Railway was the oldest in Ireland, having been opened on 17 December 1834. By the time the Queen used it, other railways had come to Ireland, and were doing good business even in the distressed 1840s. As to Kingstown (Dun Laog-haire) the Queen's reference to a covered way between train and steamer is interesting. It may have been a temporary one. For many years longer, at too many railway ports handling passenger traffic in England, such as Dover and Folkestone, the unfortunate travellers were obliged to stagger with their hand-luggage over wet cobblestones, with no shelter whatever. Often they were still being actively sick during the process. As one poor lady remarked privately: 'My dear! When at last we got off that awful boat, the quay seemed to move about worse than ever!' At Dover, the trains went to and from a bleak mole whose paltry rampart was not proof against waves breaking over it, spraying the carriages and the passengers impartially.

From these depressing things, let us go to some *post scripta*, chiefly mechanical. Motive power on the Queen's first trip on the Great Western has been noticed. That on her first ride from Scotland was remarkable in that the same type of engine – in basic design – was probably used throughout the long journey from Montrose to Birmingham. It was that generally called the 'Crewe Type', with mixed frames and outside inclined cylinders; the joint offspring of Alexander Allan (who went to his native Scotland from Crewe), Francis Trevithick, who stayed at Crewe, and William Buddicom, who went to France.

In those days, the Locomotive Superintendent of a railway often went on the royal engine and drove her himself. Daniel Gooch had done so on the very first journey up from Slough, and F. Trevithick did so on the London and North Western. On that journey from Scotland he had a bad shock when the royal train entered at fair speed on a stretch of track where the ballast had been dug out, but all was well, as with the shunted wagon in the North. Still, the journey had twice suggested the 'possibility of a long regency' to some people other than the anti-railway lobby at Westminster.

South of Birmingham, that first Royal Scotch Express was headed by the little, light engines of Edward Bury's design, based on Wolverton in the L.N.W.R. Southern Division, with which the old London and Birmingham company had started business.

The 'Crewe Type', however, had not ended in Birmingham, for John Gooch's London and South Western engines had close affinities to the design as to arrangement of cylinders and frames, and Buddicom had already gone to France, to make engines for that Paris and Rouen Railway which Louis Philippe had been tacitly forbidden to use. A very early form (by Forrester) served the Dublin and Kingstown. Something like it was soon to appear (John Gooch again, and Robert Sinclair from the Caledonian Railway) on the Eastern Counties (later Great Eastern) Railway. Was it not, of its day, a Royal Locomotive?

Reverting to the Queen's *Journal*: one likes her use of the sonorous word 'railroad'; good, reverberating English word, though now regarded as American for a 'railway'. We should have kept it!

2
THE WORLD WATCHES

For some time to come, we are still to be with Queen Victoria; also with Prince Albert who understood both technological and social evolution much better than she. The young Queen was schooled in the tenets of her mother the Duchess of Kent and of Uncle Leopold of the Belgians, and had assumed the purple straight from the dogmatic tutelage of her glum-seeming Governess Lehzen, whom she was to create a Baroness in her own right.

But the world was watching. In the 1840s, the railway had proved itself as a reliable and extraordinarily convenient conveyance for passengers, however exalted. The train was at least as safe as a ship; apparently safer, though already it had had its misfortunes. In spite of the sad end of the French admiral, railways had not yet burnt that hypothetical bishop offered by the Reverend Sidney Smith, let alone a royal personage. So, with the world, Kings and potentates watched.

There was King Ernest Augustus of Hanover, who was not on good terms with his Cousins of England. (Victoria was precluded by the Salic Law from succeeding to Hanover, which, in one of Lawrence Housman's dramatic pieces, she dismissed as 'no longer a British possession'.) Then Ernest Augustus is reputed to have been 'shoved', with the overturning of a chair, at the Christening party of Victoria's first child, by the usually patient but young and muscular Prince Albert, over a claim for precedence. But the King had already sampled the rail, and had inspected Queen Adelaide's carriage with approval. He ordered a replica to be made for his own conveyance about his kingdom. Alas, he was buying something already obsolescent! To be sure, the Great Western, the London and Birmingham and the South Western had done better than that! Other potentates were watching too, as were the railways and the manufacturers who were waiting to serve them.

During the years 1845 to 1850 – a mere demidecade – some very fine royal railway carriages were built, of an elegance, and with comforts and conveniences, not hitherto thought of by most people. The contributions of the Great Western and the South Eastern companies were especially noteworthy. A British author would like to think that these showed the rest of the world how to do it. But certain such refinements were anticipated abroad. Some of the Foreign Exalted had more imaginative ideas than those of acquisitive, but testy and rather stupid, Hanoverian Majesty in his own new Kingdom. In those days, there was no longer a Holy Roman Empire, but Austria still had an Emperor, who from 1835 to the revolution year of 1848, was Ferdinand I. For him was built in 1845 a truly magnificent royal saloon by the State Railway Company (*Staatseisenbahn Gesellschaft*, or 'STEG') which is illustrated in side elevation and plan by Dr Fritz Stöckl in his *Komfort auf Schienen* (Verlag Eisenbahn, Basle, 1970).

Its aspect in the drawings is distinctly American; (the same sort of thing was happening in Russia). That means that it was a bogie-carriage on eight wheels, with no side doors but with entry and exit by two hooded, but open, platforms, either end. Inside, it was divided into five compartments, each opening to the next. The middle one was the State saloon, which could serve for either audience or conference. It was furnished with four splendid armchairs, one to each corner, with a table in the middle, and it had three oblong windows each side. An ornamental false cornice in wrought metal filigree crowned this portion, though not the rest of the vehicle. There was a pair of double cantilevers, to match, in lieu of trusses below. It was entered, from either end, through two more private compartments. One contained a pair of half-couches or *chaises-longues* where the Emperor could relax while travelling with a good cigar and, perhaps, the Empress. The other, in opposite direction, contained two longitudinal berths; entirely necessary in an Empire stretching from the Adriatic to Poland. Then there were the two compartments abutting the entrance platforms. That at the *chaises-longues* end had four upright seats, but of comfortable sort, for the Emperor's equerries or any other immediate attendants. Its opposite number, adjacent to the other entrance, was an ante-room, containing two arm-chairs. One of these, the drawings show, contained either a water-closet of sorts or at least a close-stool. Such apparatus in disguise was very soon to appear on trains in England. The body was in Anglo-American measurements approximately 30 ft long, excluding end platforms, and rather more than 9 ft wide. It was sufficiently high for any but a very tall man to walk erect in modest headgear. The bogies were very short, like very old American car-trucks, but speeds in the Empire of those days were not rash. This must have been one of the most advanced railway carriages of its time, anywhere. As noted, it conferred sanitary security on Imperial Majesty, if not on his suite, and that was, in recent Chinese phraseology, a 'Great Leap Forward', where trains were concerned.

Charles Saunders and Isambard Brunel, Secretary and Engineer of the Great Western Railway in England, were not averse to holidays abroad, even in earliest days when Daniel Gooch was still struggling with the appalling locomotives which Brunel had saddled upon him at the beginning. As all good men make use of their holidays profession-ally, they doubtless noticed what was happening elsewhere when it came to 'shop', including the splendid Austrian vehicle just described. Long years after there was to be a close personal as well as professional connection between G. J. Churchward of the Great Western and that great Austrian Carl Gölsdorf.

Things were not quite happy about the 'Old Royal', the first Great Western Queen's Carriage which had to be altered before she used it. It is possible that an unsuccessful essay was made about 1848, for, as remarked, one has seen drawings, at Swindon, of a most extraordinary vehicle resembling neither the 'Old Royal' nor the new and indeed luxurious Queen's Carriage which was in use by 1850.

This Queen's Carriage was certainly most creditable. It was an eight-wheeler, with wood-felloed iron-tyred wheels shrunk on the axles, which were equalised in pairs with some side-play, though not on bogies as were those of the Austrian carriage. The main compartment, in which the Queen, Prince Albert, and at least some of the Royal Offspring were expected to travel, had a very long plate-glass window each side and, by means of a bulge in the sides, was made 10 ft wide. It had an entrance vestibule to itself. At one end from this was an attendant's – or possibly equerries' – compartment, complete with observation windows, and on the roof between the two was a small disc-and cross bar signal by which the Queen could – by deputy – signal 'too fast' or 'all right', display of the crossbar part indicating the former, to be observed by that Good Spartan called the travelling carriage porter who sat facing backwards on the tender, in what everyone called 'the iron coffin', (shown in the picture of Victoria's first train, Plate 1). This grim

31

sort of sentry-box lasted to the end of Victoria's reign where the royal trains were involved, at any rate on the Great Western and North Western systems. On the latter, he was done up in oilskins like a lifeboatman, sometimes being drenched when the train took up water from track troughs.

Reverting to the Queen's Carriage, G.W.R., *circa* 1850. At the opposite end of the 'attendants'' there was an ante-chamber of sorts, which old photographs show to have been partitioned within itself, while it, also, had outside access. Certainly it contained a lavatory. There survives a pedestal basin for the washing of the royal hands, with a discreetly disguised pot-cupboard below. There may have been a portable water-closet, such as had served George IV when visiting. A real one was to follow fairly soon. The vehicle was 30 ft 8 in. long with a maximum height of 7 ft 7 in. The roof was nearly flat, with no clerestory as in the 'posting carriage' type, though it acquired such in the course of a complete rebuilding in the 1880s. It was converted to standard gauge in 1889 and broken up in 1903. Internally it was very comfortably furnished in the new Victorian-Puritan style, which later would have been called 'club'. Ere its end, Dean's pendulum-link bogies had succeeded Gooch's equalised semi-rigid axles for its eight wheels.

There is a charming note in MacDermot's *History of the Great Western Railway*. Break-of-gauge bedevilled many people's journeys, from north to west especially, with the Great Western straddling a considerable portion of England on its broad gauge, while dividing the North Western, Midland and other railways from the South Western and its neighbours. With a Queen who was later to spend much of her time on Deeside at one end, and in the Isle of Wight at the other, break-of-gauge speedily became a confounded nuisance:

> The first of the Queen's northern journeys affecting the Great Western appears to have been that made in the autumn of 1849 from Scotland to the Isle of Wight. It afforded her personal experience of the inconvenience of a break-of-gauge, of which she had doubtless heard and read much. Arriving at Gloucester by the Midland from Derby, where she had spent the night, Her Majesty was of course obliged to change on to the Broad Gauge, and it may be that the new and luxurious saloon lately built to supersede the original of 1840 consoled her to some extent for the trouble.

Whether the sorrows of break-of-gauge really had reached the Queen's awareness may be scouted. This party imagines that she simply said, at Gloucester: 'What an agreeable, spacious carriage!' But the thing had to be revoked. At Basingstoke she had to change back to the narrow London and South Western, which would mean the old and small carriage she had known since 1844, and which was to have such a long and curious career, ending more than a century later on the Welsh Marches.

But to the credit of the 'narrow' railways in general, and the southern ones in particular, the South Eastern Railway furnished a beauteous vehicle in 1850. It was designed by Richard Mansell, inventor of wheels with centres of hardwood segments, superseding the earlier wooden wheels of Joseph Beattie, already mentioned. His carriage for royal travel – now developing over the narrow waters between Kent and Picardy or Flanders – had certain affinities with the new Great Western one, which antedated it on the broad gauge. Again it exemplified the scheme of having a central 'State' compartment, but this time that had a central door, and either side of this it followed the lines of a much elongated State coach. Fore and aft were half-compartments or 'chariots', one being for attendant officers and the other providing an ante-room in communication with a central one. The second-named contained within one of its corner seats – as for Ferdinand five years before – what South Eastern specifications called 'a patent convenience'. There was also a marble-topped wash-stand in the same place. The carriage was very ornate, inside and out. Externally, the 'bodies' followed traditional coachbuilders' curves, and between the curves there were in high relief semi-recumbent lions, gorgeously gilded. The carriage was naturally less massive than the Great Western's broad-gauge one, and was mounted on three axles. The main saloon was 12 ft long, 8 ft wide and 6 ft 8 in. high. Quite a civilised compartment! Decoration was rich. One has mentioned the gilded lions outside. Inside, it would have pleased George IV, had he lived to ride in a train. But if Victoria's first Great Western carriage had been pagan-bright with its paintings of the Four Elements, this South Eastern one was already going *pi*. The door leading from the main saloon to the ante-room was decorated as to its upper panel with a fine painting representative of 'Guardian Angels'. One might have imagined something like a multiplication of Janey Morris as portrayed by Edward Burne-Jones, but neither of these had quite arrived as yet. The treatment is now shown.

This carriage lasted for a very long time for, with improvements, it was a very good one. It appears in an illustrated-paper representation of the ageing Victoria receiving a prospective relative-in-law in the South Western station at Windsor, fairly late in the century. The windows with rectangular bottoms and semi-elliptical tops, and the 'chariot' mouldings, are unmistakeable. Ere that, many splendid new carriages had appeared, whether at home or abroad, and in the forefront were those for Victoria herself, whatever the Emperors of Russia, Austria, and the French might be contemplating.

There was the business of putting Queen Victoria to bed on a train. Already, as we have seen, Ferdinand I of Austria had been so favoured, and so had the Tsar of All the Russias. But in 1861 Richard Bore of the London and North Western Railway produced a carriage in which it could be done, whether she were on her way to Scotland, which she loved, or to Ireland, which she did not. For her, on such journeys, Mr Bore designed and had built at Wolverton a neat four-wheel carriage on behalf of the London and North Western Railway. It could be used anywhere from the Metropolis to the remote north-eastern Highlands of Scotland, though not, as yet, over much of the Great Western Railway, which, with gauge of 7 ft 0$\frac{1}{4}$ in., remained unique with much of the railway system of Cornwall and South Wales, dividing the other parties. What a crying pity, looking back over far more than a century, that Brunel came too late, even in the 1830s!

Late in 1856, mixing of gauge between Oxford and Basingstoke had made it possible for the Queen to travel right through from Aboyne on Deeside to Gosport for the Isle of Wight without change of carriage. The Deeside Railway from Aberdeen reached Banchory in 1853. It had a handsome station there, which at the time of writing still stands, though the lovely railway is gone. The Deeside Extension line followed in 1859, to Aboyne; Ballater, the final royal railhead, did not follow until 1866; Braemar, never. The splendid

Great Western saloon carriage, being broad-gauge, could not, of course, be used, and, with the cold and often unkind eye of historical retrospect, it may be felt that Mr Bore of the London and North Western might have produced something more spacious than in fact he did in 1861. To be sure, he was to rectify the fault some eight years later, as we shall see.

Bore's London and North Western Queen's Saloon of 1861 was, as noted, a four-wheeler, the wheels having Mansell's wood-segmental construction between tyres and centres, and was very handsomely furnished and decorated. The *Illustrated London News* went to town on it, with beautiful woodcuts and fulsome text. But it simply amounted to a 'bed-sitter' on wheels, even though its reported cost was more than £3,000, which would have bought two really nice detached suburban residences on the London peri-meter some 70 years later. The carriage was built, not at Wolverton Works on the L.N.E.R., but privately at Saltley, with Messrs Cawkwell (General Manager) and Bruyeres (General Superintendent) more or less standing over Mr Bore to give advice.

Phraseology of the *Illustrated London News* reported 'under the direction of', so one supposes that they were prompting their coachbuilder in matters of what they con-sidered 'good taste'. Bore knew how to build a carriage. This one was chiefly of oak, as to frames. Oak, incidentally, was not a good timber for vehicles expected to last a long time. It was acid, like ash, and could thus attack bolts and nuts and flitchplates and so on. Teak was found to be much better, and about this time the Realm was busily acquiring and consolidating an Indian Empire from which to get it. But Mr Bore made his carriage with a triple floor, or at any rate one containing a cork-sandwich to deaden noise. Inside the body was quilted at sides and ceiling to the same end, and by way of insulation. The main compartment contained, *inter alia*, a large sofa, which could be either converted to or replaced by a modest double bed, across one end. The other end opened into a spacious lavatory, or, as it was delicately called, dressing-room. At the end was a completely divided compartment for the sergeant-footman, the servant in personal attendance.

Possibly, at first, this person really was a sergeant, but his office was speedily assumed by John Brown, later created Esquire by Royal Letters Patent. He had become a ghillie in the Royal Forests in 1849, entered permanent royal service in 1851, and had been at once selected to lead the Queen's pony when she was wandering about the Scottish Highlands. He was promoted to the rank of Upper Servant in 1865 and became the Queen's perman-ent personal attendant. He was to become one of the most cordially disliked men in royal service, but he knew how to manage an extremely difficult widowed Queen, who would hear no ill of him, as well as knowing the rough country which she had come to adore. The Prince of Wales, later King Edward VII, could not bear him.

That great and long-suffering personage, more worthily indeed, should have a prelimi-nary note here. His father disapproved of him in the stiff German manner, though left alone they probably would have understood each other well enough. But to Victoria, he was all that a Royal Mother most disliked and disapproved of. He *liked life*, and she had her own which she exclusively understood. It became worse with the untimely death of Prince Albert in the back-end of 1861. By that time Albert Edward of Wales was just over 20 years old. His boyhood had been miserable, and so was much more to come, but he was no longer compelled to read, and be examined on, the awful works of Martin Tupper. In his baby-clothes, he had been the first Heir Apparent to ride in a train. He was destined to be the first British King to own, use and enjoy a motor-car.

At the time of his father's death, even the English Press was attacking him for his unseemly behaviour here and there. *The Times* three times requested him to consider his proper position. He was afraid of none but his mother, and occasionally rebelled. He was married to Alexandra of Denmark on 10 March 1863. She arrived in London at the old Bricklayers' Arms Station, South Eastern Railway, and there survive copies of a very fine coloured lithograph recording the detrainment of the lovely, but undoubtedly frightened, young lady. One opines that the prospect of her exalted mother-in-law, and her impending experience of the vast city with its wild crowds, scared her much more than a quiet ride in the South Eastern company's handsome royal saloon.

William Hardman in London wrote to Edward Holroyd in Australia:

> The other day just before his marriage, he was smoking in a first-class railway carriage (ordinary train) and the porter, not recognising him, asked him to show his ticket. A lady residing at Windsor told a friend of ours she was sure the Prince was a person of no mind at all, as he had gone up to the bookstall and bought a copy of *Punch* and actually paid for it himself. Perhaps you will agree with us that an unaffected young fellow who hates non-sensical dignity, smokes in the railway, and reads *Punch*, may not turn out so badly after all.

Two comments on that extract: Hardman, far from being of Radical persuasion, was a high Tory and eventually became Editor of the *Morning Post*; second, at that time, the Great Western Railway still strictly forbade smoking, not only in its carriages but even in the open air of its premises. (Was any exception made theretofore in respect of I. K. Brunel, its most eminent Engineer? He had died in 1859, and even public photography has recorded him with an anticipatory Churchillian cigar punctuating his physiognomy.)

From the Royal Humanities back to the royal vehicles and journeys! While Prince Albert was alive, journeys to and from Scotland by train were made fairly impartially by either the West or East Coast routes. Records, pictorial or otherwise, are scarce in respect of the vehicles furnished by the East Coast companies – the Great Northern, the North Eastern and the North British. Some are picturesque, like that of the Royal Family's departure from London, Maiden Lane, in 1852, just before the opening of the new and stupendous Kings Cross Station, but the rolling stock shown looks like something out of a pantomime harlequinade following the presentation of *Cinderella*.

Several ridiculous representations of the Royal Family *en route* have survived too many years; the worst – and unfortunately the most endemic, simply shows Victoria and Albert, with their rapidly increasing progeny, grouped amidst a childish representation of an elongated railway compartment crudely drawn and painted round them. The Royal Nannie is passable, with the latest arrival in her arms, and the likeness of Windsor Castle is somewhere in the scenery, but the rest is preposterous. The Great Western was a very gentlemanly company, but it must have felt somewhat *narked* in view of the beautiful carriages it really provided.

Your author is not sure as to when royal trains were first outwardly decorated. The custom, on certain lines, was to be flamboyantly observed at the end of the century. The view of the departure from Maiden Lane, Great Northern Railway, shows a Royal Standard flying from the tippety-top of the royal saloon, but the contingency seems remote. It would not have lasted long in the Great Northern tunnels.

But when, ere that, the northern portions of the incipient East Coast Route were completed with the High Level Bridge over the Tyne and the Royal Border Bridge over the Tweed, the North British Railway surpassed, surely, anything that had gone before, and much that was yet to come.

On 29 August 1850, the Royal Border Bridge was opened by the Queen. The North British Railway provided the inaugural train, and contrary to usual practice, North British motive power was furnished northwards from Tweedmouth, on the English side of the river. Berwick was properly the southern terminal of the N.B.R., unless one counted Carlisle on the West Coast, or the branch connections to the North Eastern at Hexham and Morpeth, or Silloth on Solway, all of which came later.

For the inaugural royal train, the North British company furnished a Crampton's patent locomotive, its No. 55, then almost new, which it had bought from E. B. Wilson of Leeds Railway Foundry. At short notice the Foreman-Painter at St Margaret's Works, Edinburgh, was required to paint it, all over apart from working-parts, smokebox and chimney, in Royal Stewart tartan. It was done. (Your author had it at second-hand from a distinguished locomotive engineer, D. MacAulay of the Eastern Bengal State Railway, who served his time on the N.B., part of that immediately under an old man who had seen it. Many have doubted!) But by the time the anonymous precursors of P.R.&P.O. had finished with the long-suffering locomotive, her splendid livery was so cloaked with red-velvet drapes and festoons and conventional gilded crowns, and stags and things in polished brass, that even the reporter of that most respectable paper the *Scotsman* failed to notice what was underneath them. Some time ago oneself painted this engine into a picture (a major portion of which now forms Plate 18) just to see what she must have looked like. One had adequate drawing-office guidance. The painting has been several times previously reproduced, twice in colour.

Elaborate decoration, or special painting, of locomotives was mostly exemplified in Great Britain. Elsewhere there might be some flags; even a mounting of the Papal Arms. Russia favoured evergreen garlands, which later were to adorn, by accident, a most unfortunate spectacle; but of that, more later!

American influence, through the firm of Eastwick and Harrison, and the practice of Ross Winans, was to be strong in the earliest days of Russian railroads. Winans's hand, indeed, was particularly apparent in vehicle design, with long bodies on short bogies. The Austrian carriage previously mentioned also showed it. The Emperor of All the Russias was furnished in these years with an enormous carriage on sixteen wheels, arranged in two eight-wheel bogies.

But in Central and Southern Europe, not to mention Egypt, there blossomed what can only be called the Highly Decorated Train, beside which even the South Eastern company's effort on behalf of Queen Victoria looked restrained to the point of Cromwellian austerity. Several have survived, and one of the more modest, and most charming, examples, is the carriage built for royal journeys on the nearly-new Lisbon and Santarem Railway by the Cie Générale du Matérial des Chemins de Fer, in France, in 1858. At that time Pedro V was King of Portugal, but the carriage is generally associated with Dona Maria Pia of Savoy, who married his successor in 1862. The photograph in Plate 39 is fairly descriptive, and though it shows the vehicle as it has survived, no change was made as to styling, which involved not only the primeval arrangement of three 'bodies', but an undulating underframe to match, a very rare arrangement, with the roof in harmony. From right to left in the illustration, we see the entrance vestibule, in which attendant officers sat during travel; then, in the middle, the main or State saloon, similar in outward style but longer and with no side doors. At the farther end, and similar in dimensions to the ante-chamber, is a spacious arrangement of dressing-room and lavatory, with a capacious water-tank on top. The roofing is double, throughout its witching waves, against the strong summer sun of the Peninsula, with an extra-large lamp over the middle of the saloon. This lovely old carriage is, of course, on broad (5 ft 6 in.) gauge, and one notes a marked affinity, in the design of the wheels and the suspension, with old broad-gauge (7 ft) practice on the Great Western Railway. In later years, continuous brakes were fitted, for sumptuous vehicles had long lives. The hoses are visible to the right of the photograph. With French makers the *diligence* conception persisted even longer than did the stage-coach tradition in England. Unusual, and charming, are the inverted-dewdrop quarterlights. The vehicle is lovingly preserved at Santarem.

From the ornate to the flamboyant, which was achieved variously on behalf of the Turkish Viceroy of Egypt (Said Pasha), who had things outshining those of the Sultan himself; the last of the Popes who were also temporal rulers (Pius IX); and the Wittelsbach Kings of Bavaria, the country of superb Baroque churches. Europe and the rest of the world were watching what British skill and craft might be doing for that alarming little lady who already ruled a most powerful industrial United Kingdom which, having lost its first lot of colonies to its own first colonists, was now well on the way to building up, by colonial expansion, a vast empire. Victoria was a puritan. Popes and Catholic Majesties and Eastern potentates wished for things more splendid to behold than what would satisfy this exalted but already rather austere little Queen.

Whilst, in Turkey, and as late as 1872, the Sultan Abdul Aziz was to be satisfied with a four-wheeled saloon carriage made in Birmingham (it is today preserved at Istanbul-Sirkeci and might be described as the last word in ornately uncomfortable luxury), his Viceroy in Egypt had far grander ideas. For one thing, Said Pasha liked locomotives for their own sake. In 1862 he bought a Conner express engine with 8 ft 4 in. driving wheels, intended for the Caledonian Railway, from the London Exhibition of that year. When the ship carrying it to Alexandria foundered with its precious cargo (some people nowadays have yet seen a locomotive break loose and sink the ship!) he immediately ordered another, which was duly delivered, and lasted for many years.

Ere that, he had already had two purely private locomotives from Robert Stephenson and Company, and had had two more ordinary 2-2-2 express engines dressed up in a form so regardless that it made Queen Victoria's tartan engine on the North British look, by comparison, like something serving a Scottish gasworks, save that a 'Crampton' had been scarcely suitable.

The two private tank engines had each a sort of pavilion mounted where one might have expected to see tank and bunker (well tanks were in fact used, between the frames). The most famous, or at any rate that most frequently illustrated, was a 2-2-4 built by Stephensons in 1859, with double frames, inside cylinders and a trailing equalised bogie to support the saloon part. This last was of curved-coach shape on a curved frame, as in the Portuguese carriage already noted, but it was open to the air above its curvaceous waistline and there screened each side by a pair of curtains which, half drawn together, somebody likened to a Turkish lady's trousers, though to western eyes they looked like nothing so much as a Victorian giantess's drawers, with plenty of room in the seat, hung up on the line to dry. It was a very little engine, with 5 ft driving wheels and cylinders only 8 in. by 14 in., but it was sufficiently powerful to haul, on the level lines of the Nile, a saloon carriage for the Viceroy's attendant ladies, eunuchs and others. Decoration of this, as of the other two noted, was incredibly rich, with gold-leaf arabesques on purple as to the frames, purple arabesques on silver as to the boiler clothing plates, a prodigal sparkle of more gold, and vermilion, on other portions. The chimney, crowned and polished, was fluted like a Doric column. The dome-casing, with a bell-mouth top to contain the safety-valves, was of polished brass (was it indeed gold-plated?) and had its barrel in the form of a short Etruscan column or pedestal. It seems a pity that something had not been adapted from the great temple of Karnak, which would have added classic Egyptian to the already mixed styles.

The Viceroy had already, from 1858, a magnificent saloon carriage mounted on two double-bogies, thus providing 16 wheels in all and ameliorating such inequalities as might occur in light track laid over the primeval sands of Egypt. In its middle there was an open loggia, dividing Viceregal apartments from those of the harem. This carriage lasted for an immense time. One heard of it, between the wars of 1914 and 1939, serving a very useful purpose as a mobile laboratory in Upper Egypt.

One doubts that any rolling stock in railway history could have outdone that of the Egyptian Viceroyalty in the middle of last century, but just then, the servants of the Vatican in Rome and of the Wittelsbachs in Bavaria were running it close.

Ludwig II of Bavaria was an aesthete and a romantic. Long after his death, people in Munich were to revere him as if he had been a deified Roman Emperor of the more creditable sort, even though he had beggared their exchequer. He had made his metropolis one of the most beautiful cities in the world. He had discovered Wagner and brought him to fame with all his extraordinary new music. His fantastic castles dotted Upper Bavaria. After his death, someone wrote, and published as a popular rhyme-sheet, a wondrous poem about his arrival in Heaven, to the awe, and wonder, and delight of the Celestial Hierarchy. One has seen it most piously framed in a Munich lodging briefly occupied in 1928. Of course, he had to have a Court Train.

Not that he particularly liked travelling by railway. He was wont to send it around his kingdom to draw attention to his magnificence, while he rode behind horses and used it simply as a mobile palace for provincial reception. Indeed, in the beginning, it had not been built for him at all, but for his predecessor King Maximilian and Queen Marie. Ludwig, incidentally, had no use for queens. But he delighted in his train, wherever it might be standing, and in his time it was improved and embellished – very considerably!

King Max's train, as it at first was, appeared in the 1850s. It survives now, in its ultimate glory, in the Transport Museum, Nuremberg.

This train was built, in stages, over the years 1860–5. King Max died in March 1864, when Ludwig succeeded, and in the following year his scarcely credible State saloon was ready to complete the train. It is an eight-wheeled carriage, originally on fixed axles with sideplay, set in the midst of a rake of four-wheelers. It must been seen to be believed. All the richness of Nymphenburg, Herrenchiemsee, Linderhof, and perhaps some of the phantasmagoria of Neuschwanstein seem to have been distilled into one rolling vehicle. Anticipating the arrangements of Queen Victoria's later carriages in England, the main drawing-room has an enormous central oil-lamp, but here it looks like a minor sun in the midst of a false dome gorgeously painted with allegorical figures. Outside, the the ventilating arrangements are seen to have *the likeness of a kingly crown set-on.*

In the last, to be sure, there was nothing very new. Victoria had one, on the London and Birmingham in the early 1840s; so had Maria Pia in Portugal, and that old rascal Said Pasha had several set about, but none on such a terrific scale as this. Within there were paintings, and mouldings, and carvings and gold leaf galore, as one can see to this day. Even the royal w.c. preserves its swansdown cushion, with a hole in the middle like an American doughnut. (One is reminded of Dr Samuel Johnson's criticism of such an appointment in a Dutch Embassy of his time.) The gorgeous chairs and the sofa are in buttoned-in blue satin. Outside, the train is painted in royal blue, heavily decorated and with all those elaborate mouldings and cornices gilded. One of the attendant carriages contains a small locomotive-type boiler for keeping the train warm whether a locomotive be attached or not. It is possible to pass right through the train, as in an American or Russian train of its time.

Poor Mad Ludwig! Born in August 1845, to succeed in 1864, he was obliged to recognise a Hohenzollern, William I, as Emperor in 1871. He was deposed in June, 1886, to commit suicide three days later, taking with him his unfortunate resident physician to the cold waters of the Starnberg Lake. His castles and his train survive, and a good thing too, especially in respect of the train though the castles be engaging. That train does not seem to have been much used, but certainly it was trotted out for the Shah of Persia, Nasr-ul-Deen, in 1889. (This ruler, born in 1831, visited Great Britain several times, first in 1873. On one occasion the London and South Western Railway specially named an engine *Persia* for a journey to Windsor. On his first sampling of the South Eastern Railway, it is said, he ordered the immediate execution of the driver who had brought him from the coast, for driving him too fast.) Briefly back to the Wittelsbachs: Ludwig's brother Otto, who succeeded him as King of Bavaria, seems to have been even more disastrously odd. Fortunately their uncle, Prince Luitpold, who was a tactful old gentleman, was hurriedly made Regent by anxious Government.

So, now, to 'Pio Nono'. He was the last of the Popes to be a temporal ruler. He was also the first – and until John XXIII the only – Pope to travel by train after having received the Triple Crown. In the Papal States of the 1850s, the Pope still *ruled*. He was helped by the Bonapartist French, and on that subject one can only quote, or draw from, one's distinguished contemporary Peter Kalla-Bishop, who is deep in the mysteries of both the mechanical history of Italy and the other sort. Rome's earliest railway arrangements were divers. The Rome–Frascati line was opened by the Pio Latina Railway Company on the east bank of the Tiber in 1856. Over on the west bank, with at first no physical connection, there was the Rome–Civitavecchia line belonging to the Pio Centrale Railway. Both companies, with their systems thus separated, were naturally eager to please the Supreme Pontiff. Both had built, and in 1859 presented to him, sumptuous rolling stock. Let us take first the Pio Latina company, on the east bank. (The two companies were amalgamated, with the frightful 'King Bomba's' Royal Neapolitan Railway, to form the General Roman Railways Company in 1860.) As Kalla-Bishop rather nicely remarks: 'All three Roman railway companies were French-financed, together with the gasworks. The French were not occupying Rome for nothing.' The offering of Pio Latina was probably the first eight-wheel carriage ever to have been seen in Italy, for it was a large vehicle on bogies with equalised springs. It was of most ornate style. It is recorded as having cost, in terms of £ sterling at that time, £5,500, which was a lot of money for a railway carriage in 1859, when even the mighty Great Western Railway in England was making them with *papier mâché* body panels. A good allowance of that same useful material went into this new Papal carriage, though chiefly for decorative purposes.

The vehicle had to be seen to be believed. From a spacious entrance platform with three steps down, protected by the most elegant bronze gates and railings, protected by a half-length hood, there came first a vestibule and a reception room. The latter was in fact an audience chamber with a throne, of loggia type but with an enormous drop window of plate glass each side. Passage from this led on into certain private arrangements, divided closely between a reading-room, an oratory and what was delicately called a retiring-room (wherein less exalted beings have been wont to read undisturbed to this day). Over the main, middle part of the carriage, the roof was raised above the already generous arc to form a sort of elongated Gothic dome, semi-elliptical in cross-section, and decorated inside with what have been called priceless paintings and frescoes. There were in fact several circular panels on a very rich ceiling (at least one of them cut-out and stolen in the course of the years to come). In short, the carriage was decorated as magnificently as nineteenth-century piety could desire, nineteenth-century art could achieve, and nineteenth-century industrial wealth (through France) could commission.

Still inside, upholstery is recorded as having been chiefly white velvet, which sounds like an unwise choice for a steam railway whose engines burned some sort of French coal, though white upholstery was certainly favoured by certain Italian railways for superior accommodation much later than this. In his classic *Railways and Scenery*, covering the years 1888–1913, J. P. Pearson was to complain of the dirty-looking white-satin-stuff in an Italian first-class carriage.

All decoration, inside or outside, was of extremely pious sort, and was executed in sculpted wood or moulded *papier mâché*, and variously golden- or silver-gilt. Along each side, among many other things, were almost life-size pseudo-caryatid figures of Faith,

Hope and Charity, crowned and halo'd, as sculpted personifications of Cardinal Virtues ought to be.

From Pio Centrale came a pair of carriages, very beauteous, and designed for both purposes, those of travel and benediction *en route*. Both of them were four-wheelers, and were equipped on very sumptuous lines, but structurally modest compared with such sixteen-wheeled prodigies as those of the Tsar of All the Russias, the Viceroy of Egypt, and President Lincoln in the U.S.A. One of these Roman carriages contained an entirely civilised arrangement of three basic compartments, each with a pair of long windows, and opening through, one to another. Again there was the sequence of vestibule – reception-room – reading room. In a corner of the last there was a small annexe containing either a water-closet or a close-stool, and a wash-stand (in English monastic language, rere-dorter and lavatory, for example beautiful specimens at Fountains Abbey and Gloucester respectively).

The other carriage was best described as a complete loggia-on-wheels, such as Egyptian Viceroyalty was essaying about the same time, though in this case it comprised the entire (much shorter) vehicle. This, whence the Pope gave his blessing to his provincial sheep, was decidedly ornate, with filigree gates to the steps at the end, such as the most ostentatious of American business nabobs might have envied 35 or 40 years later. Open, as suggested, at the sides, its roof, heavily gilded and corniced though nearly flat, was supported on what Philistine England at that time would have called barley-sugar columns, entirely gilt. There were curtains and drapes in purple velvet with gold-lace fringes, and when, at an intermediate stop, His Holiness appeared between the two inner columns to give a general Pontifical blessing, all went down on bended knee, including the soldiers and policemen, as excellent photographic evidence shows to this day.

Two of our illustrations, Plates 34 and 35, show the ceremony at Velletri, and the train of the Pio Centrale company, though the line is that of the Pio Latina. They had been connected by bridge over the Tiber in 1863. This unique photograph has been dated variously to 1863 and 1865, so it *may* have been in 1864, but not earlier than these three years. These three carriages were officially used by Pius IX, at one time and another, until the end of 1870, when he lost the last vestiges of his temporal power. He had been born in 1792 and had been considered a singularly liberal Pope of his time. Albert Edward, Prince of Wales (who unlike some princes was a gentleman) and Princess Alexandra (indubitably a lady) visited Pio Nono in the spring of 1871. Goodness knows what Queen Victoria thought of that visit. Evidently she had been convinced that it was expedient (though she detested the word, and reproved one of her Ministers for using it). Apart from travelling Nuncii (e.g. to Dublin) there were to be no more Papal railway journeys before the middle of the next century. They had ceased by 1871.

Some notes are deserved by the locomotive portrayed in one of these interesting views. Kalla-Bishop identifies this as having been built by Grafenstaden in France (works number 121/61) and as one of the Médoc type, bearing the General Roman Railways No. 81. As to her later history, he notes that in 1865 the Roman Railways (a new undertaking) made her No. 310 with the name *Nocera*, and after 1885, under a new 'grouping' of the period, she became No. 2037, *Camillo*, of the Mediterranean System, which named its engines as inclusively as did the Great Western of England in broad-gauge days. She ended her days some time between 1907 and 1910 as Italian State Railways No. 1369, having been No. 1309 from 1905 to 1906. Original basic dimensions included 5 ft 3¾ in. driving wheels. General Roman had forty-two of the class between 1861 and 1865, all French. There was some affinity with certain engines built in London by George England about that time. Note the forward-hinged *capuchon*, acting as smoke-deflector!

At home in Great Britain, Victoria had become the Widow of Windsor, since the death of Prince Albert. She retreated and ever retreated, with the rough, strong arm of her faithful but unpleasant John Brown to lean on. Albert Edward and Alexandra had a devil of a time. Her movements seemed, save occasionally, to triangulate Windsor, Osborne, Balmoral and – when absolutely necessary – London. She even forswore use of the East Coast line from England to Scotland because memories of Albert were apt to make her weep on the railway stations before the British People. Her Great Northern saloon carriage languished, save that the Prince of Wales found it useful when compelled to quit Sandringham temporarily for Balmoral, probably to be carpeted by Mamma. One of that carriage's last assignments (it was getting antiquated by contemporary standards) was to convey a commoner, Mr Charles Dickens, from Edinburgh back to London when he was ailing towards his own mortality. The often-execrated railway companies were full of liberal generosity to deserving citizens. The South Eastern had nearly killed Dickens in the derailment near Staplehurst, and considerably dirtied the MS. of *Our Mutual Friend*, on 9 June 1865. (Ten died, and Dickens survived exactly five years.)

Albert Edward's relations with his mother had been difficult and certainly unhappy. With the death of Prince Albert, and the Prince's marriage to Alexandra, they became less unhappy – for he knew how to enjoy the life he had been given – but in many ways more difficult. Progressively, he was required to represent the Widowed Sovereign and at the same time to suffer rebuke that was sometimes public, and which at other times seemed to leak out. Even Prince Albert had suffered, while alive and loved.

The Prince visited the U.S.A. in 1860, and young as he was, he behaved himself remarkably well, even with the brasher and therefore most vociferous elements, which welcomed a chance to get at royalty. The comments are best suppressed, even after all these years, though Hardman recorded one.

A railway adventure of the Prince of Wales in India may be remarked here, though it be out of context, for it was in 1875. There had been a row with the Queen about precedence (Heir Apparent or Viceroy?). Disraeli seems to have arranged that with admirable tact, and so the Prince went. The Bombay, Baroda and Central India Railway assembled a scratch royal train from the best – but very miscellaneous – passenger carriages it could assemble. There were even mechanical discrepancies, vehicular age-groups being already somewhat mixed. The carriages became buffer-locked, and it was quite some time before the procession managed to get out of the old Churchgate Station in Bombay. The train reached Baroda, with the Gaekwar as host. When, presumably, a happy time had been enjoyed by their Highnesses, Edward and Alexandra returned to Bombay, so loaded with presents that there was no room for the expensive packages on the improvised royal train. The worst and most obsolete third-class carriages were therefore requisitioned – and what an obsolescent B.B. & C.I. third-class carriage of 1875 was like, is best imagined after a century more. Probably rats had long consumed the grease while the vehicles were cooking in the sidings. The boxes ran red-hot after a few miles, and the sumptuous gifts had to follow on later. Later still there were to be superb royal and viceregal trains in India, not to mention the Prince's own, but the Queen Empress herself never visited her Empire, nor yet her colonies. She was, as already remarked, morbid in widowhood and unhappy at sea, and the only aircraft she knew (by sight) would have been the homely free balloon.

In America, of course, the U.S.A. never had any royal trains, though south of the Isthmus both Mexico and Brazil were to furnish such rolling stock for their briefly reigning imperial heads. Of these, more later. But in later years, Canada was to furnish some magnificent ones, and even in mid-nineteenth century – and with a bloody war in progress at that – the U.S.A. managed to produce a very remarkable Presidential Car. Mr President was at that time Abraham Lincoln, with the war on his hands too. It deserves mention as (forgive us, America!) a 'quasi-royal' car, and as such needs inclusion in this terribly selective sort of record.

Really, Abe Lincoln's car was the most remarkable vehicle of its time, *as a vehicle*, for if it did not reach the heights of decorative floridity achieved by Pius IX and Ludwig II, in terms of technical advance, it was superior to anything built for Russian Tsar or Egyptian Khedive, though the latter's carriage of 1858 was comparable. An excellent half-tone illustration, with some very interesting detail of bogie suspension, was published in *Locomotive Engineering*, New York, of September 1893, which journal is worth quoting as to several details, furnished at the time by W. H. Price, then a Master Car-Builder in Atlanta, Georgia.

Early in the Civil War, Price had been a foreman under B. P. Lamason at Alexandria, Virginia, and in November 1863, the latter began work on a car for the exclusive use of the President of the United States (or, as William Hardman in England was then unkindly calling the Great Republic, the Disunited States, for war was in full blast).

At first it was intended to be an eight-wheeler, on the bogies which had already become common in America, Russia and elsewhere, but Lamason provided a double-truck arrangement, through a pivoted truss with two more pivots below, and generous springing through both laminated and rubber arrangements, to make the car a sixteen-wheeler, with body bolsters of Ambrose Ward's patents. (Such trucks were later to be used by George M. Pullman in various cars including, for a while, the *Pioneer*, the first real Pullman sleeper, in 1865.) It was anticipated in the Egyptian carriage of 1858.

The body of the Presidential Car was clothed in iron plates – an early interpretation of the 'bullet-proof car' – and was 42 ft long inside, with a clerestory roof over most of the length. Design strongly resembled that of Pennsylvania cars of the period. Inside there were three long compartments called 'drawing room, parlor and state room', the last-named being in the middle, and all were not only armoured outside but heavily quilted and handsomely trimmed inside. In the middle of the lower quarters of each side was a moulded oval containing a representation of the American white-headed eagle, clutching the national escutcheon with clouds and lightnings, while arms of the various (presumably loyal) states adorned the clerestory sides.

War being war, this magnificent iron car was an unconscionable long time a-building, but ultimately the job was done. It was painted in dark brown, or chocolate, thus presenting a sober aspect apart from American heraldry. It was ready in February 1865.

Its history thereafter was unhappy. Ere he had a chance to travel comfortably for once in a while, President Lincoln was shot dead through the back in a box at Ford's Theatre, Washington. Ah, poor man! He never knew what hit him, though the assassin jumped over the box on to the stage and escaped, to be burnt alive in a barn, with some gloomily satisfied soldiers surrounding it outside. So Lincoln made his only journey in the Presidential Car at last, for it took him, feet-first, with the remains of his predeceased son which had been dug up, from Washington to his old home-town of Springfield, Illinois. The rather frightful Mrs President was on the train, in the Pullman sleeping car *Pioneer*. One gathers that she was the first American lady to have been allowed to occupy a sleeping berth on the rail. American puritanism had imagined all sorts of incipient immorality in the earlier days of sleepers.

Great Lincoln was not royal; by his own convictions, far from it. He always meant well and may sometimes have done badly. His sculpted likeness stands in Parliament Square, London, and is seated in Washington (does a negro boy still come daily to black the statue's boots?). So far, he has been America's nearest approach to a king, and better than some real ones elsewhere. The history of his railroad car remains sad. It went later to the Union Pacific as a pay-car. Angus Sinclair of *Locomotive Engineering* wrote that it ought to go to the Smithsonian collection, but, ephemerally preserved as a sort of minor national monument in a public park, it fell ultimately a victim to a grass fire in that park (which cannot have been properly mown) so that nothing was left of it but some scorched and soon rusty iron plates and flitches, and wheels that were not original, for it was latterly on quite ordinary American equalised four-wheel trucks.

What Queen Victoria really thought of President Lincoln cannot be properly stated, even were it known. She was by nature a Tory, and so tacitly supported the Confederates in the war which had smitten America, ultimately to their disadvantage, over nearly five years. She had been intensely unpopular with British Radical elements as far back as the middle 1850s with Albert beside her, and was destined to further unpopularity, which was to rise to dangerous heights in the middle and later 1870s. The Prince of Wales was the man, in the eyes of many, and his lovely little Alexandra captivated many more, even when she had become an old lady in another war which Victoria had deemed unthinkable. A contemporary cartoon showed Her Majesty chastising the British Lion while watched by the Emperor Wilhelm I and other approving Germans, by John Brown and other approving characters in kilts, and by rather smug Mr and Mrs John Bull who didn't quite like it. The Franco-Prussian war had not happened yet, but still it was not to sway Victoria's favours when it came. Admittedly, in British thought, the French had started it. The French Emperor, Napoleon III, had a sumptuous Imperial Train from the Paris-Orleans Company, not only with proper sleeping berths but even a *conservatory of flowers*, but he was to lose it in 1871, and the Russian Emperor was to acquire it, at a bankruptcy sale, and for a while enjoy use of the carriage bodies remounted for the Russian broad gauge of 5 ft. (This was a very slight break-of-gauge; just enough to make it awkward for invading Austrians and Germans on 4 ft 8½ in.)

Napoleon III, while he lasted, was a man of grandiose ideas, though without the ability of his redoubtable uncle. He had become Emperor of the French late in 1868, adroitly by the Republican back door. To him, Empire meant all sorts of things. When Mexico became free of Spain in 1821, Napoleon I had already been interfering – as far back as 1808 – and it was through the influence of Napoleon III that the Archduke Ferdinand Maximilian of Habsburg became Emperor of Mexico in 1864. At that same time, another new arrival was the Mexican Railway, or at least 50 miles of it, inland from Vera Cruz, under British enterprise. Of course the Emperor must have an imperial saloon. In England it was built, a large four-wheeler whose aspect suggested what the North London Railway might have built had it really let itself go, with an external water-tank on the middle of the roof. The style was that of Ashbury's in Birmingham. Dynastic Empire was short. Ferdinand-Max died before a firing squad in 1867. His carriage then became a first-class saloon, looking as English as ever, with the upper-class 'I' in an oval panel on two doors each side. It lasted for many years, then was preserved in the company's station at Mexico City, still on rails in a bay. That was its undoing. It was destroyed by a piece of careless shunting in 1949.

Let us turn, more cheerfully, back to England, and to Edward and Alexandra, newly married. If there was one thing the couple needed, it was a country house and estate not too near to either the Metropolis, or Deeside, or the Isle of Wight. The Prince of Wales picked on Norfolk. There was splendid open country, also with considerable forests; nearest in all England (though one seems not to have seen this noted before) to Alexandra's Denmark, with a marked affinity in some of the scenery.

In his minority, the Prince had been forbidden all sports except riding and shooting, so in these alone was he proficient, and North Norfolk would provide. (He was forbidden, under Baron Stockmar's advice, to read fiction. Even Scott's *Waverley Novels* came under the ban. One imagines that Dickens would have been deemed 'pornographic', on account of the elopement of Mr Carker with the second Mrs Dombey, and of the equivocal relationship between Bill Sykes and Nancy. Both characters had suitably nasty ends; Carker under a locomotive!) So in the old Kingdom of the Angles he enjoyed, from time to time, his manumission. The present Sandringham House was built in 1870, but he had escaped ere that, and the Great Eastern Railway joyously backed him up within business limits. He had bought the estate just before his marriage, and that decent, though often-lampooned railway company took him down with Alexandra on 28 March 1863. One of Robert Sinclair's very admirable express engines was painted creamy-white all over – even as to the chimney – and decorated with floral swags and garlands. In the following year, the Great Eastern furnished a magnificent saloon carriage for the Prince. It was considerably better than the London and North Western one built for the Queen in 1861, and of course less 'old-fashioned' than the spacious Queen's Carriage on the Great Western.

It was a six-wheeler, generous as to body and certainly comfortable as to appointments. It followed the royal railway convention of the time in having a main saloon, an ante-room and what house-agents still call the usual offices. The first-named was just over 11 ft long, with a sofa and four generous chairs. The water-tank at one end was outside, as in Maria Pia's Portuguese carriage, and many others about that time. Much attention was paid to superior suspension. Not only were the springs very liberal; the body was supported on the underframe by twelve rubber balls resting in hemispherical cups of iron. Lighting was by oil-lamps in the common arrangement of two small/one large for saloon carriages. Decoration was rich. There was a fine ornamental frieze outside, and the door and commode handles were gilded, with ivory grips. This carriage lasted quite a long time; in the 1870s it became an eight-wheeler, mounted on two American-type equalised bogies, admittedly so close that they anticipated the very pretty toy carriages later marketed by such German firms as Märklin and Bing. It suited Bertie and Alix.

Other railways later made extra-special carriages for them ere they succeeded, notably the Great Northern, and at the end of the century the London, Brighton and South Coast Railway made an entire train of very handsome sort, which we must notice later.

It was time Victoria herself had a new carriage, and so the London and North Western, with Richard Bore still *in praesidio*, designed a pair of such, for day and night travel with internal passage through bellows, and these were ready in 1869. The Queen had now a self-sufficient apartment on wheels, which would take her from Gosport, or London, to Deeside, or vice versa, or from Dover, wherever she wished on the rail, save in the farther West of England which was still full of unmixed broad gauge. An almost identical pair was made for travel abroad, and kept in Brussels, though that came a little later.

The London and North Western carriages – later united into one – have survived to this day, and need quite liberal attention.

They began as a pair of six-wheelers, and their connection through bellows must have been the very first in Great Britain. The Queen, be it remarked, greatly disliked going through those bellows if the train were in motion, and save in some mild emergency she always waited until the train was standing at some place like Larbert, or Carlisle, or Bushbury Junction in the English Black Country near Wolverhampton where the convoy paused in transit from Great Western to North Western, or vice versa.

A note *passim*: the London and North Western guard, or conductor, of the royal train, over many years, Donald Mackenzie, was a Scotsman and a veteran of the Napoleonic Wars in so far as he had been born on the field of Waterloo during the fighting. (His incipient mother had followed his gallant father from Brussels out to the battle, and so 'had him'!) He was infinitely more tactful – and so much more liked – than John Brown.

The two new carriages were each 30 ft long, and so ultimately made, united on one frame without those bellows, a 60 ft twelve-wheeler, though that came only towards the end of their active existence. The day carriage was divided into four compartments, the main one being $14\frac{1}{2}$ ft long and containing a handsome sofa, two easy chairs, a side table, two occasional chairs and two footstools. At one end of this, towards the night carriage, was a very spacious lavatory with two wash-basins side by side – so that the Queen and her attendant princess did not have to use the same water – and a truly regal water-closet in a vast box seat, decorated in a blue pattern as to the basin with a brass valve at the bottom, as was usually the case in good houses and decent hotels of the period.

23 Royal Hungarian State Railways: royal saloon, 1896, for Emperor Francis Joseph as King of Hungary.

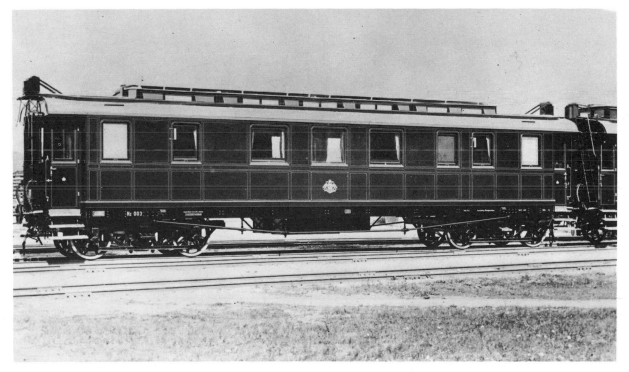

24 Austrian State Railways: Emperor Francis Joseph's living and sleeping car, 1891.

25 *left* Austrian State
Railways: Francis Joseph's
carriage, 1891. Note
Kaiser-Fauteuil.

26 *right* Heating and power
carriage for Francis Joseph's
train, 1891. Observe large
horizontal boiler.

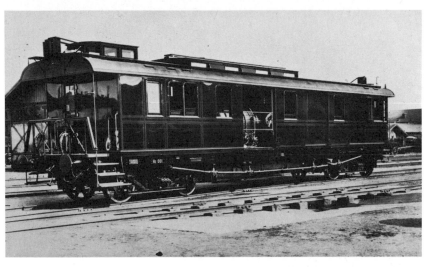

27 Envy of the German
Emperor: carriages for the
Austrian Imperial Court, 1891
and after.

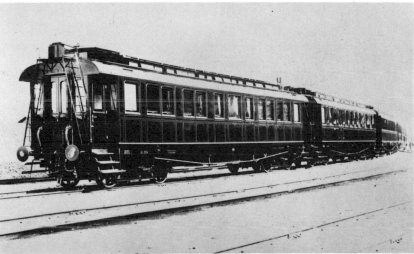

28 Sleeping car *à couchettes*, for
the imperial and royal servants,
marshalled next to the
Austrian Emperor's own
carriage.

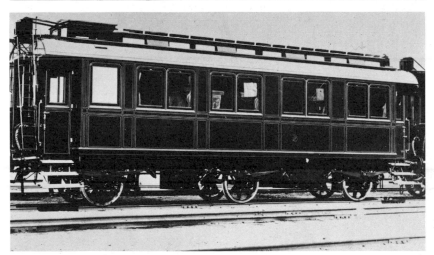

29 Austrian State Railways: Empress Elizabeth's economical quarters for writing and sleeping in the Ringhoffer saloon of 1873.

30 Reception saloon in the train of William II, last Emperor of Germany.

31 Prince Imperial's saloon, Paris–Orleans Railway, about 1860.

32 Observation car for Emperor Napoleon III, Eastern Railway of France, before 1870–1. It was later sold to Turkey, and used by the Sultan to inaugurate the main line from Constantinople to Adrianople.

33 Pio Latina Railway: bogie-carriage for Pope Pius IX, 1858.

34 *left* Pius IX's train at Velletri, Roman Railways, about 1864. The long-boiler locomotive is French.
35 *right* Velletri, Roman Railways: Pius IX gives outdoor audience.

36 Pio Centrale Railway: audience car for Pius IX.

37 Pio Centrale Railway: audience chamber in the 'loggia car', 1859.

38 Pio Centrale Railway: travelling carriage for Pius IX.

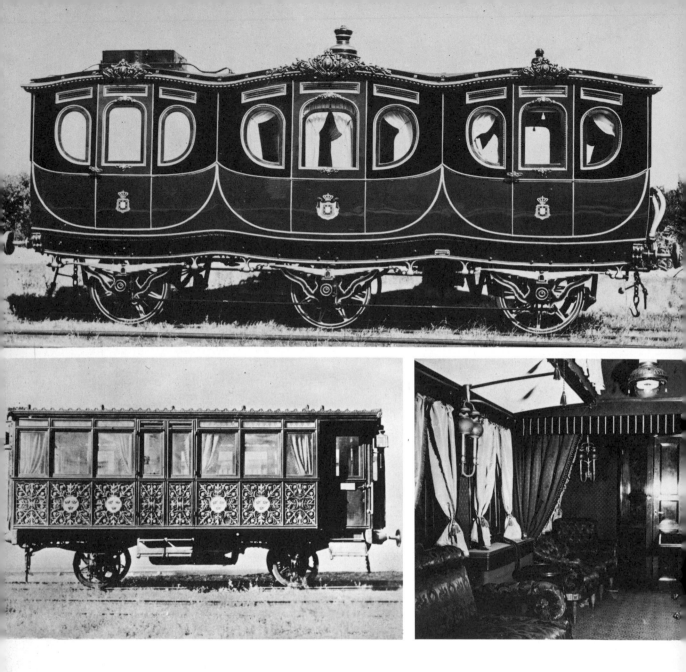

39 *above* State coach for Queen Maria Pia of Portugal, a French masterpiece of the late 1850s. Right to left are the entrance vestibule, the Queen's chamber and the lavatory, with outside access for servicing.

40 *left* Swedish State Railways: royal audience car, built in Berlin, 1874.

41 *right* Swedish State Railways: Queen Sofia's parlour, 1891.

42 Railway carriage by Alfred Stevens for King Frederick VII of Denmark, 1848.

43 Oriental Railways: saloon for Sultan Abdul-Aziz.

44 Quasi-royal: Mexican presidential car for Porfirio Diaz, built by Pullman, U.S.A. in 1898.

It was, sanitarily, an excellent arrangement if it were well built, even though in essentials it dated back to the 1770s. (Similar, though less spacious and decorative apparatus occupied the outer ends of the vehicle, for the Queen's personal servant and her dressers, respectively.) Through the bellows was the night-saloon, with two brass bedsteads; sometimes side-by-side with a space between and sometimes end-on. Next came a short vestibule with side-doors; (the day-saloon had a pair of these, and so had the servants' compartment). This vestibule opened straight into the dressers' compartment, which had four fixed sofas, two to each side. The pair of vehicles made a twin, to all intents and purposes, though with some variation as to windows. Floors were double and insulated. Sides were quilted and so were the ceilings. Lighting was variously by ordinary and large vegetable-oil lamps dropped in the usual way through roof-holes, and by sprung carriage-candles with glass bellmouth shades. There was no heating apart from the great, flat, metal 'footwarmers', containing at first water at boiling point, and later soda-acetate. These were supplied from platform vats on wheels, each having a coke stove underneath with flues passing through the water-filled heating racks. One is shown in the picture of the Caledonian royal engines at Carlisle, many years later (Colour Plate II). The train would have been pre-warmed thus, in winter, wherever the journey began (usually Windsor, Gosport or London) and fresh ones would be put in at intermediate stops such as Banbury on the Great Western, Crewe or Wigan, Carlisle and Perth. Southbound, the process was reversed. The Queen was used to cold quarters from childhood, and was most likely to complain that the place was hot and stuffy. (The palaces were often freezing.)

Through many vicissitudes, but with little improvement, this twin-carriage was used by Victoria to the last journey she was to make southwards from Scotland, before she was to die in the Isle of Wight, in 1901. It had no communication with the rest of the train except by station platform at halts, or by folding steps at some bleak place like Beattock Summit. As noted, it became ultimately a real Siamese-twin vehicle on a single frame on a pair of six-wheel bogies, with of course a continuous roof, and an artistically panelled – and to most people invisible – join, where the bellows once had been.

We shall see much more of this carriage down the years to come in this chronicle of chiefly old trains. It was very beautifully furnished and decorated in the taste of its period, which later was to be execrated, and later still deemed exquisite. Most of the coverings were in blue, white or crimson watered silk, and its external finish was superb, with all the royal and chivalrous arms adorning its white and purple-brown exterior, superbly painted by an heraldic artist, in a tradition which had gone back, in railway coachbuilding, to the finish of Queen Adelaide's carriage in 1842, and far longer in distinguished road coaches. It still can be seen, with the latter too, though both had a narrow escape many years after Victoria's death, when there was a bad works fire at Wolverton where they were preserved. The Queen was very fond of it. She would brook no replacement, and apparently no improvements which were likely to offend her eye or her habits. Of her journeys in it – or some of them – more later!

The world watched; and in some places its rulers were doing much better. The Tsar of All the Russias, unlike Victoria, was kept really warm. In such a Realm as his, for many months of the year, he had to be so!

Elevations of some of his carriages have been published from time to time, and plans as well. An elevation and section of a very large six-wheeler (a reaction from the very short bogies stemming from Winans's early influence!) built by the Moscow–Kursk Railway appeared recently in a book called *The Lore of the Train* (Tre Tryckare, Gothenburg; Allen & Unwin, London, 1971) by the present author, who cannot, however, guarantee the colours used by his gifted draughtsman, Terence Florell. Except as to the blue exterior, there was some guesswork. It seems to have been more stately than comfortable, but no doubt the beds were all right when installed. The entire body was heavily insulated against cold, and the inside walls were heavily padded, with windows few and small, as in all Russian carriages of the period. Lighting was by sprung candle-lamps (another Russian favourite, as with Queen Victoria). There was a water heater, apparently oil-fired. Lavatory arrangements were retentive, as on aircraft of today. Foul air extraction was by three immensely tall escape pipes with revolving cowls on top of the nearly flat roof. Wheels were of Richard Mansell's type with centres of hardwood segments, as in most English passenger vehicles of the mid-nineteenth century and onwards for many years. Communication with other vehicles was by gangway connections and fallplates at each end.

For many years, then and thereafter, there was a marked individuality about the Moscow–Kursk line; perhaps a remote resemblance to the Great Western in England, in that it kept itself as different as possible. Under the Tsars, Russian locomotives were frequently dark red or maroon. Later, the Soviets were to favour a rich green with red wheels, though even about 1930 there were yellow engines on the Moscow–Kursk line, recalling bygone practice on the London, Brighton and South Coast in England, and on the Netherlands Central Railway.

But old-time Germany, quite apart from the Austrian Empire, had big states, small states and petty principalities galore, ruled by several kings, one of whom was to become Emperor, as well as Grand Dukes, Prince Electors and lesser but still exalted hereditary potentates. We have noticed already that testy Majesty, King Ernest Augustus of Hanover who had a scuffle with Prince Albert. He had succeeded through the Salic Law excluding Victoria of England and, as the fifth son of George III, became the first British king (nominally at any rate) to sway a German State. He was indeed a somewhat cantankerous man. Having ordered a replica of Queen Adelaide's carriage of 1842, he not unnaturally found it somewhat inadequate with the rapid advance of coaching technology. Not that it mattered. He was much happier on a horse; he disliked railway travel, and he had certainly disliked England since that rumpus with Albert at the Royal Christening. He died late in 1851. (*What* a good thing Great Britain had not observed the Salic Law! If England had, the appalling Philip of Spain would have had England in 1558. One can think of many sorts of dynastic horrors.)

Ernest Augustus was succeeded by his son George (the Blind King) who reigned until Prussia quietly annexed his kingdom in 1866. He was to live ten years more, as Duke of Cumberland, namesake of a princely general singularly unpopular over large portions of North Britain from 1746 to this day. For the blind George V of Hanover there was furnished in 1854, from his own state workshops, a fantastic carriage on six wheels.

Compartments at each end were of elongated chariot sort, and also furnished entry. In the middle was a much elongated 'body' containing a throne room and outwardly suggesting the father-and-mother of all State coaches. These three compartments were divided by annexes of some sort, possibly containing space for necessaria and personal belongings. The carriage was about as highly decorated, externally, as anything of the sort which was to turn up until Pope Pius IX's vehicles later in the decade. Alas, poor Hanover! She had furnished a British king in an emergency, in 1715. When Prussia moved in, poor blind George ceased to be even a King.

But for long years there were to be Wittelsbach kings, or regents, in Bavaria, and more kings in Saxony and Württemberg. These, not to mention Grand Duchies such as Baden down to Principalities perhaps less than the Duchy of Atholl in Scotland, which alone in Great Britain is allowed (though not autonomous) to maintain a minuscule private army, always subject to the Queen. (Your author has known a man, an Englishman but still an hereditary German Prince, whose estates abroad supported a private army of one soldier, who apparently kept the lodge, and was allowed to have a gun for purposes of National Defence.)

The German Emperor and the Kings kept their court-trains, or at least sets of carriages, and even the lesser potentates kept their private saloons, sometimes of very handsome sort: Brunswick, Nassau, Hesse-Darmstadt, Waldeck-Pyrmont, Oldenburg (which had a very individual State Railway, all its own), Mecklenburg-Strelitz, Saxe-Weimar-Eisenach, Saxe-Coburg-Gotha and some others. There was even little Reuss which, late in the century, was to have a supposedly princely saloon which in fact was a very good side-corridor coach on six wheels, containing four 'firsts', half a 'second', a single lavatory, and entry by vestibules at each end, *D-Zug* style.

But one anticipates; there was a long way to go yet.

So there was for Victoria of All the Britons!

3
VICTORIA REGINA

Our time is now about 1870. Soon to come was the High Noon of the world's royalties, and also of the world's steam railway systems. None of the latter was yet to be challenged in their realm of heavy land transport. Nor were many of the former, apart from such things as abdications, as of Napoleon III, and an assassination or two, such as that of Alexander II who, ironically, was a singularly liberal ruler as Russian Emperors went.

For a while, however, let us make a more intimate approach to Victoria, D. G. Queen of All the Britons, Defendress of the Faith, Empress of India, first reigning monarch to order and use a real royal train in the Realm, with many other admirable qualifications. We have just seen her furnished, by her faithful London and North Western Railway, with that splendid twin-carriage, for both day and night use. It had been almost duplicated by a corresponding pair for such occasions as she wished to relax at Nice, or visit her relations and speak to Prince Bismarck in Potsdam. This pair was Belgian-built and was kept in Brussels. It could be taken anywhere in Europe except west of the Pyrenees or east of the Imperial Russian Frontier which then stretched from the top of the Gulf of Bothnia to the Black Sea, or into Greece which was to be isolated from the rest of the European system. She could go in her own personal rolling stock wherever the standard 4 ft 8½ in. gauge prevailed.

But difference in gauge brings us back to the Great Western in England, the first railway she ever had essayed. It was a long time since *all* of it had been on broad gauge. Some of it was 'narrow' (i.e. standard 4 ft 8½ in. gauge) through acquisition, or amalgamation, as of the West Midland; increasing mileage was and had been mixed (so enabling *inter alia* the through working of vehicles from Scotland to the Solent). By the middle 1870s the only unmixed broad gauge was west of Exeter and east of Falmouth and Truro.

So the Great Western company, having embarked on slow conversion in 1869 (it was not to be completed until 1892) produced a fine, new, standard-gauge Queen's Carriage in 1874. The old one on broad gauge, which had served for a quarter of a century, was packed off to Exeter to serve such journeys which Victoria might make over the purely broad-gauge South Devon and Cornwall lines. She never did so. Indeed, she liked her new Great Western carriage so well that she never again travelled on broad gauge, though for many years longer this was mixed from Paddington to Exeter, and until the late 1880s on the Windsor branch itself. It was long retained there, it is said, to console Sir Daniel Gooch who had grown up with it and always believed in it, who had first driven Victoria's engine in 1842, and latterly had been Chairman of the Great Western. The ageing, good old man lived in modest pomp at Clewer, near Bray, just upstream from Windsor, where he died in October, 1889.

The new Great Western Queen's Carriage, like its predecessor, was an eight-wheeler. It was not at first on bogies but, like many of the later broad-gauge coaches, had its wheels in semi-rigid groups of four. (That 'semi-rigid', to be sure, suggests certain gasfilled aircraft such as, in later years, the Nobile/Amundsen airship *Norge*, first over the North Pole; but here the term means that certain of the carriage axles had quite liberal sideplay.) The arrangement was not uncommon. The Metropolitan had used it since opening in 1863, and it had appeared as far afield as New South Wales at that time. W. Bridges Adams, and R. H. Burnet of the Metropolitan, had acrimonious public correspondence as to its invention.

However, to the new Queen's Carriage. It followed the general arrangement of its predecessor, though on much more sophisticated lines. Again there was the central saloon in which the Queen travelled, very handsomely furnished with the best of puritan elegance, which means opulent-but-not-gaudy. As on the London and North Western carriage of 1869, there was a large compound – one might almost call it 'multiple-unit' – oil-lamp arrangement in a big opal-glass bowl. The roof of this compartment, arched to an inside height of 8 ft 10 in., was quarter-domed at the corners of the oblong, as in the Pope's third and largest carriage on the Roman Railways. Inside height in the rest of this long carriage (by the standards of the day) was 7 ft 9 in., and original length 43 ft. The same dimensions applied laterally, for as previously, the body was slightly bulged in the middle. Comfortable compartments were furnished for equerries and ladies-in-waiting, fore and aft of this, with their own side-doors, and with their lavatories at the extreme ends, as on the London and North Western. The Queen's compartment had its own vestibule and, symmetrically arranged, the regal lavatory. The latter was designed, with artistic prudery, to resemble other arrangements, the washing equipment being within a marble-topped console-table and the w.c. enclosed, almost eighteenth-century style, within an apparent sofa. Externally, the vehicle was beautiful to look upon, with identical sequence of windows and panels from one end to the other, helped not least by the Great Western's incomparable livery, having 'tea-brown' lower quarters and mouldings, all picked out in gold, while the waist, upright and top quarters between the mouldings were in very pale cream, less yellow than in last years of the Great Western company (long after the Queen's death) but richer than the rather cold-looking 'spilt milk' of the London and North Western, which indeed had a faint admixture of blue.

These, Great Western, and London and North Western, were the two most important vehicles used on British railways by Queen Victoria during her long widowhood, and she became very fond of them, her liking being quite peremptorily expressed whenever there was any proposal to improve them, according to the advance of technology, coaching and craft. There were to be others, elsewhere; but the North Western one was invariably used for long night journeys, while the Great Western served by day in the West and South of England. It was often on the London and South Western to and from Gosport, and on the South Eastern to and from Dover. Still there were the carved and gilded lions' heads on the headstocks.

The South Eastern saloon of 1851, as noted, lasted a very long time. In 1877 the London and South Western, not infrequently used between a private station at Nine Elms and Gosport for the Isle of Wight, built a neat but stingily appointed six-wheeler, not to be improved upon until 1885. The Great Northern built a beautiful twelve-wheeler in 1889, but the Queen seldom, if ever, used it. The Prince of Wales, who had a more modest thing also from the Great Northern, came to fancy that initially intended for Victoria. He had been favoured already by the Great Eastern, and more than once by the London, Brighton and South Coast with its excellent access to the finest racecourses in the South of England.

Generally, the Queen's journeys can be fairly evenly plotted. On the negative side, as we have seen, she never went west of Exeter by train after 1873–4, and probably not for some time previously. She disliked the idea of going to Ireland, and avoided her Third Kingdom. For some reason or other, she disliked the London, Brighton and South Coast Railway. It is recorded that she had been 'publicly insulted' in Brighton; further, she had not the Prince of Wales's fondness for Epsom, Goodwood, Plumpton and some other places, while her love for the Isle of Wight was easily served by the London and South Western. For the most part, her railway journeys were on a rather complex inverted letter Y, with trimmings. From London to the Deeside for Balmoral, in North Eastern Scotland, it followed the route of her first (southbound) Anglo-Scottish railway journey, including the Trent Valley line from Stafford to Rugby through Lichfield. (This had been opened as far back as the summer of 1847, by Sir Robert Peel.) The Queen seems not to have liked Birmingham, anyway; she took great offence once when the Lord Mayor tried to introduce her to the Coroner, and remarked that it might have been the Sanitary Inspector next (cf. Lawrence Housman again.)

Between Windsor and Gosport it would be by the west curve at Slough and thence by Reading, Basingstoke, Eastleigh and Fareham. Most elaborate was the route from Gosport to Deeside (ultimate terminus, Ballater). First, the London and South Western was responsible for the Queen in her London and North Western royal train, though with its own motive power as far as Basingstoke. The Great Western took over in the South Western station, for its own was a small terminus under a typically Brunelian timber-barn roof. (Not that the South Western establishment, over many years, was a place a man might hanker for, though it had for a long time a station bar open to the platform. The Great Western men called it Blaze-'n-smoke.)

Now came a long Great Western hike, though not necessarily disagreeable save for the fact that in winter months the train was likely to be perishing-cold all the way to Scotland save for the panacea of footwarmers on the floors. Behind Great Western locomotives, the train loafed up by way of the Reading West curve, Didcot and Oxford, to Banbury, where it was by usual schedules high-tea-time, and everybody got out to enjoy this as best they might, and the train, in cold weather, received more footwarmers. Wise railway officers, seniors of whom always accompanied the train, were wont to stock up with hampers and a reasonability of bottles.

Still in charge was the Great Western company. After Banbury, a general retirement was usual among exalted and distinguished travellers. Blinds were down and all grew progressively quieter as the train, at its regulation slow trot, made its way into the Black Country.

Bushbury Junction was a bleak spot about Wolverhampton, where the Great Western joined its old enemy the London and North Western with which, in those parts, there had been pitched battle, in the not-too-distant past, for British railway companies were not averse to such over junctions and matters of disputed running-powers.

But now, while the Queen perhaps gently stirred in her brass bedstead under the hooded lamps, the Great Western engine came off, and the London and North Western engine came on. Uniformed railway staff also changed, though officers might travel far over 'foreign' mileage, and the royal servants went all the way, officially on active duty for as long as the journey lasted.

Over many years, Bushbury Junction involved the advent of that man with a singular history, the Royal Conductor, Senior Guard Donald Mackenzie. The superior rank of Conductor had been created back in 1865, jointly by Neele of the North Western, Ward of the Caledonian and Croll of the Scottish Central companies. It was bestowed on senior guards.

From Bushbury Junction, the long and now darkened caravan heaved itself onto the old Grand Junction line and trundled northwards by Stafford, Crewe and Carlisle, which last might be reached in pitchy darkness, or in early dawn, or at first sunlight, according to the time of year. There the London and North Western part of the journey was over. The Caledonian Railway took over, with new engines. They would certainly be in pairs, apart from the advance pilot engine, to go up from Beattock to the summit at the head of Annandale in Scotland. At Carlisle the black engines drew away and quietly retreated: the blue ones came on. Sooner or later the stirring Queen would call for her early-morning beverage, to be quickly supplied by John Brown, who kept the necessary equipment for what soldiers and others have long called brewing-up, in that very little cubby-hole at one uttermost end of the rolling-establishment which housed also his scullery sink and his water-closet, facing each other across the vehicle, 2 ft 8 in. long between partitions and less than 8 ft wide inside. Nobody seems to have considered this arrangement curious.

Usually at Larbert, or Greenhill, in Central Scotland, the Queen would send for her dressers and her ladies-in-waiting, so that she should look entirely respectable by the time the train reached Perth. So far, the strictest privacy had been preserved. Sightseers had been shoo'd away at Basingstoke and Banbury. All had been quiet and retired at Crewe, Wigan and Carlisle. But at Perth the train made quite a sojourn, during which it was swept, cleaned and more or less garnished while the entire party had breakfast. At first that morning feast – and many people needed it after the long rumble from Banbury on the Great Western – was served in the old boardroom of the Scottish North Eastern Railway, which became moribund as such when the Caledonian company expanded its empire. The Queen would have some finishing touches put to her *toilette*. There survives the delicate china apparatus whereon she hung her rings while she had a good wash, which the royal saloon, being without any proper means of heating water beyond the humble kettle-on-a-stove, could scarcely furnish.

Gladly the anxious officers and others in the *entourage* applied themselves to a sideboard laden with buttered eggs, devilled kidneys and bacon, veal cutlets, stuffed tomatoes, good sausages, and – this being Scotland at last – lots of lovely fish, and oceans of tea or coffee according to taste! They had to look sharp, for the Queen was often a small eater, and apt to indicate, by a small but regal gesture, that breakfast was over.

Perth, too, was the scene for a reception of the principal railway officers who, whether or not they had been on the train all night, had to be formally presented to her. Even after the Caledonian company had absorbed its northern neighbours, the Scottish Central and the Scottish North Eastern, there were three companies in occupancy at Perth, which came to possess a vast and splendid General Station; the Caledonian itself, the North British and the Highland. By the Highland it was reached with running powers south of Stanley Junction. For the North British it was simply a terminal junction, and that company had no part in the normal working of the royal train by the West Coast Route. But it was the largest railway in Scotland and its Chairman over the years 1866–82 was John Stirling of Kippendavie. He was a most remarkable man. Though a partial cripple, and defective as to eyesight, he was at once amiable and clubbable of manner, very shrewd in business whether as to land or its necessary transport, and had a brave heart in all things. In his old age, his company was smitten by the appalling Tay Bridge disaster of 1879, but though stricken, he would not die until a new Tay Bridge was on its way. A Scottish Episcopalian, he may have been a crypto-Jacobite, as his Scots enemies darkly whispered, even after all those years since 1746. But since the Queen rather sentimentally recorded in her Diaries that she was an ardent one, that should have been all right, and she graciously received him when he came to make an elegant fuss of her at Perth.

G. P. Neele, the London and North Western Superintendent, who accompanied the royal train over many years, detested Stirling. Apparently he considered that the proceedings were none of the North British company's business, and that the presence of its Chairman, whom he insisted in his *Reminiscences* on calling 'Kippen Davie', seemed presumptuous. Looking back, one fancies that there was some class jealousy in this, as well as inter-company feeling. Neele was East Anglian commercial bourgeois in origins. Stirling of Kippendavie and of Kippenross had been a laird since succeeding in boyhood, with his roots deep in the rich Links of Forth. He had promoted the Dunblane, Doune and Callander Railway in his own country; he had been one of the big men of the Scottish North Eastern, getting good terms on its acquisition by the Caledonian. So the supposition that his presence was irrelevant was erroneous.

While breakfast was being taken, and greetings were being made on the red carpet, the royal train would have its water-tanks filled up after the long night run. Until the middle 1860s, its only lavatories had been in the Queen's Carriage and in a couple of saloons. There had to be rather embarrassing 'comfort stops'. These were bad enough at intermediate stations, themselves insufficiently provided, but it was much worse when the Queen's whim decided that bed-time should coincide with the stationless Summit, above Beattock. Lytton Strachey, writing his *Queen Victoria* long years after, remarked that the royal train remained for long immune from modern conveniences, and when it drew up on some border moorland . . . the high-bred dames were obliged to descend to earth by the perilous footboard, the only pair of folding steps being reserved for Her Majesty's saloon.

Favoured companions at that time were the Duchess of Athole and Lady Augusta Bruce. The latter seems to have been a lady of splendid presence, much bigger than the little Queen. Even the discreet Mr Neele allowed himself to record that 'Mr. Christopher Johnstone, a very short, sturdy man, highly amused us by relating his struggles to "push-up" Lady Augusta Bruce into her saloon on one of these journeys.' He gave credit to Dr Jenner for urging that *all* the train should be suitably provided. (Sir William Jenner, 1815–98, was Physician to the Queen, 1861; Bart., 1868; K.C.B., 1872 after bringing the Prince of Wales through typhoid; P.R.C.P., 1881.) As we have seen, it was not until 1869 that the attendant ladies could occupy the same vehicle as the Queen.

After the breakfast reception at Perth, the character of the royal journey underwent a

Slough, G.W.R., 13.VI.1842

C. Hamilton Ellis

I *The Queen takes a train*

Our scene is the 'up' station at Slough on the morning of 13 June 1842. Persuaded at last
by Prince Albert, Queen Victoria uses the Great Western Railway to reach her capital from
Windsor. Daniel Gooch, thin as a pole under his top-hat, stands dutifully on the footplate of
his latest express engine, the *Phlegethon*. Beside the tender is one of the Queen's Equerries in
the full-dress uniform of the Grenadier Guards. Isambard Brunel, the company's great
engineer, is just saying: 'Colonel Arbuthnot! Pray don't step back too sharply!' The
company's police (inspector and two constables) stand rigidly to attention.

II *Diamond Jubilee, 1897*

The scene is Carlisle, Citadel Station at sunrise. Queen Victoria is going to Balmoral to relax after London celebrations which have been gratifying but tiring to an old lady who has reigned for sixty glorious years. The two Caledonian Railway locomotives by John McIntosh, named *Jubilee* and *Victoria*, wait to take over the royal train from the London and North Western, after its long rumble through the night. The North Western engines will have been *Greater Britain* (painted red) and *Queen Empress* (painted white), the two companies having thus achieved a sort of locomotive tricolour, Caledonian locomotives being blue anyway. Note the footwarmer-man beyond *Jubilee* !

marked change. There were no more drawn blinds. The Queen was clearly visible to her subjects, sitting close to the window on a blue watered-silk chair. The citizens of Forfar, Stonehaven and lesser places turned out to see her go by. At Ferryhill Junction, just south of Aberdeen Joint Station, where the train usually reversed, to be taken over by Great North of Scotland engines, there would be a real crowd, cheering and waving flags, for even in her years of seclusion the Queen was much more popular with the Scots, who thus saw her moving about, than with people in the South, to whom she seemed to be sulking in her mournful weeds. The Deeside people, to whom she was at once a living reality as something of a vested interest, received her joyously, and she smiled on them, instead of wearing that tired-and-cross expression which appeared even in royal portraiture.

For these, and all the British royal journeys, the most elaborate safety precautions were taken. The country's railway operations had advanced from the primitive, through time-interval working, to the block system with interlocking of signals and points and elaborate telegraphy, but still normal methods were not considered sufficient for royal progress. (As far as one has ascertained, Victoria never travelled by ordinary train, though, as noted, she had made do with an ordinary first-class carriage on her first journey south from Scotland.)

An elaborate schedule was always drawn up, and other traffic had to keep to the wall. In early days, goods trains had to be stationary on approach of the royal train while passenger trains slackened speed. Far from being relaxed with the advance of improved signalling, continuous brakes and other improvements, this rule was made more strict. A pilot engine preceded the train, 15 minutes in advance, and before that came, all facing points and crossing gates must be locked; also, all goods movements must have *ceased*. The line was under patrol throughout. During Fenian troubles in later years, lookout men were placed within sight of each other over many hundreds of miles from south to north. The train and its occupancy were strictly programmed, with a preliminary plan circulated, showing where each carriage was marshalled, and where each personage or person was to be placed. Senior officers of the railways concerned usually bedded down on either side of a first-class compartment, or on facing sofas in a saloon carriage. Sleeping cars having arrived in 1873, these were cautiously introduced to the royal trains, but they provided uneasy rest. One's frock-coat and boots might be shed, but one might need to be correctly on parade at dead of night; certainly if anything went wrong, as it sometimes did and also to be on the safe side even if it did not. G. P. Neele seems always to have been up when the train stopped, and had many encounters with John Brown who sat up with his boots on, and conveyed remarks pungently paraphrased by himself. Neele called him the Queen's 'coarse phonograph'.

Victoria was certainly aware of the elaborate precautions made on her behalf, and at one time publicly desired that the same should be done for all her subjects, a nice and pious wish which, if carried out, would have caused the entire railway system of Great Britain to grind to a halt. Using a modern expression, 'work to rule' would have been a mere picnic, by comparison.

But accidents on the railway, which could and did happen ever since the *Rocket* had run over Mr Huskisson in 1830, moved her to grief expressed in angry broadsides.

She had no idea of *how* a railway was worked; only as to how she considered it *ought* to be worked.

An annoying year was 1873. Four were killed on the Great Western and North Western joint line near Shrewsbury, through a broken axle, on 8 May. On 21 June there was a derailment on the Midland near Higham, Derbyshire, through a broken tyre, with two killed. Much worse befell on 23 August at Wigan on the London and North Western, when a night Scotch express divided and scattered its battered carriages all over the platforms. There were thirteen dead, including nobility and gentry known to the Queen, such as Sir John Anson. She became restive.

More troubles! At Retford, junction of the Great Northern and the Manchester Sheffield and Lincolnshire lines, a collision killed three on 23 August, and on 2 September a derailment on the North Eastern killed three more. Yet another three, all passengers, perished on the London and South Western on 9 September. It could scarcely have been blamed on the company, save that its carriages of the period were light and flimsy things, like many other people's. A runaway bullock had jumped a gate at Peasmarsh Crossing near Guildford, to encounter an up Portsmouth train. The engine successfully reduced the poor beast to beef which, however, was still in such substantial joints that the vehicles in rear went off into a sandbank. (The Inspecting Officer for Government recommended cowcatchers!)

The Queen arose in her wrath. W. E. Gladstone, whom she greatly disliked, was in power at that time, so she may have had some grim satisfaction when she wrote:

> *Queen Victoria to Mr. Gladstone.*
> *Balmoral,*
> *October 3rd. 1873*
>
> *The Queen must again bring most seriously & earnestly before Mr. Gladstone & the Cabinet the vy alarming and serious state of the railways. Every day almost something occurs & every body trembles for their friends & for every one's life.*
>
> *The Messenger has been (since the accident to the bridge was completely repaired) repeatedly several hours late; the post never comes in 2 days running at the same time; trains arriving in Edinburgh & London are 2–4 hours late. In short it has come to that pass that the Govt must consider what penalties and restrictions can be devised by Parlt to ensure safety to life.*
>
> *If some people were punished for manslaughter who neglect their duties – or if a Director was bound to go with the Trains we shld soon see a different state of things! There must be fewer Trains, – the speed must be lessened to enable them to be stopped easily in case of danger & they must keep their time.*
>
> *The gtest safety wd be however in having separate lines for luggage. This ought to be insisted on.*

(This is from correspondence between the Queen and the Premier, published in the *Sunday Times* in the early 1930s. The present author made the abstract for the *Railway Magazine* of September 1933, and thus far disclaims plagiarism.)

Alas, such pious wishes never could have been carried out! To make a comparison with transport conditions just over a century later, they were tantamount to requiring parallel motorways for private and coaching, and for freight traffic, with speed limits of 50 and

35 miles an hour respectively, to permitting but one aircraft to land or take off at an airport in 20 minutes, and with our present railways, to quadruple existing double track and to double all single track. But the Queen struck home truly on one point, that of punctuality. In the eyes of many people, her sympathies were strongly pro-German, and oneself remembers from one's own youth that express trains in Germany seemed rather slow compared with the British and French, but that they kept time to the second, with the exception of things like the westbound Orient Express which had been floundering about incalculable places in South-eastern Europe.

Quite some time before the Queen's interesting suggestion that a Director be bound to go with the trains – which would have necessitated an astronomical increase in seats on the companies' boards – a *Punch* cartoon had illustrated a patent railway safety buffer. On the front of a locomotive was a comfortable leather arm-chair, with a prosperous-looking man at ease in it with sherry and a cigar, and an unworried expression on his face. Long, long years later, in 1921, Lord Herbert Vane-Tempest, a director of the Cambrian Railways, was killed by a head-on collision between two of his own company's trains at Abermule, Montgomery.

As for the prosecution for manslaughter – or culpable homicide in Scotland – various poor wretches had faced that before, and were to do so thereafter.

Minor *contretemps* there were indeed on the royal trains, especially on that long, long hike from Solent to Deeside, making full demand on such General Managers as Sir William Cawkwell and Sir George Findlay of the London and North Western, and their Super-intendent G. P. Neele, and on their colleagues of the South Western, Great Western, Caledonian, and Great North of Scotland. We learn most from Neele, and truly the London and North Western people seem to have borne the brunt, though the Caledonian certainly had its troubles at one time and another.

There was the business of the electric bells, which were in the first pride of their recent invention. One can see early examples of them to this day in the surviving London and North Western Queen's Carriage; enormous things on top of boxes, like part of the works of a handsome parlour clock.

In 1868, even before the appearance of the new and luxurious twin saloons, bell communication from the Queen's to the dressers' carriage had been installed, by Martin and Varley. Martin, thick with the Press, had rather indiscreetly communicated this fact to the newspapers, which caused some departmental displeasure in advance, but he was bidden to the royal saloon at Windsor, at the start of the journey north, and graciously required to explain how the bells worked. He was Telegraph Superintendent to the L.N.W.R. and was, in Neele's words, 'in the seventh heaven'. But in the night, the thing 'conked', and there was sore trouble at Perth in the morning. Princess Louise, during the early morning, had been obliged to alight during a stop and call the dressers. Martin had been guilty of a breach of etiquette by informing the newspapers, but it put poor Mr Varley, the electrician, in a most embarrassing position. To William Cawkwell, the North Western General Manager, he tried to explain something about batteries having been overcharged. Cawkwell would accept *no* explanation. Varley's bells and batteries were cleared out of the train, not to reappear for a long time. Sir William Cawkwell, as he became, has left a photographic likeness resembling that of the more benevolent sort of druid, with a long, straight, white beard. But his wrath on this occasion seems to have been memorable. Of what sort, or temperature, of carpet Martin had to endure for his indiscretion, is outside your author's records.

Then there was the ill-advised attempt in 1884 to light the train by compressed gas. All went well on a northbound journey as far as Oxford. The Queen became aware of an unusual glare (the globes were not frosted), and she was furious. She demanded the instant removal of the new gas-lamps and their replacement with her old oil-pots, which, as the same lamp-holes were being used, was quite impossible. Neele could only suggest that the gas be turned low, while Her Majesty made do with the old candle-lamps till bed-time.

After that the oil-pots returned. They are still there in the preserved carriage, as well as some ornate electric reading lamps which miserably languished until Edward VII succeeded, and made use of them for as long as he tolerated his mother's old carriage, before being furnished with new rolling stock in 1903. A quaint thing is that the London and South Western company had provided the Queen with gas-lamps since 1887, and with electric ones in 1897; but as only day journeys were involved between London and Gosport, the chances are that she never noticed these offensive luminants. The Hampshire tunnels were not very long.

Yet the old-fashioned arrangements preferred by the Queen were far from infallible. John Brown was the invariable bearer of evil tidings in this respect, and paraphrased the Queen's complaint into a more pungent Doric. One night in particular was not comfortable on the train going north. Dutifully Mr Neele got up and out at Wigan to see that all was well, and encountered Brown on the platform. To Neele's inquiries, Brown replied angrily: 'No! The Queen says the carriage is shaking like the devil!' Neele was surprised, for he had had a smooth ride so far. There was more trouble at Perth. The oil-lamps had somehow leaked in the saloon.

Going south on the night of 17 June 1873, an appalling oversight was discovered when it was too late. The Queen wanted to read herself to sleep, and the candle-lamps were empty. There was a worried conference down on the ballast at the summit of Beattock bank. Richard Bore, the distracted carriage superintendent of the L.N.W.R., knowing the unlikelihood of carriage candles being immediately obtainable out on the bare mossy mountain suggested that, as the train was already delayed, it should run on to Carlisle and be supplied there. It is a long way, to be sure, from 'Summit' to Carlisle. John Brown said flatly: 'The Queen says the train shanna stir a fut till the lamps are put in,' and, noted Neele, *it had to be done*. One can only surmise, though it be not recorded, that a special stop was made at the bottom of the long hill, where Beattock Station had an omnibus service to Moffat and, one supposes, some supplies necessary for that homely conveyance.

Then there were *smells*, even in years which had seen much improvement in sanitation. On the train they could come from various sources, but usually two; a hot bearing or box on engine or vehicle, or from *something nasty in the carriage*. The former was no joke, indeed. A burning axlebox in its way anticipated the stench of badly-managed diesels in our time, yet the Queen seems not to have noticed it on the night of 24 August 1890, even though it was most unfortunately under her night saloon. The motion of the train, of course, put her to windward, and when the train stopped it was dealt with as quickly and silently as possible while the Queen, it was hoped, slept.

In the morning of 30 August, 1892, after breakfast at Perth on a journey from Gosport to Balmoral, one of the engines was the offender, on the Caledonian. Neele recorded:

> For some time prior to our stoppage we had detected the pungent smell of hot oil . . . at Forfar the train pulled up. 'The Queen wants to know: *What gars this stink?*' is John Brown's remark as we pass along the platform by the side of the Queen's saloon. It was certainly a most offensive smell. The locomotive was detached and we travelled with one engine the rest of our way to Ferry Hill.

Though the ferocious Dugald Drummond was already gone from the Caledonian company's Locomotive Department, no doubt there was a very bad time, under his successor John Lambie, for some people.

Not only the Queen expostulated about such things. On 17 November 1892, the Ladies of the Household complained that they had not enough sleeping berths to go round on a southward journey. C. A. Park, who had long succeeded old Dick Bore as Carriage Superintendent, promised that all would be well when they reached Perth.

But the girls were evidently irritated, perhaps with cause; for Neele recorded of this journey:

> At Carlisle the complaint from the ladies broke out again – one of them complaining of a 'deadly smell' in the vehicle. Dr. Reid left our friendly little supper table in the refreshment room and undertook to act as Inspector of Nuisances.

One has found no further record, but it may have been a dead mouse, judging by the lady's definition. Mice were apt to explore seldom-used railway carriages, such as special and family saloons, after crumbs, and then to die of starvation while holed up behind panelling or upholstery. From personal experience, one small mouse could make temporarily intolerable a fair-sized room in a fine seventeenth-century house, when it died in a cupboard. One's dog flushed a live one in a third-class carriage of British Railways' Southern Region, as recently as 1950.

Mice or no mice, 'smells' on the royal and other trains were often caused by what Victorians delicately called 'bad drains'. One would have thought that a train, with neither sewer nor cess, would have escaped. But at that time, and often for long after, the chutes under the water-closets were far too short, and often very carelessly arranged. On the rebuilt 1869 royal saloon of the London and North Western they remain like bent iron spouts turned inwards, with no regard for track water-troughs, and little for equipment set at a lower level. Those at the ends, for servants, dressers and ladies-in-waiting, were above the bogie frames. This was a common fault on many old express trains. Supposed unmentionability often entailed neglect of these things. Sir Edwin Chadwick had gone for the municipal and domestic sanitation of those days, but he let the trains go by.

We are not yet done with these purple-brown passages. The Queen had lost her beloved

Albert through such things – or neglect of them – and she nearly lost Albert Edward of Wales through the same visitation, typhoid, contracted at the most respectable house of Londesborough Lodge, late in 1871.

In 1890 the Queen and her party, for the first time, had breakfast in the new and magnificent Station Hotel at Perth, instead of in what had been the Scottish North Eastern boardroom and its committee rooms. The train was run into the 'east platform'. The now ageing Queen had complained about the stairs, and so she was able to move to the breakfast table 'on the flat'. There were probably sighs of relief also from the more elderly members of her *entourage*. But on the return journey southwards, on 29 November, there was a sad bother.

It seems impossible that anything should have been wrong with this new hotel set up so auspiciously by a joint consortium of powerful railway companies. The city's water supply had been a model ever since the building of Adam Anderson's beautiful Regency Classical Water House early in the century. But that autumn there were dark rumours of an outbreak of typhoid there. Possibly infection had been brought by a carrier, as by passengers on air-liners in our own time. However it may have been, the hotel was quarantined against the Queen. For the railway journey south, from Ballater to Windsor on 29 November, instructions required that the train be halted at Perth 'for dinner in the carriages', and that only 40 minutes would be allowed instead of the usual 55 minutes. (Service was, in fact, to be accomplished in 48 minutes.)

Sir Henry Ponsonby, as usual over many years, was responsible for arrangements on the Queen's side. G. P. Neele, trying to speak to him about this new scare, got through to Balmoral on the strange, new telephone but met with an obstacle other than electrical. The intelligent head switchboard girl (probably the only one) complained to Ponsonby: 'I cannot understand him. He speaks English.' Be it remembered that while Neele's speech was somewhat East Anglian, the poor girl's was possibly very academic English indeed, taught by a Gaelic-speaking dominie to her Gaelic-speaking self. (John Brown's, be it noted, was rather a rough sort of Lowland Scots with, perhaps, a broad seasoning of Buchan.) Victoria, who picked up some oddments of Gaelic because she loved the country, would have understood. The reference in Neele is further interesting in recording that from the very beginning of such things, the telephone switchboard was a girl's preserve. Even a long-ago engraving in the *Engineer* shows the girls sitting up, most respectably in their bustles at their switchboards; some of them wearing *pince-nez* like equally respectable schoolteachers.

The railway up Deeside never penetrated beyond Ballater, though Braemar – and even Tomintoul and Speyside – were mentioned at one time and another, as the Great North of Scotland Railway cast longing eyes at a potential independent route to Inverness; if only to spite the Highland Railway, for such a line could not have been very remunerative.

The Prince of Wales could not bear John Brown, and he had some reason, for the Queen had a habit of sending Brown to *summon* the Prince, and we have noticed already something of his style in paraphrase. Housman's dramatics should not be discounted; his integrity was undoubted, however embarrassing, and King Edward VIII, soon after his accession in 1936, 'gave him the green light' in his old age. One of the many small acts described just such a domestic difference at Balmoral, at the end of which the Prince said that since Mamma and he could not agree, he had better cut short his stay at once. On his withdrawal, the Queen sent Brown (who had been listening out of sight behind the Queen's garden pavilion) to order that *no* carriages were to leave the royal stables until she gave permission. But as Housman remarked, Albert Edward had a mind of his own. He sent a runner to call the station fly (a 'hired conveyance') and H.R.H. took the night train for the South, a procedure which H.M. afterwards described as 'most extraordinarily improper'.

John Brown was ultimately gathered to his fathers, as even faithful servants must be, and was succeeded by his understudy whom Neele usually, punctiliously, referred to as 'the Munshi'. His name was Abdul Karim. He claimed to be the son of a surgeon-general in the Indian Army, though in fact the father seems rather to have been a quite ordinary Indian apothecary. His title meant 'the Teacher' and for some years the Queen seems to have regarded him as a sort of *guru*, or holy man. He had an *entourage* of his own. To those who murmured, foremost among whom, as might have been expected, was the Prince of Wales, the Queen uttered bitter condemnation of what she regarded simply as racial prejudice. *She* was Empress of India!

When it came to attending the royal train, Abdul Karim intimated that his own personal attendants, being of varying caste, would need three separate compartments. Already he was making himself quite as unpopular as Brown had been in his prime, with equally protocol-ridden railway officers and servants. They had become at least accustomed to the rude Scotsman. With this haughty Indian, it was another matter. They made a compromise on two compartments instead of three. There was more fuss when the Munshi requested and required suitable accommodation for his family. Worried railway officers from Gosport to Ballater were preparing for the commanded provision of a sort of mobile *seraglio* when it transpired that the virtuous but arrogant man (an Oriental in his own country, if he be anybody particular, must be assertive or else despised) merely needed decent night-lodging on the train for his wife and one dusky, smiling daughter. With sighs of relief the officers of several railway companies decided that in spite of differences, this dark gentleman would do, for as long as he properly looked after the old and sometimes difficult Queen.

Enough has been remarked already to show that Victoria detested any changes in her personal comfort which were not absolutely necessary, and that if that were so, it had to be imperceptible to her, unlike those gas-lamps at Oxford! The Great Western Railway quietly put its Queen's Carriage of 1874 on to the shorter sort of Dean bogie, with pendulum-link suspension. The London and North Western made various applications of Webb's radial trucks under the twin-saloon, which itself suffered an awkward accident in June 1881. The London and North Western Railway at that time was messing about with mechanical – as opposed to powered – forms of continuous braking, thanks to its Chief Mechanical Engineer, Francis Webb. On the way down to Gosport with the as yet empty royal train, and probably through snatch in Webb's awful chain-brake, the permanent coupling between the twin saloons was broken, and the bellows between the two bodies were pulled out like a concertina at a rather drunken village party. However, things were patched up and a successful departure was made from the Clarence Victualling Yard. Such *contretemps* were possible, though otherwise absent as far as one knows, until the Queen's Diamond Jubilee year of 1897, when at last the two old 1869 bodies were put on to one twelve-wheeled frame with the North Western's incomparable bogies, and there were no longer any bellows to be pulled out.

Still Her Majesty wished for no really new carriages. The London and South Western company, whose royal equipment was quite archaic even when one allowed for the six-wheeler of 1877, built two very handsome eight-wheeled double saloons on American-type equalized bogies, in 1885. Each had two long compartments, sumptuously furnished in overstuffed, bobble-draped style, with two full-width lavatories and a reasonably spacious servants' compartment. The South Western company was not above using them for other purposes. Both of them, plus the six-wheeler of 1877, formed the decorated inaugural train to and from Launceston, Cornwall, on 21 July 1886, when the Queen certainly was absent.

But in the following year she celebrated, with great pomp, her Golden Jubilee. It was the first time since her widowhood that she had really come out into the open air of her kingdom, or so people thought in England.

The South Western celebrated by putting a very large clerestory on top of one of these carriages, with pendant gas-lamps. Ten years later, it was the other one's turn. This received a flattened semi-ellipse to its new roof, and electric lighting, as previously noted, and bellows at one end for connection to a kitchen car. Neither vehicle is much associated with the Queen, though they lasted for many years and were to be seen on the reception of foreign royalties at the South Railway Jetty in Portsmouth Dockyard precincts. The older one is shown in Colour Plate III, leading in a train ordered for Alphonso of Spain who came courting Princess Ena in 1907. Its rather altered twin-sister would be the third vehicle, adjacent to the kitchen-brake. These, and the older six-wheeler, vanished during the 1930s. No more royal rolling stock was ever built by the London and South Western.

A very remarkable royal vehicle was built, however, by Cravens of Sheffield, in 1883. It was designed by Thomas Parker of the Manchester, Sheffield and Lincolnshire Railway (he receiving a handsome gratuity for the job); it was officially allotted to the South Eastern Railway, and it was sent immediately to Calais on the Northern Railway of France for the service of British Royalty abroad. It was intended for, and frequently used by, the Prince of Wales, for the Queen already had that Continental version of the London and North Western twins. Its curious origins were due to the overlordship of Sir Edward Watkin. He was, at that time, in control of both the Manchester, Sheffield and Lincolnshire, and of the South Eastern Railways; in his way as powerful as Sir Richard Moon of the London and North Western from 1861 to 1891, and in retrospect – though they differed considerably in character – as unpleasant. Railway etiquette – also in its way – was as strict as that of the Court. It would have been most improper for one railway company actually to *build* a carriage for another; hence custom being given to Cravens and a fee to Mr Parker. (A decade before, the London and North Western Railway had been in legal hot water on account of having built locomotives for its allied and indigent neighbour, the Lancashire and Yorkshire Railway.)

It was a splendid vehicle on two six-wheel bogies, 58 ft long, 8 ft 6 in. wide and 12 ft 6 in. to the top of its clerestory roof which rose, oblong, from half-domes, in the lower deck, at each end. It was arranged rather ship-fashion, with four main compartments whereof the principal one was 11 ft 10 in. long, three lavatories, and quarters for someone who would not have been John Brown for as long Albert Edward used it. Lighting was by both pot-lamps in the roof and more civilised ship's lamps (kerosene) in gimballs at the sides. (Electric lamps also were later added.) This carriage, which eventually passed to Southern Railway ownership, lasted until 1929, though latterly it was not much used. Later, as we shall see, it was involved in an attempted assassination.

Such indeed befell even on the most respectable Great Western Railway in its station at Windsor, by Roderick Maclean on 2 March 1882, after the Queen had quitted the G.W.R. royal train and entered the carriage to drive to the castle. An illustrated-newspaper cutting of the period showed Maclean being hurried away in a police vehicle, with sturdy Oppidans of Eton running alongside, trying to lynch him. McGonagall, that lovable world's-worst poet, committed the event to deathless verse. Who could have foreseen that one of the world's most disastrous assassinations, historically, that of Francis Ferdinand at Sarajevo in the summer of 1914, was to involve a motor car? There had been four previous attempts on Victoria, starting in 1840.

Another beautiful twelve-wheeled royal saloon was built by Cravens, this time for the Great Northern Railway, in 1889. One has seen it described as a 'Queen's Saloon', but here again it seems to have been appropriated chiefly to the use of the Prince of Wales, who had an official, but distinctly inferior, one already. It lasted for very many years, and when the London and North Eastern Railway had been formed in 1923, it was allotted after a while to the Southern Scottish Area (the old North British Railway) as an officers' saloon. One has seen it being trundled over the Forth Bridge behind a tank-engine in the 1920s, and last saw it, still in such service, in a corner of Edinburgh Waverley Station, about 1960. It ended its days in Galloway, minus its wheels, as a place of worship for a minority congregation. A quaint destiny, perhaps, for a vehicle which in its time had not only conveyed but pleased a Very Exalted Personage who was at once sporting, uxorious, a colossal trencherman and a smoker of tremendous cigars! So was Edward VII, as he would become!

For Albert Edward, already elderly but still in his dynastic minority, the London, Brighton and South Coast Railway built a complete and very beautiful train in 1897, his mother's Diamond Jubilee Year. The Great Western simultaneously built one for her too, all new except for the Queen's Carriage with which she would on no account part. These two trains made a dead-heat in being the first complete, indivisible rakes (the American word is 'consist') to be built for the exclusive use of British royal personages and their guests. Even the Queen's vast caravan on the London and North Western, while based on the famous twin-saloons, was made up from a mixed collection of sleepers, saloons, coaches and vans, the best available at the time and presenting a somewhat up-and-down appearance in consequence.

Let us take the Brighton train first. Attention to the Great Western one can be deferred until we come to the events of the Diamond Jubilee. R. J. Billinton of the L.B. & S.C.R.

was an old Midland man, and people were not surprised when his new royal train of five vehicles, beautifully symmetrical, presented on top a uniform line of deeply arched clerestory roofs, the first on that railway apart from Royal Mail sorting carriages and Pullman cars (which last were prefabricated in the U.S.A. in classic-American style). At each end of the train were 'brake-firsts', each consisting of a long van section, with liberal ducket-lookouts at the outer ends, and two very liberal first-class compartments with a pair of lavatories between. (The Brighton company made unusually comfortable first-class carriages, even though its suburban and country third-class was something of a reproach to it.) Then, moving towards the middle, came two double saloon carriages. All these, and the Prince's saloon also, were 52 ft long and 13 ft 1 in. high, but the latter was 8 ft 9 in. wide, on two $11\frac{1}{2}$ ft six-wheel bogies, whereas the others were only 8 ft wide, and mounted on four-wheel bogies.

There was no corridor through the train, and that omission was no fault of the Brighton company. The Prince, on being consulted as to the design of his new train, had indicated that while travelling, at least, he wanted to be left alone. Lighting was electric, from generating equipment in one of the vans (a common Brighton practice at that time). Furnishing was opulent, in Pall Mall rather than Osborne or Balmoral style. Again one can sympathise. The window glasses were elegantly etched round the edges. The clerestories to the roofs were coved inside, American-fashion. The Pullman company called that the 'Empire roof' though with what reason one knows not. Victoria, Empress of India, never sat under it; nor did the unfortunate Napoleon III of the French; nor did far-eastern Sons of Heaven, as far as one is aware.

Though its earlier journeys were chiefly concerned with sporting events in the South of England, this lovely train, all in varnished and gold-lined mahogany, was to serve on many other distinguished occasions down to the 1920s. The London, Brighton and South Coast company, to the very last in 1923, mounted splendid arms in full blaze of heraldic colours, on the front of its royal trains.

You shall hear more of this train later. For the present, let a few more Victorian royal journeys be considered, including one which was – though people did not know it – to be sadly inauspicious. The latter part of the nineteenth century saw the closing of several water-gaps in the existing railway system by construction of great and splendid bridges. Tyne, Tweed, Tamar and Menai had been thus dealt with in the 1850s. There remained Tay and Forth in Scotland, subject to bleak ferries as alternatives to rather circuitous through services by railway. The Forth ferry, to be sure, had been the first train ferry in the world, devised by Thomas Bouch, but in normal traffic it took only goods vehicles while the passengers shivered and lost their breakfasts.

To Bouch also was entrusted the first Tay Bridge, under the North British chairmanship of our old friend Stirling of Kippendavie. It was ready in 1878; a long, slim, single-track structure from Wormit in Fife to Dundee Esplanade, so narrow that, except in the high girders over the fairway, the train seemed to be miraculously rumbling on nothing over nearly two miles of menacing-looking estuary.

Menacing indeed, though the trouble was fated to come not from the sea but from over the mountains!

On 1 June 1878 the first Tay Bridge was opened. On 20 June 1879 the Queen, returning from Balmoral, had the royal train diverted over the North British Railway, south of Kinnaber Junction, via Montrose and Arbroath to Dundee, so that she could see the new prodigy. At Dundee, Tay Bridge Station, she did not get out, but enthroned on the now familiar blue watered-silk chair she received the Provost of Dundee, Thomas Bouch, who had designed the bridge, and the North British Chairman Kippendavie whose afflicted frame was at last filled with his cup of joy as he presented the others. The Queen congratulated Bouch and bade him join the train for Windsor, where he knew what was coming. With rich yellow North British motive power unusually heading the white North Western train, she was carried slowly over the bridge. Down in the firth, the training ship *Mars* fired a royal salute. The train then went via the Devon Valley and the Stirling and Dumfermline lines to rejoin the Caledonian main line. It made its usual dignified rumble southwards through the night. In Windsor Castle next day, Bouch bent his knee, received the Royal Accolade, and rose a knight.

On the afternoon and evening of 28 December 1879 came that ferocious storm from over the great hills, buffeting the ancient capital city of Perth, roaring on, down to Dundee and the ocean, with unroofed houses, fallen chimneys, dispersed hayricks, and damaged persons and beasts in its wake. It struck the bridge in a tremendous gust just after seven o'clock while the evening mail train was even in the central high girders. The bridge broke. It fell. All were lost.

It was a national disaster, and was treated as such. When all inquiries were over, the broken Bouch retired to a small house at Moffatt, where he faced his end.

What Victoria had to say is not, to our knowledge, recorded. This was far, far worse than those railway misfortunes of 1873 which had directed her grievous ire against Mr Gladstone and his administration for their supposed indifference to such things.

As remarked before, it was Stirling of Kippendavie who, sickening to his last, waited to see through the building of a new, and much more substantial, Tay Bridge. It was under him that contracts for a suspension bridge over the Forth, also designed by Bouch, were expensively cancelled, and new plans authorised and drawn up.

There was less regal enthusiasm for the new Tay Bridge. The Queen had been horribly shocked by the accident. But the New Tay Viaduct Act received the Royal Assent in July 1881. W. H. Barlow, who had been on the Board of Three inquiring into the accident, and his son Crawford, were designers of the new bridge, which was to be on double track and of very robust sort, a little way upstream from the stumps of Bouch's bridge, which had been finally demolished down to those. Needless to say, there were different contractors, the original ones having disimproved Bouch's faulty design by abominably bad work. The new Tay Bridge was opened for passenger traffic on 20 June 1887. The Queen had gone south on June 16 and did not return to Balmoral until August.

The great Forth Bridge by Fowler and Baker, not so long but far more stupendous, was finished in 1890. It was the biggest bridge in the world. Each of its main spans, at 1,710 ft between cantilever towers, was 115 ft longer than the single suspended span of the Roebling bridge across the East River between Manhattan and Brooklyn (1883).

The Forth Bridge was owned by a joint Forth Bridge Railway Company, sponsored by the North British, North Eastern, Great Northern and Midland, all of which would greatly benefit by it. In a howling gale on 4 March 1890, a royal train steamed onto the bridge, headed by North British locomotive No. 602, which had been built in 1886, and, by virtue of this occasion, became for some years the N.B. company's royal engine. She was driven (doubtless under guidance) by the Marchioness of Tweeddale, wife of the Company's Chairman. On the train was Albert Edward, Prince of Wales, in all his stately port, attired in a long ulster (for, indeed, the weather was quite abominable) and a tall silk hat which somehow stayed on amid the tempest. Guided by a character generally named Cork George by reason of his artificial leg, the Prince alighted and ceremoniously drove the last rivet. Everybody cheered against the wild wind and rains, then gratefully got back into the train, which proceeded north. Queen Victoria afterwards made Sir John Fowler, senior designer, a baronet; his partner Benjamin Baker and the contractor William Arrol became knights, and a baronetcy was conferred on Sir Matthew Thompson, Chairman of the Forth Bridge Railway Company.

Cork George was to live on, and look after the bridge at least until 1923. To this day one can see an iron cottage, high up among the girders. N.B.R. engine No. 602 was thereafter adorned as to the driving-wheel splashers with the Prince's insignia of the Bohemian Three Feathers earned by the Black Prince at Crecy in 1346. Your author encountered the old engine at Riccarton Junction in 1926. She had served well.

On 19 June 1891 the southbound royal train from Ballater was diverted so that Victoria could see, slowly and at close quarters, both the new Tay Bridge and the Forth Bridge, 15 minutes being allowed to each, with stops thereon. The North British at that time had no General Manager. John Walker had died suddenly at the South Western's Waterloo Station in London. Neele noted:

> I had the pleasure of travelling with Lord Tweeddale and Lord Elgin and we had a very sympathetic chat as to the loss they had sustained . . . and they very openly discussed with me the qualities of two or three of the names of officers they had under consideration as his sucessor.

Good old *Premier Line*, with all its pretensions! The North British never had been its ally, far from it! But the N.B. thus sought consultation with the Superintendent of its old enemy at Euston. The L.N.W.R. had long been a very businesslike undertaking, and wise in the ways of commerce. The thirty years' command of the stern and upright Sir Richard Moon, who *was* the North Western, left their mark, and for many years longer. Lord Stalbridge, who was to become Chairman, seems to have been a much more human character than Moon. For one thing, he once said publicly that he had loved trains for their own sake since boyhood, and that in presiding over this magnificent railway company he had fulfilled his most glorious dreams.

Back to G. P. Neele. Early in the morning of 21 May 1894, he was northbound with the royal train at Carlisle. The Queen had visited the new Manchester Ship Canal, and did not turn in until 12.37 a.m., while the patient Neele patrolled the draughty platform, for the train must not move until after the Queen had passed through the bellows. He had taken cold badly, and was in great pain by the time Perth was reached. At Bridge of Dun he had to quit, handing over to C. A. Park, the Carriage Superintendent, and telling John Brown who was up, as usual, whatever the hour. It was five in the morning, with three hours to wait for the first southbound train. Stationmaster Mann, a kind old man, locally famous as a bone-setter, looked after him. Neele had been a railwayman since 1847 and was still tough. He recovered, cheered by a sympathetic telegram from Balmoral.

It was soon after this that the twin saloons were at last united as a long twelve-wheeler, and the detested bellows vanished.

On 21 June 1895, G. P. Neele made his hundred-and-twelfth, and last, journey with the Queen; a southbound one. At Ballater, Prince Henry of Battenburg conducted him, before starting, to the Royal Saloon, and formally introduced him to the Queen:

> Her reception set me at once at ease. Looking at me with her full blue eyes she said she was sorry that this was the last time I should accompany the train: that I had travelled many times in charge of it; that I had also on many occasions taken care of members of her family, and that she would wish me to have some record of them; turning to a large framed engraving – which stood raised up in the carriage – she added that she would like me to have that representation of them. I thanked Her Majesty and told her that I had only done my duty, but that it had ever been a most pleasurable duty. She accorded me a most pleasing smile and said she would shortly send me some further souvenir. Princess Beatrice was in the saloon as well as Prince Henry of Battenberg. This unexpected interview thus came to an end – the Directors and officers of the Great North [of Scotland] wondering what could give rise to the delay in obtaining the usual signal to start.

The engraving was after Tuxon's group showing the entire Royal Family at Windsor, at the time of the Golden Jubilee of 1887. Neele was glad to have it, a signed artist's proof, but he found the signature 'L. Tuxon' insufficient to his liking. Sir Fleetwood Edwards obligingly took it back to the Queen, a little later, and she gladly wrote on it:

Presented to G. P. NEELE, ESQ.,

BY VICTORIA, R.I., 1895

The 'souvenir' came soon after: a rich and massive silver tray, boldly engraved with the names of recipient and donor. The Royal Household presented a silver Monteith bowl, again suitably inscribed, and bearing thirty-five names, headed by those of the Countess of Antrim and the Duchess of Atholl. They did not include that of John Brown, but that of the Munshi Abdul Karim was there, just after that of the Queen's doctor, Sir William Jenner.

So the good old Superintendent retired happy. Like all truly senior railwaymen, he received *The Clock* on retirement.

The year 1897 saw the Queen's Diamond Jubilee. She had reigned for as long as George III, and on the whole very much more successfully. He had lost the first British Empire, or most of it, and she had gained the second. Also, after long middle years of unpopularity through public indifference and impatience with what seemed morbid widowhood, the once young and fecund Faerie Queen had emerged again as a Royal Grandmother, respected and loved by many.

The British railway companies, as far as lay in their power, reacted joyously to this Jubilee. Only the Great Western, however, was able to do anything particular. It was the first railway Victoria had ever known, and deserved its privilege. It produced, as previously noted, an almost completely new royal train. The qualification must be made because the Queen flatly refused any visible interference with her own quarters. The invisible parts, however, could be managed. The Queen's Carriage of 1874 was lengthened at each end. It was mounted on a new frame, with much longer bogies (10 ft wheelbase) and the length over body increased to 54 ft. Opportunity was taken to provide double doors to the Queen's vestibule. At each end (though not for the use of the Queen) were bellows, giving through passage to the rest of the now sumptuous train for the *entourage*. The new vehicles, all electrically lit, were of the clerestoried type favoured by William Dean and his carriage man James Holden since the early 1870s for the best Great Western stock. (Holden, incidentally, had lately gone to the Great Eastern at Stratford, but his styles in coachbuilding lasted on the G.W.R. into the early 1900s. The entire rake formed the first royal corridor train in Great Britain, though the principle had appeared, with intermediate gangways between vehicles, on both the Great Western and the Great Eastern in 1891. Apart from the rejuvenated 'Queen's', the vehicles were five. There were two brake vans with limited passenger arrangements, two corridor saloons and one corridor coach, the latter having what the Great Western company called a 'semi-saloon' (equivalent to two compartments with a central gangway) and five ordinary compartments with end lavatory; all, needless to say, of first-class sort. This carriage was specially requested for the benefit of distinguished Eastern visitors who expected exclusive quarters. Some years after the Great Western royal train had served its time, and had been discarded, your author encountered what seemed to be this carriage on an up South Wales express: Swindon to Paddington in the middle 1940s. Official explanation told that it was a duplicate. All these vehicles had half-domed ends to the clerestories, contrary to the usual Great Western practice at the time, as had a few other saloons including the official Directors' one (which fortunately survives on the Dart Valley Railway in South Devon).

Certainly, it was a lovely train to look upon! The majestic aspect of all Great Western express engines, from first to last, gave its progress noble port. So it was ready for the Queen's Diamond Jubilee celebrations in London, and took her up to her Capital for these. Not only the locomotive, but also the tender, mounted massive castings of the Royal Arms, each side, in correctly splendid heraldic colours. Further, a large Royal Standard was hoisted on a jackstaff at the very front. This arrived at Paddington somewhat worse for wear, but its tatters are lovingly preserved to this day like ancient standards and colours in the Chapels Royal.

As yet the London and North Western Railway was not allowed to build a new royal train, though C. A. Park had long had his ideas on the subject, ultimately to be carried out for King Edward. Victoria's twin-carriages were, as noted, united on a twelve-wheeled frame which must, from memories of London and North Western twelve-wheel carriages, have made it very comfortable indeed without disturbing the Queen's furniture and other domestic arrangements, except for the better.

Metropolitan festivities notwithstanding, nothing could keep the Queen for long from her beloved Highlands, and off to them she went, with a sigh of relief, as so often before. Good Mr Neele was gone. Rough John Brown was gone, but there were still the London and North Western, Caledonian and Great North of Scotland Railways to carry her, and the silently omnipresent Munshi to attend her. Princess Beatrice, as she knew already, would have her mattress put on the floor beside the Queen's bed to be closer if she was not well.

Now the London and North Western Railway, unlike some others, did not elaborately decorate the royal locomotives with heraldic achievements in painted cast-iron, waving flags and festoons of bunting. Its business with the Queen was usually at night anyway, and the North Western was a pragmatical company. Nevertheless, when it came to the Diamond Jubilee year and the journey northwards, it made a show. There were two fairly new, and very magnificent compound locomotives by Francis Webb, the company's autocratic locomotive engineer, named *Greater Britain* and *Queen Empress*. The latter had already been to the U.S.A. and back in 1893, for the first of the World Expositions at Chicago, and while in America had worked her way back from Chicago to New York by the Water-level Route hauling two London and North Western carriages, a sleeper and a coach, as well as some truly American Wagner sleepers. (Wagner was a rival of G. M. Pullman, and they quarrelled over their business, patents and contracts. Wagner was fated to be killed in one of his own cars on the New York Central.)

To take the Queen to Scotland in her Diamond Jubilee Summer, the strict old L.N.W.R. – even through the person of its coldly austere Chief Mechanical Engineer, Francis Webb, unbent. London and North Western locomotives, since the beginning of the 1870s, had been painted in what somebody called, very happily, 'blackberry black' with a discreetly rich lining-out. Now from Crewe issued forth *Great Britain* in bright scarlet ('Post Office red' was specified) and *Queen Empress* was painted white. Borders indeed were variously lavender and purple and there were some gilt lines as well as other picking-out. This meant that from London to Crewe the Queen had what was then a giant engine painted red, from Crewe to Carlisle a sister-engine painted white, and from Carlisle to Ferry Hill Junction, Aberdeen, the engines would be blue, Caledonian locomotives being so anyway. (Great North of Scotland engines were then a fine rich green. Is it possible that a railway in so Protestant a quarter of Scotland, not so very far from where Archbishop Beaton had been assassinated, tacitly represented Ireland? Of course not! My picture (Colour Plate II) is an endeavour to recapture the scene at Carlisle, at first sunlight of a Border morning. There stand the Caledonian's royal engines of John McIntosh's first Dunalastair class, *Jubilee* and *Victoria*. Ahead of them, out of the picture, is the company's single-driver No. 123, of 1886, which has survived and which for many years was the pilot engine to the royal train north of Carlisle. Incidental to the picture are the mixed gas-globes and pendulous electric-arc lamps of the period below Carlisle's superb station roof; the wheeled and fired-up vat for fresh hot 'footwarmers' (to the right of *Jubilee*'s buffers), and the Cheshire cat, doubtless an immigrant from Crewe Refreshment Rooms. Many of these cats went great distances up and down the railways as stowaways, as on ships, to settle with good-natured – and grateful – cooks, waiters and barmaids. Queen Victoria was very fond of cats.

As to the electric-arc lamps, with their violet-white glare, Robert Louis Stevenson had already written, somewhere, that they furnished ideal illumination for a mortuary. All the same they made very good lighting, in buildings or streets, over many years.

But Victoria was a game old Queen, and was to see in the new century before she was done. She gave her name to an entire era of English – and British – history. Looked at socially, rather than historically, the Victorian Era really began with the Great Exhibition of 1851, and ended with the outbreak of war in 1914.

Early in 1901, with the South African War rather frustratedly raging still, the Queen was obviously ailing. (She never *failed*.) The time was at last out of joint for her. The Empire was hers and came before all things. But the Bible-thumping righteousness of the South African Dutch was nearer to the heart of her private ethics, and she could do nothing about it. Nearer to her heart too (though lately she had been angry with him) was her grandson William II of Germany than her son Albert Edward who was to be her successor.

It was time to go!

On 18 January 1901 came the Press Bulletin announcing that the Queen was ill at Osborne. The Prince of Wales was hurriedly summoned to her bedside. (He travelled to Portsmouth Harbour in a three-carriage reduction of his train built in 1897, with the twelve-wheeler in the middle.) So was the German Emperor. On 22 January she died.

There followed ten days of elaborate preparations. They involved the improvisation of two hearse carriages, both furnished by the Great Western Railway. The latter's regular royal train was to be used from Paddington to Windsor, with the Queen lying in her old saloon of 1874. Another Great Western saloon served the same purpose from Gosport to London (Victoria) being marshalled third from the engine in the new King Edward's London, Brighton and South Coast train, just ahead of his twelve-wheeled saloon. This train was otherwise augmented by one reserve first-class coach, and a first-and-second-class composite for accompanying soldiers. The route was to begin on the London and South Western Railway, but with the train being attached to a London, Brighton and South Coast engine at Fareham.

On 1 February, a brilliant winter afternoon, R.Y. *Victoria and Albert* brought the royal coffin across the Solent from Cowes to Royal Clarence Yard, Gosport. The sun went down in a glow of red as the ship berthed, then grey mist fell, and darkness.

There had been some intention of landing the coffin at the South Railway Jetty in Portsmouth Dockyard, and on 28 January a trial run was made with the train on the Dockyard branch, to test clearances on curves. The Brighton company had produced an elaborate chart of the train, with its extra vehicles, to show where everybody of the large party should find his place. Then and thus the troubles began. For when, the Dockyard branch having been turned down, the train was taken round to Fareham, and there reversed to get it to Gosport, it was of course the wrong way round according to the plan; second, while the platform at Royal Clarence was just long enough to take the basic train of five carriages, it was much too short when three more had been added. Contrary to the promise of the previous evening, the weather was very bad, rain coming down in torrents. Through it rushed and floundered and silently cursed the royal and distinguished mourners, including the Kaiser, seeking the accommodation which was precisely contrary to its expected place. The South Western locomotive (No. 555, fitted for both vacuum and air brakes for such workings as this) move the train back when the first lot of the company had sorted themselves out – and in – so that the rest could enter the three coaches which were presently at the front. The lack of internal corridors did not help matters. Fortunately the King was up in London, waiting to meet the train there, or his wrath would have been dire.

At 8.53 a.m. the train pulled out of Royal Clarence Yard, eight minutes late already (with some reason, as we have noticed!) At Fareham the South Western engine came off one end of the train, and the Brighton one, the 4-4-0 No. 54 *Empress*, came on at the other. (The two engines were respectively of Adams's class A 12 and Billinton's class B 4.)

There was more trouble at Fareham owing to delays in testing the brakes. The pilot engine (No. 53, *Sirdar*) was sent off correctly in advance. On the train engine (which was draped in purple along the handrails), were R. J. Billinton himself, with his Outdoor Locomotive Superintendent, J. Richardson, Driver Walter Cooper and Fireman F. Way. The train left Fareham just ten minutes later. Richardson said to Cooper that he was, for Heaven's sake, to try and make up some time, as the King would be furious if he were kept waiting at Victoria.

The route was via the northern spur between Cosham and Havant, then wholly on the Brighton company's line through Chichester, Arundel, Horsham, Dorking and Mitcham Junction. Victoria Station was to be reached at eleven o'clock. In fact, such was Cooper's handling of the *Empress* that arrival, far from being late, was two minutes early. There had been some very fast running, such as the Queen had never known in her lifetime. William Willox, then Northern Divisional Engineer of the London, Brighton and South Coast Railway, often recalled his anxiety as the train went romping down the Holmwood Bank with the Dorking reverse curves just beyond the tunnel at the bottom. All was well! The waiting King was unruffled. The Kaiser was as delighted as a boy, sending an equerry to congratulate the driver at Victoria Station in London; one of the nicer gestures, which he could make, when pleased.

Following the sporting behaviour of the London, Brighton and South Coast Railway, after its muddles with the London and South Western company, the funeral *cortège* across western London had other delays ere it reached Paddington, where an eight-vehicle augmentation of the Great Western royal train was drawn up at Platform 9, beside the big carriageway, whereon was partially mounted also a sort of grandstand. The train was headed by the *Royal Sovereign*, which name had been borrowed from a slightly older engine (one of William Dean's bogie-single-drivers) and bestowed upon his new four-coupled engine *Atbara*, thus temporarily renamed. (The G.W.R. did this sort of thing, then and thereafter. Conversely the Brighton engines used to Victoria, *Sirdar* and *Empress*, were well known to your author as *Richmond* and *Princess Royal*, at least until 1923.) At long last was heard, approaching and swelling, the band playing Chopin's *Marche Funèbre*, adapted for brass and drums from the slow movement of the Sonata in D Minor. (Handel's *Saul* was usual at the time.) Otherwise solemn stillness brooded over Brunel's splendid station until came clashing of arms, the clumping of booted feet and the harsh words of command; the scuffling and generally discreet vocal exchanges attendant upon entrainment, and the bearing of the very little royal coffin to the catafalque in the Queen's Carriage which had been in use since 1874.

Many had tried, and some had succeeded, in getting admission either to the stand in the cab-drive, or on to the long footbridge. One such spectator was Norman D. MacDonald, Scottish advocate and indefatigable follower of railways and all their works. Just in front of him were, briefly, the new King and the German Emperor. He heard Edward VII say to William II: 'Come along! Hurry up! we are twenty minutes late already!'

A pilot train had quietly gone forth in advance, carrying Field-Marshal Lord Roberts and the G.H.Q. Staff, behind the engine *Baden-Powell*. The royal train proper was about as crowded as any such train ought to be. In addition to officials, royal footmen and attendants in the leading vehicle, and German soldiers, the Chairman and General Manager of the Great Western (Earl Cawdor and J. L. Wilkinson), seven interpreters and the rear guard in the last, there were thirty in the corridor coach, chiefly military, and twenty-five, entirely military, including two Dukes, one Greek count, two Earls, one other Peer of the Realm and one knight. Third came the old royal saloon. The Queen's coffin was guarded by the Duke of Norfolk and the Duke of Portland, and the Earls of Clarendon and Pembroke. In its ancillary compartments were at the forward-end H.S.H. Prince Louis of Battenberg, Count Gleichen, Admiral Sir M. Culme-Seymour, Vice-Admiral Sir J. Fullerton and Major-Generals Sir H. Ewart and Sir J. MacNeill. At its after-end were eight more very distinguished personages: the Duke of Buccleuch, the Earl Waldegrave, Viscount Valentia, Field-Marshal the Rt Hon. Viscount Wolseley, Lord Belper, Sir Arthur Acland-Hood, Bart, Lieut Col. H. T. Fenwick and V. Cavendish, Esquire. Next came that saloon which later, the old Queen's Carriage now being obsolescent, was to be appropriated in more recent times to the King's use. Therein rode King Edward and Queen Alexandra, with the German Emperor, the Duke of Connaught, the Duchess of Fife, Princess Victoria, the Duke of Saxe-Coburg, Prince Charles of Denmark, the very youthful Crown Prince William of Germany, Princess Christian, Prince Arthur of Connaught, the Duchess of Argyll, Prince Henry of Prussia, Princess Henry of Battenberg, the Crown Prince of Denmark, the Duchess of Saxe-Coburg, the Duke of Albany, and Princess Adolph of Schaumburg-Lippe.

In short, as far as this carriage was concerned, it was a family funeral party, as was proper. In the next carriage there were three more kings, of the Belgians, the Hellenes and of Portugal, with thirty-five other royal Archdukes, Dukes, Hereditary Princes and others, including the Duke of Fife, who, being a relative in-law, was thus separated from his Duchess who rode with the King and Queen. To the seventh carriage were introduced the Duke d'Alençon and five ladies, including the Duchess of Buccleuch. In view of the crowded state of the previous one, it is possible that some polite adjustments were made. After them came the German soldiers and the senior railway people, as noted. The front guard was T. King, the rear guard was W. J. Fowler. The engine was driven by the Great Western's senior top-link driver David Hughes. A contemporary portrait shows him bearded (as were most locomotive drivers at that time, but in the style favoured by King Edward and the New Prince of Wales) and attired in uniform somewhat resembling that of an American admiral. The photograph was probably taken when the King, in

July 1901, invested him with the Royal Victorian Order.

Back to Paddington on that memorable afternoon. The funeral train was booked to leave at 1.32 p.m. It left at 1.40, an effort by no means bad in view of King Edward's impatient complaint to the Kaiser just in front of Mr MacDonald's speiring ears. The engine mounted the great castings of the Royal Arms, each side of the smokebox, as had been carried at the Diamond Jubilee, but this time draped in purple, and on the front was the Queen's Cypher surrounded by a wreath. Driver Hughes took the train quickly and decently down, through Slough where the once young lady had first taken a train, round the Slough east curve and so to the Great Western station in Windsor, where the wretched Maclean had tried to shoot her dead many years before. The royal standard went up to half-mast on the top of the Round Tower.

Even there came something of *contretemps*. All the way down, faithful servants of the Great Western company had been standing beside the line at 25 yard intervals. But the royal horses defaulted for once. It was bitterly cold. The hawsers attached to the gun-carriage bearing the royal coffin were stiff with frost. The impatient horses started to kick and plunge, and had to be unharnessed. Good sailors came to replace the horses, and to replace the hawsers the Great Western company resourcefully requisitioned all the communication cords from the carriages on the station sidings. The sailors then hauled their dead Queen by these.

So the great Queen, who had given her name to a millenially brief but most important phase in social, constitutional and economic history – *Victorian* – and to its sort of life in English-speaking countries; to a State in Australia and to a city in British Columbia, and to many other places including railway stations from Manchester to Bombay, made her last journey by train fifty-eight-and-a-half years after her first, and was laid beside her beloved and patient Albert for the first time since the end of 1861. In her lifetime, the railway had risen from being a noisy and dirty form of industrial machinery, to become something that was part of the lives of people all over the world.

As suggested, all the ticklish horrors of rigidly observed protocol and orders of precedence had been involved, with the usual corollary of horrors, which was the funny side. Something of this has been indicated, but one of the funnier things has been mentioned already by Paul Dost. Let it be recalled from the very surface of his *Red Carpet*!

Ferdinand of Bulgaria (who so liked driving locomotives as did Boris after him) came to England for Queen Victoria's first Jubilee. So did the Crown Prince Francis Ferdinand of Austria, who was to have a fateful end some years later in Sarajevo. Order of precedence was rather uncertain. Ferdinand was not yet king, though his father Alexander of Battenberg had been deposed the year before. Francis Ferdinand was certainly not Emperor of Austria, and indeed never would be so. Both the young princely hopefuls headed for London via Calais in their respective saloon carriages, which were to be marshalled at the head of the regular express. Ferdinand of Bulgaria was naturally first on the train. Next came passage of the Austro-Hungarian Empire. Francis Ferdinand insisted on his Right of Precedence, which meant that his carriage be marshalled ahead of Ferdinand's on the long train. The fact that there would be reversals later on was immaterial, and doubtless unconsidered. At Vienna West, of course, the Heir Presumptive simply commanded, and the thing was done. But the Bulgarian Ferdinand as simply chuckled and said to his sergeant-footman: 'Just see that the doors to the bellows are locked! We don't want all sorts of people traipsing through the carriage!' So it was done, and when Francis Ferdinand wished for his dinner he had to wait until the train was standing somewhere, and then walk along the platform to the diner. Both Highnesses had chosen the ordinary express, and so it *went* like an ordinary express apart from extra rolling stock attached by the way.

It is Paul Dost's story, to which one can only add the old English epithet: 'Foxy Ferdie!' In many years, the Orient Express and its siblings were to produce many curious stories.

Other acknowledgments must be given. The *Railway Reminiscences* of G. P. Neele, sometime Superintendent of the London and North Western Railway, have given very substantial help. They were published by McCorquodale of London in 1904. In the *Railway Magazine* of March 1940, there was an article entitled 'Queen Victoria's Funeral Journey', based on the researches, memories and reports of the late John Pelham Maitland and the late William Arthur Willox, and of Charles E. Lee, all from the Southern Railway or its constituents. One remembers old friends and colleagues. A splendid facsimile of the Great Western company's programme and chart for the last journey, in 1901, was printed in George Perry's *The Book of the Great Western*, published by the *Sunday Times Magazine*, London, in 1972.

4

INTERMISSION

Victoria, Queen Empress, had reigned a very long time, during which she had been intolerant of any change that could affect her personal habits. Most of the rolling stock assigned to her became in consequence more and more old-fashioned. But still the world watched, and had been watching for nearly as long as that reign. While it watched, many of the world's railway administrations produced much more advanced versions of what their rulers ought to use in railway conveyance.

In Russia, the converted vehicles from Napoleon III's train became obsolescent. Variously new rolling stock was built for the Tsar. That current in the 1880s was to suffer sad damage and even disintegration on 29 October 1889, when the Imperial Court was returning to Moscow from the Crimea. The train consisted of ten vehicles, whereof the first was a luggage van and the second carried fitters and travelling workmen. In the third was placed the Minister of Transport, perhaps on the premise that if anything went wrong, he would be early smashed up, and that therefore nothing would go wrong. There were also many soldiers who, with the workmen, were about to suffer severely. The kitchen car came fifth, the 'buffet' – in fact a kitchen service car – sixth, and the dining car seventh, having in rear of it the Princes' car, Imperial car, and one for the personal Court. The royal engine proper, next to the train, was an ordinary 2-4-0 express locomotive, but for the sometimes abrupt changes of gradient in the South, a massive helper had been added; one of those 0-8-0 outside-cylindered engines which once were innumerable in Russia, as in Central Europe. A good intention; but, to draw a Victorian English parallel, it was rather like heading the London and North Western royal train down from Shap behind two Webb compound engines, with a 'heavy coal' leading. Further, South Russia did not furnish quite such substantial permanent way as that between London and Carlisle.

Down the hill went the train, faster and faster until the small wheels on a relatively long rigid base of the leading engine mounted the rail-head on one side, and dropped from it on the other. The rails broke, or went snaking out on either side. The train piled up behind the engines which ended in drunken attitude on the embankment, crowned by evergreens and other adornments like Bacchus and bacchante before them.

Twenty-one of the company were killed, for the old wooden carriages – oldest behind the engines – broke up abruptly. (Paul Dost, in his remarkable book *Der rote Teppich* (*The Red Carpet*) (Frankh'sche Verlagshandlung, Stuttgart, 1965) gives ultimate casualties as 22 dead and 36 severely injured.) The Tsar, Alexander III, and the Tsarina, had gone into the diner and were at their coffee when the crash came. They were scarcely hurt, but the Emperor's principal personal servant, and his favourite dog, were both killed. One old account described Alexander as having been splashed with blood and coffee. Russia being Russia, sabotage was instantly suspected, but it was not so. (An English railway-man's verdict was true enough: 'Eight-coupled running fast downhill on bloody-awful permanent way!')

'Eight-coupled', of course, meant in the Europe of those days the simple 0-8-0. The magnificent 'Mountains' (4-8-2) of America and France, the splendid Austrian 2-8-4 with the Helmholtz bogie, the American 4-8-4, and others comparable were as yet far ahead in the coming history of railway mechanical engineering. Those were to be de-

signed as express engines. But someone had fallen down badly in the Russian State Locomotive Running Department; and someone decided that suicide was the only way out of
such trouble as was to gather after the initial one. So he took it. Peace be to the old bones
that once, suddenly, framed horrified flesh! Of what happened to the unhappy enginemen, whose most important train had run away with their engines, one has no record at
this stage, long ago as the thing was.

This seems to have been the only serious accident to have befallen a complete royal
train. As noted, there had been threats to such in the past, even in respectable Victorian
England, and as we have seen, Victoria had two narrow escapes from accident even on
her first journey from Scotland to England in 1848. Sometimes royal personages were
involved in accidents when their special vehicles had been attached to ordinary express
trains. Paul Dost mentions a few.

Many years later the Prince of Wales, son of George V and briefly Edward VIII of
Great Britain, on his world tour of his father's Empire in the beginning of the 1920s,
was to be overturned, and to rise smiling from one of the uppermost doors of his carriage
which was lying down in dry Western Australian grass. (West of Kalgoorlie, speeds were
scarcely reckless, nor east of it, on broader gauge, for that matter.) Delays through accident
in advance of royal trains were indeed recurrent down the years. The South Eastern and
Chatham Railway had quite a spectacular collision, though without serious hurt except
to the locomotive of a down express coming into Tonbridge, in Edward VII's time, just
when His Majesty was on his way to the Continent (see pages 135–6). 'Teddy', who, as
noted, was much annoyed at any sort of unpunctuality, had to be re-routed, but he was
ever a great gentleman, and at once required truthful information as to whether any had
suffered badly. He had already faced, as Prince of Wales, attempted assassination on a
train in Belgium. Victoria had faced the furious fanatic several times; indeed, during the
Fenian threats, intimation had been passed that her train would be blown up. Two pilot
engines were therefore provided, so that the second might touch off the bomb. The
enginemen knew of this and, as Neele remarked, they took their lives in their hands.
Fortunately nothing happened. It was a soldierly thing to do.

But for as long as Victoria lived, ambitious designers for the British railway companies
had found their style cramped by her habitual preferences. It was not so abroad. Sumptuous rolling stock was being built for the Kings, and for the two Emperors, William II
of Germany and the legendary, if ageing, Francis Joseph I of Austria Hungary. The
latter had a vast realm, and unlike Victoria's it was geographically all in one piece. He
was not only Emperor; he was also King of Hungary. His dominions included Bohemia,
Moravia and Ruthenia – the frame of the future Czechoslovakia – a substantial slice of
the long-dismembered kingdom of Poland, while what was officially Austria proper
stretched down to the Adriatic. His Government's attitude to the Balkan countries was
sternly paternal, which was to lead to dire trouble for everybody later on.

Travelling about his vast realm entailed provision and standards on a scale which
Victoria never knew or wished to know. His magnificent vehicles were variously built,
but the finest of them, which were to last to the end of his reign, came from his Bohemian
Provincial Capital, Prague, where were the works of the great coachbuilding firm of

Ringhoffer. This already had built wondrous vehicles for public service, such as early sleeping cars which were fairly often patronised in the South, for it was a long and mountainous way from Vienna to Trieste and back. Such vehicles had appeared as early as 1858, when Pullman was first having ideas in America and, in Great Britain, 'twin-sticks' with their intermediate cushion were a luxury to be hired on the Irish Mail and the night Scotch expresses, from and to London.

During 1891 Ringhoffers produced one of the most superb trains in the then known world, the Americas included, for Francis Joseph and his suite. At that time the Wagons-Lits company was really arriving with its sumptuous public vehicles, and the Orient Express was becoming a legend. Closed-end vestibules, interconnected, were being demanded by citizens of the U.S.A. In Europe, Germany had begun to produce the *D-Zug*, the complete corridor train with entry at ends only to each carriage, and completely closed connection between them. The Austro-Hungarian imperial train became its most magnificent example and remained so for as long as the Empire lasted. Altogether, and ultimately, there were some twenty vehicles available for its make-up. The most interesting are illustrated, both by photograph and diagram and plan, in Dr Fritz Stöckl's work with Claude Jeanmaire, *Komfort auf Schienen* (*Comfort on Rails*), published by Verlag für Eisenbahn und Strassenbahnliteratur, Basle, Switzerland, 1970.

The carriages were generally clerestoried, though sometimes partially, as in what English-speaking Europeans called *the van*. This had a little power station, with boiler and vertical steam engine, to generate power and heat throughout the train. This engine compartment quite necessarily had a clerestory over it, for it must have been awfully hot inside. This was on two four-wheeled bogies, and included complete arrangements for the head conductor, including a roof-lookout or, as England would have called it, a 'birdcage'. There was a fairly large luggage compartment, with small living compartments for the staff at either end. The outer end had an open platform, old-style, but towards the rest of the train there was a proper closed vestibule. Next to be considered, though relatively plebeian as to service, was a six-wheeled side-corridor coach with four full compartments convertible into double-berth sleepers *à couchettes* a-nights, and – as in several others – an elevated guard's seat in a 'birdcage', for the immediate court servants. Next, the Emperor's private saloon. Like the six-wheeler, it was of pure *D-Zug* pattern, and was 15·3 m. over headstocks and 2·85 m. wide in the main body, containing the usual lavatories at each end, with medial corridors between, plus a very small compartment containing a sort of *chaise-longue* for the night-servant. Between these offices were three much more liberal compartments, crowned by clerestory which did not extend for full length as to the body. There was the Emperor's bedroom, extending full-width, and thus not passable save by equerry and servants, 3·27 m. long and containing a liberal bed, some chairs and a corner lavatory basin; then the *Salon Seiner Majestät* with sofa, three arm-chairs, a desk with office-chair to it, a table, and another *chaise-longue*, of the sort called, in Austria, *Kaiser-Fauteuil*. In the clerestory were two handsome electroliers (there being one, and a bed-lamp, in the sleeping compartment).

The first electrically lit railway vehicle in the world had been a Pullman car, American built, but on the London Brighton and South Coast Railway in England, supplied by

III *The King of Spain calls*

Through the Hampshire chalk north of Winchester roars the royal train of the London and
South Western Railway! Alphonso XIII of Spain is paying one of several state visits to
Edward VII and Queen Alexandra, for he is courting Princess Ena (a delicate piece of
dynastic gallantry, on religious grounds). The South Western company has done its best, for
the locomotive, built by Dugald Drummond in 1905, is almost new, while the royal saloons
(first and third in the picture, with a kitchen van between) date back to 1885. Since then one
has acquired a clerestory and the second a semi-ellipse with electric lighting.

IV *The end of an era*

The scene is York, on the North Eastern Railway, south of Poppleton Junction. The Prince and Princess of Wales, on the train and bound for Tyneside, are soon to become King and Queen. Wilson Worsdell's North Eastern locomotive shows the shape of things to come, for she is a giant of her time, the year being 1900. She *could* have done better with a bigger boiler. The vehicles are unashamedly Victorian; indeed, the leading one is a rebuild from a Stockton and Darlington antique, and has been included in the royal train as a saloon for the North Eastern company's officers in attendance. Somewhere behind the train is the noble skyline of York.

Fauré cells under the body, ten years before. One must say that France had done the lighting, and thus must claim full share in the honours.

Next came the Equerry's compartment which, historically, is very interesting. The Austrians (or Bohemians who built it) called it *Adjutantscoupé*. It was 2·47 m. between partitions, with an arm-chair, an occasional chair, and two small tables or desks, but on the other side of the passage there was what America, long after, was to call a roomette; a very small longitudinal compartment still comfortably containing a bed.

Next came a carriage, very similar in outline and arrangement, for the immediate Royal Suite, which included two of the top-drawer sort of compartments in Wagons-Lits style, two more of the secondary sort, both portions being flanked by side corridor, and between them a full-width saloon, with two sumptuous fixed seats, four arm-chairs and a table. 'Offices' were more or less as before, and there was a clerestory except for the outermost portions, one of which had another guard's, or brakesman's, section, with a lantern look-out overhead.

Then came the imperial dining saloon; a *diner* to challenge the world, even where Mr Pullman was Satrap. There was a vestibule at one end only, that towards the carriages just described. It led into what resembled two bays (American: sections) of a British, or Wagons-Lits, Pullman car, having four arm chairs each side, with tables between them, giving eight seats in all. This was the smoking-room. Beyond that, going inwards towards the middle of the train, was the *Speisesalon*, the main dining-room, with fourteen chairs back-to-windows, and two at each end of a long central table, with two electroliers over-head. Beyond this again was a service compartment with a hatch to the dining-room, and like it and the smoking-room, occupying full width of the vehicle. The dining saloon was 7·39 m. long between partitions, and the preceding smoke room 5·07. All these were very handsomely decorated, as someone remarked much later of an Austrian departmental dynamometer car which had been inherited, as a vehicle, from the sometime imperial train.

Through the bellows, after that, came an enormous kitchen car, with the usual vestibules but otherwise with side corridor throughout. The qualification is necessary, for Europe's first corridored 'dining-set', used on the Great Eastern service between Harwich and York in and from 1891, comprised first-, second- and third-class vehicles with bellows all on one side. The main kitchen, more or less in the middle, was 6·9 m. long between partitions, opening towards the dining saloon into a dishing-up compartment with china cupboards, 3·67 m. long. At its other end the carriage had an entirely civilised sleeping compartment for the head cook and his assistant, followed by the overstepped arrange-ment of brakesman's compartment and staff lavatory, the former approached by steep steps over the latter and with yet another roof-observatory, before the next vestibule connecting with that of the following vehicle in this considerable *Hofzug*.

Now, as suggested, the Emperor was also King of Hungary, and as a kingdom, Hungary also had to produce a royal train, which was normally to be used east of Vienna. It included a very magnificent King Emperor's saloon, this time on two six-wheeled bogies, and rather more ornately decorated outside than the Austrian one. Again, ironically or no, it was built by the Czechs of Ringhoffer's establishment. As the world had previously watched what happened in England, Eastern and Central Europe now had been watching what happened in Francis Joseph's Empire. Not least Ferdinand of Bulgaria, whom angry Englishmen were later to call Foxy Ferdie! (The imposing Battenberg nose had something to do with the nickname.) He had some beautiful carriages made for him, but his favourite place was on the locomotive. Perhaps the first royal 'locomaniac'? His successor King Boris was to be as much – perhaps even more so! Both loved to drive 'real engines'. The dynasty survived the war of 1914–18 and – more irony – King Boris was ultimately to disappear in the course of something unpleasant happening to an aeroplane when Bulgaria was more or less compulsively allied to Hitler's Germany. (It was Hobson's Choice; on the other hand lay Stalin's Russia.) The Nazis seem to have found Boris a nuisance.

Of Romania's rolling stock one recalls, from years long ago, that it was generally Austro-German – i.e. *D-Wagen* – in design. The locomotives were often of Prussian sort, though express engines included a rather ugly version of the natively beautiful Maffei Pacific from Bavaria. The royal rolling stock of the late King Carol and his son Michael was decidedly Francis-Joseph in style. The rather short windows with longer panel-space between, in the Romanian saloon of 1896, however, rather suggested Russian practice. This vehicle was an eight-wheeler, clerestoried except as to the vestibules, as in many Austrian ones.

The Austrian Emperor, scarcely a happy potentate for all his many years, used to go and relax at Bad Ischl in the Salzkammergut. The Salzkammergut Local Railway (0·760 m. gauge) provided a suitable carriage for him, and long after the Emperor and his brief successor were gone, this was turned into a motor-railcar of agued sort. When even the Salzkammergut Lokalbahn died (and how glad one is to have known it!) the car survived, and went to the Styrian Provincial Railway.

There was no more love lost between William II of Germany and Francis Joseph of Austria than there was between the former and Edward VII of the United Kingdom, but the first-named watched the second with what may have been some envious interest. All three were Emperors; the first two on a Metropolitan scale, though William had some parts of Africa, while Edward had India. William *must* have a new imperial German train, and so it was. The admirable *D-Zug* style was followed with the most important carriages on six-wheeled bogies. There had been some predecessors. As recently as 1958 the present author encountered a handsome eight-wheeler – by then a first- and second-class composite coach – whose vestibules and rectangular-ended clerestory suggested Old Prussia, on a semi-fast train of the Westphalian Provincial Railway, that remarkable undertaking which was to continue furnishing modest main-line service without State interference or sequestration, through all the hazards of *Kaiserzeit*, Weimar Republic, *Hitlerzeit* and war. This engaging vehicle, after a brief and not very meritorious shot with this party's camera, was whisked away. 'That?' said somebody, 'Oh, that was once a *Speisewagen des Deutschen Kaisers*!'

So it was! As far as one could see, the dining saloon had become second-class (the hard sort in later German terms) while the first-class compartments had been improvised from kitchen or service quarters. Nice old carriage! One wishes one had gone to investigate Warstein in it, but one was obliged to return to Soest on the last available train that day!

But in the 1890s, more vast and elaborate vehicles were being furnished for the German Emperor, on long six-wheeled bogies, with the diner as a sort of banqueting hall, and a style of decoration throughout which Potsdammed the late Ludwig II's travelling Nymphenburg. Gorgeous inside, it was outwardly a very elegant train indeed; restrained, too, like the rolling stock used by the Russian Emperor, on both broad and standard gauge, between his empire and the warm southern regions other than the Crimea. (South from Warsaw there was standard gauge.) Of the last official assignment of the German Emperor's train, more later!

One notices in all these trains, as of those which served Queen Victoria, that what Daisy Ashford long ago called the 'State Compartments' went full width. None but Imperial Majesty could pass right through; not that he was normally likely to do so. The German Imperial Train had a livery of its own; rich blue in the lower quarters and spilt-milk above, though it is suggested that during the 1914–18 war it was at some time painted in chocolate, which would have made it look less conspicuous to possible raiding aircraft. The Kaiser was already aircraft-conscious, and his early pride was in Zeppelin's superb airships. (As a weapon these proved a failure, though scarifying a-while. Count von Zeppelin was saddened; his aim was an *air liner*!)

The last of the German Emperors loved big, imposing things, as he loved big ships, big parades, grand uniforms and grandiloquence. So did his Uncle Bertie, Edward VII of the Britons, when it came to good living. The Kaiser had a liking for quick change acts, too. In *Our Railways* (Cassell, 1896) John Pendleton recorded that on the short journey from Windsor to Paddington in 1891, the German Emperor joined the Great Western train in a tweed suit and left it 'in the striking uniform of the Queen's Dragoons'. When he visited Deeside in the North, he would appear there as a 'best-dressed Highlander', he having received special licence to wear the Royal Stewart tartan, which incidentally is allowed to all British subjects. It is a good thing that his grandmother was not to see what was to follow. We always called him *The Kaiser*, and one notes that to this day Victoria is referred to, in Germany, as *die Queen*. In his book *Komfort auf Schienen*, Dr Fritz Stöckl has captioned an illustration of the Prussian royal train as *Preussens Glänz und Gloria*. Certainly, it was at the time all that the Emperor could have wished. The last time he used it will be described later.

Alphonso XIII of Spain had succeeded as a very little boy, to become like so many royal personages, a prisoner within a system, just as do promising Marxists and others in later years than his. One has not heard that, like the monarchs of Bulgaria, he was wont to insist on driving his own engine. The Duke of Saragossa, however, assumed that privilege, and from Don Gustavo Reder came the deathless story about the arid wastes of an up-platform at San Sebastian. Formalities were going on-and-on-and-onner (acknowledgment to a parodist of Longfellow!) until the Duke, leaning out of the cab of a substantial North of Spain express engine, bawled out: 'Buck up, Alphonso! We're two hours down already!'

It is time to look at some of the quasi-royal trains, though still there were some real ones in unlikely places, not least in Brazil. The Monrovians, whether of the U.S.A. or of the 'Latin' republics, might disapprove, but there it was! Consequently, we must look first to the North of England. The City of Lancaster had long been a dreaming old has-been place when, in 1863, there was founded the Lancaster Railway Carriage and Wagon Company, which was to build vehicles for places all over the world, from the tramway of its own ancient City-Palatine to the real East, and for Australia. Also, it found good custom in South America, where many of the railways were built by British contractors and owned by British companies.

Brazil had become a Portuguese colony in 1530. Independence was declared in 1822, and the Regent was declared Emperor Pedro I of this vast dominion. He abdicated in 1831, and Pedro II reigned, through many stormy South American troubles, from the end of another Regency in 1840 to deposition in 1889, when Federal Republic succeeded.

This younger Pedro latterly enjoyed use of an imperial train, thus sharing with the unfortunate Maximilian of Mexico the distinction of having been the only imperial or royal personage in the Americas south of the Canadian border. For his personal conveyance by railway over the Minas and Rio line (metre gauge) of the 1880s, there was a handsome bogie eight-wheeler, very British-Colonial, 40 ft by 8 ft internally, and divided in the middle by its *necessaria*. There were principally furnished a compartment rather like an English family saloon with chairs, two long sofas facing a folding table, and fixed end-seats; and a sleeping compartment with convertible longitudinal berths. The roof was clerestoried with pendant kerosene lamps. Entry was by platform and hood at each end, old-American and British-colonial fashion. England was to build South American carriages on such lines for many years after.

Pedro II was the last South American monarch. But the new Spanish-speaking republics in their turn were watching. None was more proud than Argentina, or as it was then generally called by the English-speaking peoples, the Argentine Republic. A very large proportion of its railways had been built by British contractors, financed by British capital, and equipped by British engineers. Lovely locomotives from Manchester and Glasgow powered them. The vehicles were likewise British; British in style though American in arrangement.

Brown, Marshall and Company of Birmingham built and supplied a splendid pair of 'twin saloons' for the Argentine President of the time. (Both the Brazilian and the Argentine carriages were illustrated in the old *Railway World* (ultimately *Transport World*) of June and August 1892. At the previous date, this periodical was known as the *Tramway and Railway World*. One treasures one's old copies.) They were shallowly cambered as to the roofs, but with clerestories majestic and deep. One of them had middling-narrow vestibules at both ends (something between the full-width and the true narrow of North America. (Such vestibules were soon to distinguish the new British royal trains of Edward VII, who, all too briefly, was about to come into his own.) The second Argentine Presidential carriage had the vestibule at one end only, and at the other an elegantly balconied platform, such as would have done credit to the most ostentatiously opulent private cars of North American business nabobs. The fully vestibuled carriage contained a state dining-room with chairs for twelve including head and foot of table, about a superb double ellipse. Panelling was an Italian walnut including the ceiling, which was double in the lower decks. Lighting was by very ornate

45 *above* Queen Victoria, King Louis Philippe and Prince Albert on the London and South Western Railway, 1844.

46 *below* Royal Wedding, 1863: arrival of Princess Alexandra of Denmark at Bricklayers' Arms, London on 7 March, for her marriage to Albert Edward, Prince of Wales, later King Edward VII.

47 Wedding of the Duke and Duchess of Edinburgh: Queen Victoria greets the bride, Grand Duchess Marie, daughter of Tsar Alexander II, at the London and South Western station, Windsor. The carriage is the South Eastern Railway's royal saloon of 1850. (From the *Illustrated London News*, 14 March 1874.)

48 Borki, South Russia, 1888: Tsar Alexander III has a narrow escape. Twenty-one of the Imperial Suite, including soldiers and workmen, were killed. The Tsar escaped with bruises, covered with blood and coffee, his butler and his dog being abruptly dead. (From the *Illustrated London News*, 17 November 1888.)

49 Queen Louise of Denmark supposedly *en route* with her grand-daughters, the Princesses Victoria (left), Maud (perched) and Louise of Wales. The carriage is in fact a lifelike Danish mock-up, about 1881.

50 Arrival of the King of Portugal at Portsmouth, South Railway Jetty. Left to right: H.M.Y. *Victoria and Albert*, a Portuguese battleship, and the Great Western Railway's royal train.

51 Arrival of the Shah of
Persia, Portsmouth, 1902:
London, Brighton and South
Coast Railway's royal train,
with engine *Empress*.

52 *above* H.R.H. Albert Edward, Prince of Wales,
visits North America in the 1860s. Left to right are the
youthful prince, the Duke of Newcastle and General
Williams. The carriage was specially built by the Grand
Trunk Railway of Canada. One should note the early
adoption of semi-elliptical roofing and the very nice
mounting of the three feathers of Bohemia and Wales.
(From *Illustrated News*, New York, 1868.)
53 *right* Affectionate greetings between quarrelsome
relations? Edward VII and William II at Cronberg,
11 August 1908.

54 Last Journey of King Edward VII: Paddington station, 20 May 1910.

55 Funeral train of Edward VII. Engine, *King Edward*; identifiable vehicles from the tender are: royal brake, 'Windsor saloon', 1897 coach for suite, 1874 Queen's carriage as hearse car, two more saloons and a royal brake of 1897, followed by another 'Windsor saloon'. The train was reputed to have conveyed more rulers than any other in history.

56 Anhalt Station, Berlin, 1889: reception of Humbert I of Italy by William II of Germany. Note American Pullman cars in background.

57 October 1913: left to right, Archduke Francis Ferdinand, Crown Prince of Austria and William II of Germany kissing Lady Chotek's hand. Prussian royal train beyond; Persian carpet below.

58 Sarajevo, Bosnia, July 1914: Crown Prince Francis Ferdinand and his wife Lady Chotek leave a train for the last time in their lives. General Potiorek, military governor of Bosnia, is on the right.

59 End of the Habsburg Empire? The attitude of the soldiers suggests it! Charles I, the last Emperor, is alighting from the Hungarian royal saloon, possibly at Buchs.

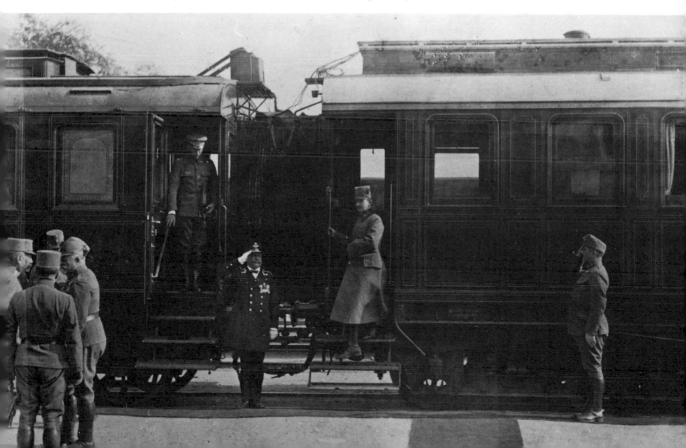

60 Arrival of the royal train at Hyderabad, on H.E. the Nizam's Guaranteed State Railway, January 1889.

61 *left* King George V and Queen Mary on the East Indian royal train, 1911.
62 *right* The Delhi Durbar, 1911: George V and Queen Mary being received by the Viceroy, Lord Hardinge of Penshurst.

63 Great Western Railway, Reading West, 22 June 1938: The original *Windsor Castle* (G.W.R. No. 4082) heads the 1903 London and North Western Railway royal train. It is going dead-slow owing to bridge repairs just ahead.

64 George V and Queen Mary, with Sir Felix Pole (in spectacles) general manager of the Great Western Railway, and others on engine *Windsor Castle* at Swindon, 1924.

brass kerosene lamps, with sprung candle-lamps at the sides. This dining-room was 20 ft long by 10 ft wide inside, and adjoining it were a 'buffet' (rather a service room for dishing-up) and an ample kitchen.

The other carriage had a full-width reception room entered from the open end platform, and thereafter it was of side-corridor type, containing a writing-room, a spacious bedroom with a full-size wooden bedstead, a dressing-room and lavatory, and a drawing-room containing an open fireplace with a black marble overmantel and a great parlour clock (necessarily with a watch movement) to match. At the end next to the vestibule leading to the diner was a compartment for the President's personal servants. All the decoration throughout was extraordinarily rich in contrasting woods with heavy velvet and brocade drapes. The two carriage bodies were each about 51 ft long, and 10 ft 6 in. wide outside, that last dimension comparing with the largest coaches built for broad gauge on the Great Western in England during the 1870s. The pair, coupled up, had an overall length of 122 ft including vestibules, platform and buffers. Each was on two four-wheeled equalised bogies set at 39 ft centres. Bogie wheelbase was 6 ft, which seems rather short, especially for running on the 5 ft 6 in. gauge of the major Argentine railways. Though a 'quasi-royal' pair, these carriages deserve some notice as having been, probably, the most elaborate railway passenger vehicles yet built by British works, certainly in the late 1880s.

The open drawing-room fireplace was much liked, and in later years when new Presidential stock was built for Argentina, this feature persisted. The whole outfit was a Victorian stylist's dream on wheels. It was also, in conception, entirely English (not even British) with seasonings from the Palace of Westminster, Eaton Hall, and some other places, and any sort of English-Puritan restraint was absent. The Argentine Establishment was evidently captivated.

At this time – and we are still on Republican ground – the great Business Nabobs of the U.S.A. were blowing up in most exuberant fashion, and every sort of privileged citizen, from Mr John Pierpont Morgan, to some small-town mill-owner who had 'struck lucky', had to have a private car, usually built by George M. Pullman's establishment. Pierpont Morgan once arbitrated in a dispute between the Pennsylvania and the New York Central Railroads. His fee came to three million dollars. Later, and most laudably, he became patron in America of that great composer Sibelius, who noted that the Morgan private car had an open fireplace burning balsam logs. All the American business rajahs of the period had each a private car (one – two – several). So did the heads of railroads (on company expenses) whether they commanded something like the Union Pacific or the 'Erewhon Short Line'. The Association of American Railroads would give them free hauls and no payment of fare anywhere, which was more than Queen Victoria could command. Some of them exemplified splendour too ostentatious for an Empress, and indeed the American rajahs' wives often dictated such things. Pullman was usually the manufacturer, in fact the Pullman company down by the shores of Michigan built up a pool of magnificent cars for hire by the visiting rich; further, Mr President, or Presidential aspirant before an election, would hire a complete and splendid 'consist' for a whistle-stop electioneering campaign, the rear observation platform providing the rostrum wherever the train halted.

These things rose to their zenith about the turn of the century and continued for a very long time thereafter. One's readers must be referred to a sumptuous illustrated book, *Mansions on Wheels*, by the late Lucius Beebe (Howell-North Press, Berkeley 10, California, U.S.A., 1959). (His books, and those he wrote in collaboration with Charles Clegg, are glittering mines of information in such things.)

While English coachbuilders had pleased South American Presidents and a Brazilian Emperor, and even, one hopes, that ill-fated Emperor of Mexico for a while, when it came to Mexican Republican Presidency, North America won. Since the sad end of President Lincoln, and the building of G. M. Pullman's first entirely original car, in 1865, the name of Pullman had become a legend. Nothing would be skimped in any sort of Pullman car for which anyone was prepared to pay. American Pullmans were being prefabricated and then erected in Europe, from Derby in England to Turin in Italy.

Western royalties were no strangers to North America, even in the late 1860s. For one thing, Victoria was Queen of Canada, though, unlike her great-great-grand-daughter Elizabeth II, she never went there, let alone to the U.S.A. which would have been to her unthinkable. Albert Edward, Prince of Wales, went over in 1868, and for his use the Grand Trunk Railway specially built the most magnificently princely sort of car people could imagine, and without Mr Pullman's appointment at that. Full details seem to be little if at all available, but the *New York Illustrated News*, a very respectable periodical, published a delightful cut of him in the G.T.R.'s splendid car, carefully watched over by the Duke of Newcastle and General Williams. What can be seen of the car has been very carefully drawn. It had a semi-elliptical roof, unlike Pullman's style, with the Three Feathers won by the Black Prince as a prominent feature in the decoration. H.R.H. Albert Edward, who went south into the U.S.A. seems to have enjoyed this trip very much indeed. It was one of his glorious escapes. In Sir William Hardman's letters are some snide quotations of *gauche* remarks south of the 49th Parallel about 'licking you Britishers'. These Albert Edward probably took as pepper in his nice stew, which he found most refreshing, while Hardman as an English Conservative hated all Americans unless they were the best sort of Confederate.

Ten years later his brother Arthur, whom one's own generation always knew as the Duke of Connaught, also was allowed over. Vanderbilt did the best New York Central resources could produce. It seems to have been a lovely car of the American clerestoried sort, with a splendid iron stove amongst all the carpets, and ships' lamps on either hand.

Much later Prince Henry of Prussia (who somewhat resembled George V of the United Kingdom and Nicholas II of All the Russias) was to receive the full Pullman treatment. The trip cost him 56,655 Marks (say £3,000). The Pullman rolling stock produced in 1898 for the President of Mexico would not have displeased all the Vanderbilts, Huntingtons, Morgans or whoever in the U.S.A. from the Atlantic to the Pacific, nor even their demanding ladies. Each of such cars contained – within the liberal longitudinals of some 80 ft – everything that could be put on one vehicle. Even the German Emperor – who was well provided by then – might have envied. One wonders whether the first and last Emperor of Mexico might have haunted the train. Of course, it is impossible. The year 1898 was a long time since he had been shot dead by his own soldiers, and his own carriage was still there to haunt, on the then British-owned Mexican Railways. This one was on the National Railways of Mexico.

Back to Europe. There was nothing in the private-car line, in all Europe, to compare with what went on in America. On the Continent, Baron Rothschild had several private carriages. They were splendidly appointed but somewhat austere, whether in Austria or on the Northern Railway of France, which seems to have been largely owned by the family. There was even a Rothschild Saloon in England, on, of all lines, the Metropolitan Railway. It could, and did, move when required between the deepest City of London, through the Underground, and thence out into equally deepest Buckinghamshire where, at one time, his lordship drove four-in-hand with zebras, or at any rate with three zebras and a large wild ass.

In mid-Victorian years, the Duke of Devonshire had a saloon carriage on the Furness Railway, and Sir James Ramsden, who quite autocratically ran that railway, had another. By appearance Ramsden's was the more comfortable of the two while the Duke's, in some ways, was the more advanced, having long windows, end entry and some sort of a clerestory roof (possibly just an elongated roof ventilating deck) but both had become archaic ere the century drew to its close. Photographs have lasted.

The Duke of Sutherland was immensely rich, and liberally enough he had financed a handsome slice of the Highland Railway in Scotland – the Duke of Sutherland's Railway over about 17 miles from Golspie to Helmsdale – it being thus a private undertaking. He also subscribed £60,000 (to the Highland Railway's £50,000) to the Sutherland and Caithness Railway. His ancestress-in-law the infamous Elizabeth, Countess of Sutherland, had systematically depopulated the country. The subsequent Dukes (c. 1833) had truly tried to make amends by the means and morality of the time. The Highland Railway was the working company of these, but the successive Dukes kept the right to work, as well as own, special rolling stock for private journeys, with right of way subject to public service requirements, north of Inverness. There were two successive locomotives named *Dunrobin*, and there is photographic record of three private saloon carriages, two of which still exist, one in England and one in Canada through the vagaries of organised preservation. The second locomotive *Dunrobin* also went west, to British Columbia, with the smaller saloon carriage (probably the one and only four-wheeler B.C. ever saw on rails). We shall note these carriages in the next chapter.

Lastly to this brief portion – two curiosities, one tragic. President William M'Kinley of the U.S.A. was assassinated at Buffalo in September 1901. Sometime private soldier in the Civil War, and later Major, he was by then a portly and rather severe-looking elderly American gentleman, clean-shaven with white hair. With Pullman or Pullmanesque rolling stock, the Vanderbilts' New York Central did their best for what was left of him. It was a costly funeral, as indeed Queen Victoria's had been, earlier in the year. He had named after him an exceeding-high mountain in Alaska.

Let us close with a sort of harlequinade. Albert Edward of Wales sometimes complained that he spent his working life thanklessly representing his Exalted Mother, laying foundation stones and opening things. One of those things was the first of the London tubes, the deep-level underground railways with electric power which were pioneered in London. That was the City and South London Railway, which for over 30 years was worked by little gin-bottle locomotives hauling very cramped cars. One cannot imagine Queen Victoria on the tube, but Edward went bravely down. He officially inaugurated the C. & S.L.R. on 4 November 1890. Its locomotive No. 10 was named *Princess of Wales*, and so remained, through rebuilding in 1905, into your author's childhood. The line was reconstructed in the early 1920s, and the little engines then vanished, save for one (somewhat cannibalised) which went to the Science Museum in London, and another which for some years adorned Moorgate station on the Metropolitan Line and was sadly burnt in one of the air-raids on London in the 1940s.

A much more imposing and sophisticated tube in London was the Central London Railway. That too was opened by Albert Edward, in 1900. He had a ride on it, declared it open, and at the ensuing feast at Wood Lane, near Shepherd's Bush in London, made what Michael Robbins of London Transport has described as one of his shortest public speeches. His Royal Highness seemed to have been out of temper. He was elderly, and his Exalted Mother did not improve as she became aged, doting more and more on her favourite grandson, the German Emperor. Having made that short, testy speech, he indicated firmly that the proceedings had gone on long enough, to some people's disappointment and even consternation.

Though the Central London Railway was quite luxurious compared with the City and South London, it had – though indefinably differently – likewise a most peculiar smell. Incipient Majesty had just discovered the delights of the motor-car. Soon he was to receive at long last his manumission, and soon after that he would be able to enjoy the use of far more magnificent trains on the British main-line railways than Victoria had known, or would have accepted. For the present, two tubes were enough! (Two more had appeared in the meantime; the Waterloo and City in London, and the Glasgow District Subway.) Indeed those tubes, and their followers, were soon to become very useful to millions of his subjects. Edward VII's grandson, later to be briefly Edward VIII, was quietly to sample the Bakerloo and others.

A less glum concluding note, anent my picture of 'what a lovely train!' (Colour Plate IV.) This scene, admittedly imagined though correctly documented, is near Poppleton Junction north of York, on the North Eastern Railway, on 20 June 1900. The Prince and Princess of Wales are making for Tyneside. Their train is headed by Wilson Worsdell's ten-wheeler No. 2010, then quite new. Among other flags she bears, on the offside of her noble bosom, the Prince of Wales's Standard with its white label, and its Welsh Arms in the middle. The Prince's saloon is the varnished-teak carriage, of Great Northern design, fourth from the tender. The leading vehicle is a North Eastern officers' saloon, rebuilt from a Stockton and Darlington relic built in or before 1871. As far as one can see, the fifth vehicle is a North Eastern saloon, with an early example of the deeper semi-elliptical roof. (The Great Northern semi-ellipse was much depressed, and little, if at all, superior to the cambered shape used by most other British railways of that time.) The North Eastern Railway, be it added, made uncommonly good carriages over many years, as did the Midland.

A fine photograph of this train leaving York on that same occasion in 1900, taken by the late Dr Tice F. Budden, has been published several times. Some 70 years ago it appeared as an early F. Moore coloured plate in the *Locomotive Magazine*, but there the colour lithography disappoints. Nor is it wholly accurate, for it shows all the carriages except the leading one in varnished teak. At that time, all wholly owned North Eastern rolling stock was red.

Faintly on the extreme left of this picture can be seen the black-topped white funnel of a river steamer paddling up the Ouse to Poppleton. (In the painter's youth there was the tall-funnelled paddle-steamer *River King*, which made for a much jollier summer evening out than some pub near the Shambles or Mucky Peg!) The figures in the painting are quite fictitious, though costume is studiously correct for the period. For the rest, there is a fine slotted-post semaphore of a sort to which the North Eastern company was to remain faithful over many years yet. (One saw such at York (Layerthorpe), on the Derwent Valley Light Railway, quite recently, with a borrowed diesel below.) The locomotive, here portrayed, heralded what was then a new phase, that of the *Big-engine*. The vehicles belonged to a dying one. There was of course to be some overlap between the two; indeed as late as 1926 one was to be astonished at the truly Victorian rolling stock on the all-night train from Perth to Inverness, some of the worst of which had started from Buchanan Street, Glasgow, to contain its uncorridored inmates for over seven hours.

Francis Joseph of Austria was by persuasion a Spartan also, and with all the sumptuosities with which the various Austrian railways were ready to, and did, provide him, he may have wished to be a sort of Leonidas. For years he would not go properly to bed in a train, demanding instead one of those extensile arm-chairs – already noted – which Austria was to call *Kaiser-Fauteuils*. Then, growing elderly, he admitted a military camp-bed, like that great General the Duke of Wellington in England. Was it latterly so? Paul Dost remarks on an ordinary metal bedstead, of the sort in which (usually in iron and brass) many burgess couples and many more proletarian ones in the West were happy throughout their conjugal lives. Dependent upon the quality of the mattress, such could be very comfortable, if not latterly stylish! In Great Britain, Edward VII and Alexandra were to be quite happy with silver-plated ones, at least on the royal train overnight!

5

HIGH
SUMMER

High Summer it was indeed! The world's railways, mostly steam-worked but with electric traction insidiously advancing, whether under great cities or through great mountains, were to mount to the top of their form, especially during the quarter-century from 1901 to 1925.

So also at the top of their form, up to 1914, were the royal heads about the world, though some were to fall by the way, like Charles I of Portugal and his Crown Prince, assassinated together in 1908, his second son becoming Emanuel II, only to be deposed in 1910.

As head of the British Empire, Edward VII sat firmly at last, many people being more than glad that they had a king for a change. Royalty sat firmly elsewhere too, for the most part, and for such important dynasties as those of the Habsburgs, the Wittelsbachs, the Bourbons, the Romanovs, the Hohenzollerns, and even that House of Savoy, some time of Sardinia in name, which had been so ably supported by such diverse characters as the shrewdly liberal Cavour, the military hero Garibaldi, the fire-eating General Bixio who had to be obeyed like God, the Marxist Mazzini, and many others. There were the older aristocrats of royalty in Denmark, and those Bonapartist upstarts, the Bernadottes, in Sweden. There were immensely rich princes in India and elsewhere, though they were not kings or emperors, as were the celestially born Mikado in Japan, or that sad Son of Heaven in China, whom the old Empress dominated far more cruelly than Victoria had tried to dominate her own children, so often found so *tiresome*.

In Russia, the brilliant Muscovite Court felt much more secure than it really was. Things like the *Potemkin* Mutiny and the first attempts to achieve universal suffrage came, and were dealt with more than somewhat severely by mounted Cossacks and quick-firing guns, for long ago Peter the Great had invented a system which, had he known it, was to outlast the Tsars, and still does so in Russia and elsewhere. How ironical that while the rest of the European publics trembled at the thought of underground *Nihilism* in Russia, that statistical old bore Karl Marx had surmised that that same Russia would be the last redoubt of imperial repression! He had been a poor lodger in England for a long time, and he is buried here, where he thought his Great Idea would first be born out of admittedly appalling slums in London, Manchester and other places.

In all the British Realm and Dominions, and in then increasing Colonies, as noted, there were some sighs of relief on Edward VII's accession. Here was a real man at the head, with ideas extraordinarily advanced by conventional Victorian standards. He was 'every inch a King'! Racing became truly the Sport of Kings. He persuaded the old Austrian Emperor to motor. Even the vagaries of his private life were engaging, for so many people had long been doing that sort of thing on the quiet, and both truly and in the burgess *argot*, Queen Alexandra was a very great lady. He could not bear his nephew, William II of Germany, and even Victoria had severely reproved the Kaiser for what she considered, to herself, a most impudent telegram of congratulation to President Paul Kruger in South Africa, over the war which had been brewing up there for some time.

The Carriage and Wagon Departments of several British railways had been spoiling to produce new and worthy things in the way of royal rolling stock. As we have seen, the Great Western had just managed it by way of the Diamond Jubilee, although the Queen had demanded the retention of her old carriage of 1874. The Brighton company had managed a complete royal train too, though obviously for the new King while he was yet Prince of Wales. For him, also, the Great Eastern had lately provided some handsome club-like carriages to serve its Sandringham and Newmarket occasions. Now, for Edward VII and Alexandra, two railways prepared and built complete royal trains which were entirely new. They were, respectively, the London and North Western, and the South Eastern and Chatham (the latter a combination of the South Eastern, and the London, Chatham and Dover companies' systems under a Managing Committee). A little later, the Great Northern and the North Eastern, as partners in the East Coast Route from London to Scotland, jointly built two superb twelve-wheel saloon carriages – King's and Queen's respectively – which were to run in conjunction with a very special saloon and special service vehicles. The Great North of Scotland Railway built a special king's saloon, convertible for either day or night use. Three Irish railways – the Great Southern and Western, the Midland Great Western and the Great Northern (Ireland) built royal saloons of most sumptuous sort, and even the little Belfast and County Down built something of the kind, which it afterwards used as a special saloon, much favoured by the richer sort of golfers of a Saturday.

First, to the old Royal Mail Route, West Coast to Scotland and also including the Holyhead line of the London and North Western Railway. In this case, there had been what might, with respect, be called a guinea-pig carriage, and it was of the sort one has already called quasi-royal. The Dukes of Sutherland we have met already, as aristocratic railway magnates with private running powers north of Inverness, two successive private locomotives, and a private station at Dunrobin, north of Golspie. To the end of the 1890s, the Duke had used a six-wheel private carriage with electric lighting from batteries as well as oil-pots for service if anything went wrong. It had convertible day- and night-berths like a Pullman sleeper but without the folding upper bunks. Though a nice carriage, it was becoming somewhat *vieux-jeu*. In 1900 came something much more luxurious. Though he owned an important link in the northern main line of the Highland Railway, the Duke went for his new design and construction to the London and North Western, whose Carriage Superintendent, C. A. Park, had already produced some handsome sleepers and some truly beautiful dining cars. After all, the Duke's longest habitual railway mileage was between the South of England and the North of Scotland, much of which was owned by the North Western company. Like the Prince of Wales to the London, Brighton and South Coast in 1897, he made one stipulation. There must be no connection by bellows with any other vehicle. The Duke had sampled American private cars, and he wanted something like those. He got one. (It still exists; a beautiful relic!)

It was an eight-wheeler on 8 ft bogies at 39 ft centres, and the body was 57 ft long by 8 ft 6 in. (maximum; the end vestibules were 5 ft 9 in., being thus neither 'wide' nor 'narrow' by American Pullman standards across the water, while the body was necessarily narrower and not so high). Height to top of clerestory was 12 ft $7\frac{1}{2}$ in., so the carriage could go anywhere in Great Britain within reason on the standard gauge. (The Tunbridge Wells and Hastings line of the South Eastern was unreasonable, owing to stingy construction as to clearances, and remains so to this day, worked by singularly *mean* diesel multiple-units, though that is not the fault of B.R., Southern Region.) Inside, the carriage contained what Americans called a master-bedroom with a double bed, and a single-bedded one, still fairly generous, and each with an adjoining lavatory, all flanked by a side corridor. Over full width was a combined dining and parlour compartment with a central table, 13 ft 10 in. long, of very comfortable sort. Beyond this to one end were a pantry and a sort of servants' cubby-hole, and at the other, beyond the sleepers, were another lavatory for general use and, as in the older carriage, a compartment containing two Pullmanesque 'sections' with extensile seats for bedding down, but no upper berths.

The original official photograph, and a plan, were published in the *Locomotive Magazine* (London) of July 1900, ironically facing an article on a singularly Spartan-looking third-class carriage wherein the Holland Railway had managed to cram eight compartments and (courtesy title) a lavatory on to a three-axle wheelbase.

The importance of this ducal carriage (and of a modest but quite sumptuous four-wheeler which one imagines the Duchess using for local calls north of Inverness) is that they set the contours of the new and splendid royal train which C. A. Park was only waiting to build for King Edward VII and Queen Alexandra. Their style was pure London and North Western, and its finest example as yet. The livery was composite; below the waistline it was *Duke of Sutherland's Green* (something between dark-olive and holly) while the upper panels were that spilt-milk white favoured by the North Western company, mouldings being very handsomely picked out and lined in gold leaf. The roof decks were white, Wolverton fashion. Lighting was electric, and original heating by a self-contained high-pressure hot water system.

Now Queen Victoria was gone, Mr Park was given his head with the new train for Edward VII:

'Now, Sir; as to the style of decoration?'

'Make it like a yacht's!' intimated the Defender of the Faith.

And so it was. Really, it was a superb train!

The two most important carriages made a pair of stately twelve-wheelers. The time was 1903. All the carriages were to be built at Wolverton, that old intermediate station of the primeval London and Birmingham Railway, where had grown up a significant, if not particularly beautiful, English industrial town, even possessing steam trams, which of course came under London and North Western Railway auspices. (The Wolverton and Stony Stratford steam trams perished with the General Strike of 1926.)

The new royal saloons were 'King's' and 'Queen's', each with appropriate night arrangements. Queen Alexandra had her silver-plated bedstead protected from draughts by a silken tent, which after Edward's death in 1910 was fairly soon ordered to be removed by Queen Mary. Each carriage was an apartment in itself; each an enlargement of the Duke of Sutherland's carriage, this time with the vestibules having double doors and with full communication to the rest of the train; each was 65 ft long by 9 ft wide and was mounted on six-wheeled bogies of 11 ft 6 in. wheelbase at 43 ft 6 in. centres. Those bogies of Park's time at Wolverton have never yet been bettered in your author's travelling experience; one simply 'drifted along' with them, as on a film of oil, or in a 'levitated train', by which one does not mean a hovercraft, ingenious invention though it be.

Looking back over years remembered since the summer of 1911, one recalls few things on rails equal to a London and North Western six-wheel bogie, under a carriage. One was Belgian, in 1958, quite by chance, oneself having been slung off an international express on the next road for not having a reservation.

So no wonder the London and North Western 'royals' of 1903 were to be in service for such a long time! Your author's experience was with old twelve-wheeled diners. The North Western vehicles were, by our supposed standards, of antique sort. The Belgian train was spacious but otherwise ordinary. Quaint! But technological flukes of history have been like that!

Anyway, Edward and Alexandra, in their time, clearly rode more easily in their splendid carriages than most people about the world, whether exalted or otherwise.

To three generations of Englishmen and Scotsmen, their style – that of the post-Victorian London and North Western Railway company – was so familiar as to make description an impertinence to such, as in telling an American citizen about Pullman-Standard in words of one syllable, during the same period. 'Yachtlike' had been the King's requirement as to decoration. The bodies were entirely wooden, with that elegantly modest clerestory which C. A. Park provided only for his most imposing vehicles, such as diners, sleepers and saloons, and – to assist internal daylight – in some parcels and luggage vans. The contour was the same as the Duke of Sutherland's later carriages. (Park's Travelling Post Office carriages had, by contrast, skylights.)

External style is adequately shown in the original official photographs and, apart from painting, in the vehicles themselves, which are still preserved. Inside, perhaps, one might call it 'Forsyte-Adam', and to one born in that first decade of this century, it was a relief alike from 'Heavy Victorian' (c. 1876) and from William Morris's awful chairs. (*He*, however, designed lovely prints and wallpapers!) The saloons, in this party's opinion, were very good to look upon. There were day- and night-saloons for the King and the Queen in each of these splendid twelve-wheeled carriages. Maximum length between partitions was 17 ft 7 in. while the width, except over vestibules, was 9 ft inside. The King's carriage had a 10 ft smoking-room with deep green leather arm-chairs, sufficiently spacious to take the vast bulk of Edward VII in his latter years. Appropriately a splendid twelve-wheeled dining car, which had won *Grand Prix* at the Paris Exhibition of 1900, was assigned to the new royal train. Like most royal diners, it included a long table with handsome chairs around, as well as another compartment arranged in ordinary dining sections for those who sat below the salt. Reverting to the smoking-room, this was much occupied by the King on daytime journeys, apart from mealtimes, in the consumption of immense cigars. (In later years, George V and Queen Mary were equally fond of it. Queen Mary was usually the more visible of the two, contentedly having the morning sherry or puffing that after-dinner cigarette which so scandalised militant anti-smoking American ladies many years ago.)

At the turn of the century, the London and North Western Railway had already a number of decidedly elaborate family saloons, for both day and night travel, which could be hired by the rich of all classes. These were increasingly used for the conveyance of the royal suite, but with the appearance of the entirely new royal saloons, Wolverton

Works produced what were to be always known as 'semi-royals', of uniform contour but with rather shorter bodies on four-wheeled bogies. The obvious prototype was the Sutherland saloon already noted, but from this they differed in having end vestibules and bellows connections. Lastly, there were several royal brake vans, of the same clerestoried shape. Two of these were describable as brake-firsts, for they contained four-berth compartments like French *couchettes* for off-watch members of the train crew. One van contained in addition a crew's messroom with a gas-cooker, and telegraph and telephone offices, for the train could be connected wherever it stood. It also had a house-telephone, to which the equerry on duty, having portable apparatus, could plug in wherever he happened to be on the train. The other 'brake-first' contained a 50-volt electric generating plant and heating boiler, for such times as the train was parked at night on some remote siding in the course of extended tours. 'Semi-royal' carriages, by the way, were often used for conveying distinguished or even exalted visitors to and from royal residences that might be remote. One was normally set aside for hire. Twelve first-class fares to any station in Great Britain, so long as destinations were not up some corkscrew branch-line like Whitby-Pickering on the North Eastern, or meanly constructed main-line such as the South Eastern company's to Hastings, could secure it, so long as the point of departure was on the London and North Western – or possibly the Caledonian – system.

A specimen train for one of the royal migrations between London and the Deeside in Scotland usually comprised eleven vehicles of the types described. It would tare – i.e. without passengers and luggage – about 430 tons. On the greatest British railways, lightness was all, and weights being relative (if it came to hitting anything else) this was as substantial as a comparable American train of wooden cars weighing nearly twice as much. (The heaviest Continental European vehicles of the period came somewhere between the two.) Two locomotives, not very large, could take this over the most formidable climbs in Northern England or in Scotland without anxiety. A London and North Western official photograph of the train, admittedly including some of the old family night saloons rather than 'semi-royals', showed it headed by the superheated 4-4-0 engines *Coronation* and *George V*, both of 1911, which should have had no trouble with it. Early in Edward's reign, on 8 October 1903, two somewhat smaller, unsuperheated Webb compounds of the Alfred the Great class, had happily taken the train from Carlisle to London, $299\frac{1}{2}$ miles, without a stop, regally rumbling through gaunt Wigan and the rat-ridden canyon of Crewe as well as roaring over the top of Shap.

This beautiful train was to last many years, and such alterations as took place in its arrangement will be mentioned later. Meanwhile, several other railways were to provide new rolling stock for official royal journeys, and far from least in importance, though relatively small, was the South Eastern and Chatham, a combination of the South Eastern and the London, Chatham and Dover companies' systems. Already, as noted, there were special royal saloons kept for British Royalty at Calais and Brussels, but it was high time that something new could be laid on between London, or Windsor, and Dover. When it came, some bitter commentator said that now should all rejoice at the first new train to be seen in South Eastern England since the death of the Duke of Wellington. That was somewhat unkind, for the South Eastern could and did build very good carriages when its bank balance would allow, and the impoverished Chatham had done its best, even being one of the first to light its expresses by electricity.

In style, the South Eastern and Chatham royal train had much in common with C. A. Park's on the North Western, apart from external painting, which was a reddish maroon, picked out with gold leaf on the mouldings. The special carriage for Edward and Alexandra, having the unique number 1 R, was distinctly like a North Western 'semi-royal', though even shorter – 50 ft compared with 57 – and it had a bellows gangway for service access at one end only. There was a clerestory somewhat similar in shape to the North Western type, with half-domed ends, while internal decoration and furnishings might have come from the same designer. Like the North Western, the South Eastern saloon was built in 1903. The second-named was for daytime use only, for this was long before the days of the Dover–Dunkirk train ferry, and its two main compartments were fairly obviously 'King's' and 'Queen's'. Trimmings were green – green satin cushions, and fixed upholstery in green fabrics and leather. The King's favourite smoking arm-chair, by appearances, was a duplicate of the North Western design; indeed one suspects more than a little entirely friendly collusion between Harry S. Wainwright at Ashford and C. A. Park at Wolverton. Why not, indeed? No two British railways could have been less in rivalry than these. The South Eastern's 1 R was only 8 ft 1 in. wide, so if needed it could be taken to Hastings via Tunbridge Wells without trouble. It was on two four-wheeled bogies of 8 ft wheelbase at $33\frac{1}{2}$ ft centres.

The largest compartment ('Queen's') was 17 ft 1 in. long. There were two lavatories; the King's was bypassed by a short corridor. The Queen's, at the 'blind' end, was of full width. Both contained box-seated valve water-closets, distinctly superior to the North Western's, and most other railways' mobile specimens at that time, though the chutes below were arranged as badly as ever. After sampling hers, Queen Alexandra initiated complaint that it was cold and hard, so Mr Wainwright most thoughtfully had the seat covered with suède leather before the next royal journey on the South Eastern. This intimate comfort lasted until someone stole it in the 1940s. Strange lore lingers long in railway works. Your author had this from an old specialist who had attended Southern royal trains for many years.

Another curiosity *passim*: By seniority Harry S. Wainwright had succeeded as Loco-motive, Carriage and Wagon Superintendent of the united South Eastern and Chatham, though he was essentially a carriage man. Most of his locomotive design was by Robert Surtees, his Chief Draughtsman, who came from the London, Chatham and Dover. Wainwright gave the engines a livery and a brassy finish both showy and stylish, as can be fully appreciated in certain treasured survivors.

The rest of the South Eastern and Chatham royal train consisted of two corridor saloons, a coach with side corridors but with bellows at one end only, a non-gangwayed saloon, and two saloon-brake carriages thriftily converted from two of the company's best 'brake-thirds', as used on the Continental expresses. These one remembers as being supplemented sometimes by a six-wheeled brake van.

Though the colour of the S.E. & C. carriages was latterly described as 'Wellington brown', one recalls that this took on a rather redder tinge on the royal train. That, like the London and North Western one, was to last many years and, latterly painted green with white roofs, became the Southern Railway's official one in the years after 1922. The beautiful – but non-corridor – Brighton one, with its limited availability, might be described as having gone into private business, to be dispersed over both the Eastbourne and the Tunbridge Wells lines for some years. Probably the last assignment of the South Western saloon (built in 1885 and rebuilt in 1897) was the wedding journey of the Duke and Duchess of York, later King George VI and Queen Elizabeth, from London, Waterloo, to Bookham early in 1923, modestly headed by an M7 0-4-4 tank engine.

Back, however, to that wonderful year of 1903 when King Edward was not only emancipated but reaping certain harvests from earlier sowing of popular sympathy and affection! While under him the twice-yearly Victorian visits to Balmoral were reduced to one, in early autumn, the Great North of Scotland Railway gladly provided a royal train of its own, or at any rate a very nice convertible day and night saloon carriage which could be combined with the company's best first-class rolling stock to provide one. Though modest in dimensions, it was extremely well arranged and of some elegance. It was to survive the King, latterly as a reserve saloon carriage, for many years. The Great North of Scotland Railway, from the 1890s onwards, under William Pickersgill made excellent carriages, including indeed the first of the corridor type for purely internal service in Scotland. The royal saloon was the only Great North carriage ever to have a clerestory roof, which was not much favoured by Scottish companies, and never for ordinary coaches (as on several English and many German and Scandinavian railways).

This G.N.S. carriage was 48 ft long and 8 ft 6 in. wide, on 8 ft four-wheel bogies. Its main compartment was 16 ft 5 in. long, with folding tables on each side, two sofas and four arm-chairs. One sofa could be replaced by a bed for night travel. There was the usual smoking-room at one end, an ordinary compartment with corridor access, an attendant's compartment and a pantry with a cooking stove, and sufficient lavatory arrangements. Lighting was electric (the G.N.S. *never* used gas), heating originally by closed-circuit hot-water arrangement, as in old Pullman cars. External finish was the best possible under Great North standard style, viz. white upper panels and a dark plum colour in the lower quarter, handsomely moulded and lined-out. The train's first assignment including this new carriage, which the Great North simply and indeed primly described as 'Saloon No. 3', was to take the King from Ollerton (on the then Lancashire, Derbyshire and East Coast Railway) to Ballater, after the races at Doncaster. The journey was made by day, which Edward VII preferred when possible, and, most unusually, reversal was not at Ferry Hill Junction but in the old Aberdeen Joint Station itself, where the Lord Provost was introduced to the King. Ballater was reached correctly on time at 6.10 p.m., which was in nice time for dinner at Balmoral. In 1906 the train was laid on to take both Edward and Alexandra from Ballater to Aberdeen to open new buildings of the Marischal College, thus celebrating the 400th anniversary of that city's great University. Most unusually for those parts, as opposed to the South and West of England, the locomotive was very gaily decorated and adorned with flags.

Before we leave the Great North of Scotland Railway, notice should be given to a possibly unique service: 'The Messengers'. King's, or Queen's Messengers filled an office as old as such hills as Royal Personages ever beheld in all the world. Passing by the Pharaohs to the country presently involved, a King's Messenger of King Corbreidh Gald of Scots (Tacitus' 'Galgacus') doubtless helped with the total disappearance of the Roman Ninth Legion, which marched out of York and never returned from some place near Lockerbie. By the time of Queen Victoria, nearly eighteen hundred years after, such had become respectable and highly educated diplomats who travelled, wherever possible, by steam conveyance or navigation.

When Queen Victoria first moved into Balmoral, her dispatches had to be brought to and from her over the mountains north of Perth. It involved a 2,000 ft summit on the road, and the Queen's Messenger certainly enjoyed no sinecure in bad weather. The old Deeside Railway, later absorbed into the Great North, winded custom, and pragmatically approached the Queen's Private Secretary, who in 1864 was General Grey. It undertook to take the dispatches from Aberdeen to Ballater, and vice versa, at £9 2s a day, in 3 hr 40 min., with 15 min. allowance for road–rail transfer at Aboyne. The contract was awarded. The 'Messengers' ran on the Deeside line from 8 October 1865 onwards, later to and from Ballater. The running of even special trains on Sunday agitated the more extremely Calvinistic congregations of those parts, but they continued, as did H.M. Mails. Ironically, Victoria herself considerably approved of the 'Scottish Sabbath'. In one's own time, the 'Messenger', going south in the afternoon and coming back in the morning, had one of the older Great North express engines heading one of its handsome composite corridor coaches plus two or three humbler vehicles for those of the public who cared to make use of such desecrating services.

As to recorded rolling stock, we are still in 1903, in which year Edward VII and Alexandra went to Ireland. Since her younger days, Victoria had shunned her Third Kingdom, which, indeed, had preferred Elizabeth, Empress of Austria, who was not only a Catholic but a great horsewoman, naturally endearing herself to many in what was ultimately to become a republic.

For journeys between Dublin, Belfast and Derry, the Great Northern Railway (Ireland) provided from the best of its existing rolling stock a train of seven vehicles, including a twelve-wheeled dining car, connected up to two saloons improvised from other dining-car stock and entirely refurnished and decorated by the famous Dublin firm of Millar and Beatty for the King and Queen respectively. The King's saloon, like the diner and a coach for the suite, was clerestoried, with the half-dome ends to the upper deck favoured by both the Great Northern companies, of England and Ireland respectively. Appointments were extremely sumptuous in high Victorian style, with much velvet, bobbled curtains below massive pelmets, and very rich panelling. The King's saloon had been a 45 ft diner. The Queen, being a *petite* personage, was accorded a 42 ft saloon with a plain roof. The King's main compartment was 19 ft 4 in. between partitions, and 8 ft 4½ in. high inside. Standard width was 9 ft, which was modest for carriages running on 5 ft 3 in. gauge, and lighting was electric throughout, the G.N.R.(I.) having been another brave pioneer in the general provision of this. Like the Great North of Scotland, and the London, Chatham and Dover Railway in England, but far unlike its English namesake, it never lit any vehicle by gas, though the homely oil-pot persisted on its older local trains (even on its first restaurant car in 1895).

In your author's memories of Ireland, the G.N.R. was a favourite, but he is bound to say that the most imaginative flights on that occasion in 1903 were by two more southerly railways; the Great Southern and Western, and the Midland Great Western. The former was the largest railway undertaking in Ireland. With amalgamations, it came to stretch not only from Dublin to Cork, Tralee and remoter Kerry but crosswise from Rosslare in the south-east to Sligo (via Limerick and Claremorris) in the north-west. Outwardly, the saloon built for Edward and Alexandra was handsome but conventional; a fine eight-wheeled vehicle with a clerestory roof of rectangular profile, 50 ft long, 8 ft 9¼ in. wide and 9 ft high inside. Its decoration was taken in hand, or at any rate advised upon, by the artistic wife of one of the company's nabobs, and Sibthorpe and Company of Dublin, a firm which already was grandly decorating some of the railway's best dining cars with an Italian artist to beautify, did the same only even more so with the royal (or as it later became, State) saloon. Internal decoration of the main compartment, 17 ft long, was Art Nouveau with a seasoning of 'Celtic Twilight', for on the bulkheads within the clerestory, the gifted Italian gentleman had painted circular panels containing, respectively, likenesses of an Irish harper and a piper. Panelling was full of restless curves, and flowers suggesting Morris wallpapers; upholstery was of the satin-striped sort, distinctly Regency; and why not? For 'Prinny' had been the first of the Hanoverian Dynasty to take the slightest interest in his Irish subjects and, incidentally, was the only one of the Four Georges to hold Court in Scotland, either.

There were two smaller compartments, intended as smoking-room and boudoir, each 10 ft long. The former's style was described as 'Francis the First', and though one doubts that that exalted and uxorious Majesty would have recognised it as such, one could imagine his substantial ghost sitting in one of its appropriately substantial leather arm-chairs with his even more substantial and still-mortal host (who loved France), discussing Life.

Queen Alexandra's *boudoir*, in which, possibly, she merely left her hat and coat, was – in the slang of a slightly later period – a 'peach'. It was 'baroque', of the nicest kind, and one of the very best examples, successfully carried out, of an old style grafted into new usage. Once, long ago, your author sat at the back of a box in the Residenztheater, Munich, for his first experience of that favourite Mozart opera, *The Marriage of Figaro*. This railway compartment was not unlike that box, only somewhat bigger!

All gone, now! (Except that lovely theatre!) The Great Southern and Western royal carriage ultimately became the Irish Republic's State Saloon. Its decorations were sadly 'modernised' to three-star hotel standards; even the clerestory was cruelly sheared off in favour of an ordinary G.S.R. standard semi-ellipse. The thing was that it was reported a much better-running carriage, less likely to run hot in its boxes, than that now to be mentioned.

That was the splendid royal saloon designed under Edward Cusack of the Midland Great Western Railway, for a tour from Dublin to Galway and Kenmare, and a trip into Connemara. Once again, as on the Great Northern, Millar and Beatty were the furnishers and decorators; but there was no question of improvisation here!

As suggested, the vehicle was entirely new in design as well as construction, and it was intended for official use of the then Lord Lieutenant of Ireland thereafter. It looked very much bigger than it really was, for its body measurements came to about 56 ft by 8 ft 8 in. with an inside height of 8 ft 5 in. It was on two six-wheeled bogies. Design of coachwork was rather different from British and Irish conventions of the time. The corners were rounded off and the semi-elliptical roof was half-domed at each end. One of those ends was 'blind' and designed as a closed observation room with windows on three sides. This was quite short; just enough for looking at the mountains of Connemara; 6 ft 6 in. between partitions, like a generous third class on the Midland Railway in England. Next came one of the most magnificent reception saloons seen on a train in many years, if any at all. It was an inch short of 19 ft long. Millar and Beatty had designed it in the form of a pillared hall in miniature, with Corinthian columns flanking it on either hand, and with cornices and internal pediments to match. Really, it was superb! One has seen it, as beautiful as ever, many years after, and is not needlessly gushing now.

Beyond this, utility prevailed over 9 ft 8 in., longitudinally, with a vestibule and a lavatory, with a fine pedestal water-closet in a blue pattern. Next came the dining-room, 15 ft 1 in. between partitions and similarly Corinthian in style, though less successfully so than in the reception room. (All the same, it must have been a nice place in which to eat and drink when sovereign duties had been done.) Beyond this again came a 4 ft 6 in. kitchen, out of which a bellows gangway led to the next vehicle. Such a kitchen may have been more accurately described as 'pantry' or (horrible term) 'kitchenette', but if more imposing things were likely to be required at the royal table, the admirable Midland Great Western Railway had some beautiful dining cars, capacious in kitchen. All attendant vehicles were painted in royal blue with white upper panels, which for several years was the 'Midland's' standard livery for main-line vehicles; the locomotive was the stately 4-4-0 *Celtic*, built the year before and one of the largest engines in Ireland at that time, likewise painted blue. It was a lovely train!

At this same time, a double journey was made over narrow-gauge, which in Ireland was 3 ft, and that was on the Letterkenny Railway which was worked by the Londonderry and Lough Swilly Railway. Even that had no suitable rolling stock for royal patronage, though from as recently as 1947 one recalls that it had comfortable first-class carriages. So the L. & L.S. company was lent a saloon carriage by the Belfast and Northern Counties Railway from its narrow-gauge line between Ballymena and Larne. It was of what Englishmen then contemptuously called 'tramway type' with open-platform access, but it was nicely done up and given comfortable chairs and so-forth. Edward and Alexandra seem to have been quite contented with it.

One is reminded that abroad there were indeed royal tram-cars. Such were known in the Netherlands. The *tramweg* was then part of the Dutch way of life; receipts went slightly down in very hard winters when the citizens put on their skates and took to the hard-frozen canals instead, but not otherwise until the bus came! Paul Dost in his book *Der rote Teppich* (*The Red Carpet*, published by Frankh of Stuttgart in 1965) not only describes fabulous royal trains but royal trams too, with illustrations. There was a sumptuous one on the

Vienna City Tramways, and also on the Vienna–Baden line. The Hohenzollerns had a ride on the Rheinuferbahn (Cologne–Bonn) which, however, was and remains something most closely approximating to an American 'Interurban', such as did such good work in the U.S.A. before the Motor Mania came to possess the West.

We have noticed already how, in London, Edward VII as Prince of Wales opened two of the first deep-level underground electric lines and emerged from the second somewhat out-of-temper. His nephew William II of Germany was much interested in such things, and in 1908 sampled the Berlin equivalent from Leipzigerplatz to Reichskanzlerplatz. With his phobia about infections, he was no more pleased than his Uncle Bertie in London. 'No person, ever again,' he said, 'will get me into this germ-carriage! ('*In diese Bazillenkutsche bringt mich kein Mensch mehr hinein!*' Quoted by Paul Dost.)

British railway companies had not yet done all for Edward VII that they could and would. In 1901 the Great Eastern had built a rather beautiful clerestoried eight-wheeler for Queen Alexandra; gas-lit and more club than boudoir, much of it in blue morocco. Serving as it did the royal estate of Sandringham, through a rather sumptuous little station at Wolferton on the King's Lynn–Hunstanton line, the Great Eastern company had long regarded Edward as a favourite as well as an exalted customer. Certain of its best locomotives were unofficially commissioned in a sort of Royal Reserve. One was a pioneer oil-burner, the T19 class 2-4-0 *Petrolea*, in Edward's last years as Prince of Wales, and during his reign as King the best of the Claud Hamilton class 4-4-0 were thus selected. (This practice persisted into London and North Eastern days, with 'Super-Clauds' appropriately maintained and elegantly finished.)

But with that Accession, the English partners in the East Coast Route were at last able to produce, jointly, something rather adequate in the way of King's and Queen's saloons, for day or night travel.

Between York, where the North Eastern Railway built its carriages, and Doncaster, where the Great Northern built everything mobile ('Doncaster Plant' was no merely ostentatious title), were mutually co-operative feelings, and the two works set out to build an entirely harmonious pair of royal saloons, for King and Queen respectively. They had worked like this before, in the provision of vehicles for the East Coast Joint Stock, which the North British company also built in Scotland, to Great Northern designs. But when it came to these new 'royals', North Eastern design was more than fairly apparent in the finished vehicles.

Both were, by British standards of the time, enormous carriages. Clerestories were *out*. The former North Eastern carriage man, David Bain, had gone to the Midland. H. N. Gresley was in command of the Great Northern Carriage Department. The deeply semi-elliptical roofs, with half-domed ends, were characteristic of his practice. The new royal saloons had these, while their steel underframes, each in the form of an inverted bowstring girder, were latest North Eastern practice, also used on some new dining cars. The varnished teak finish outside was both Great Northern and East Coast Joint. The style of the panelling was North Eastern. It was beautifully lined-out in gold leaf.

Outwardly, the two carriages were almost identical; each was 67 ft long, 9 ft wide (outside) and an inch short of 13 ft high; each was a pair of 12 ft six-wheeled bogies set at

45 ft 6 in. centres; each had vestibules with double doors at either end. The King's saloon (Doncaster's contribution) had a day saloon 17 ft 6 in. long, a smoking-room, and another big compartment which could dine six by day and contain the King's bedstead at night. There was a dressing-room and an attendants' compartment. Lavatory arrangements were spacious. This vehicle ultimately (under the London and North Eastern Railway) became the Queen's saloon, while the North Eastern became a joint one. It still survives in service at the time of writing, one of the oldest, and still one of the most handsome, British railway carriages in use. The usual run in recent years has been between London, Liverpool Street, and King's Lynn for Sandringham (the old private station at Wolferton having suffered oblivion with the Hunstanton branch).

There were several very advanced features in these two carriages not least in their electrical equipment. There was a closed ventilation system, which further warmed the air in winter. Some of the rooms had indirect lighting from tubular lamps above the cornices. There was some modest use of electrical cooking appliances, the first in the country on a train. Decoration was describable as 'richly restrained'. After an ornate phase, new Great Northern carriages were distinguished by marked plainness, sometimes ascribed to the austere tastes of that promising young man Oliver Bulleid, who was at first under H. A. Ivatt, titular head of Doncaster, marrying his daughter, and then under Gresley as his successor.

Hitherto, East Coast royal vehicles had been distinctly old-fashioned (see Colour Plate IV of the train leaving York). Now, as on the West Coast route, a number of special, or 'semi-royal' eight-wheeled saloons appeared. Their styling was Great Northern. They, too, were arranged for either day or night travel, and could be hired by wealthy notables or invalids. While the half-domed elliptical roof was used, it contained a sort of false clerestory with sliding ventilators, to which air was admitted from slots under the cantrails to the space between inner and outer roof. Construction of all these took place during 1907 and 1908.

No more royal carriages were to be built for British service over many years, while some of the old ones fell variously by the way. Queen Victoria's famous 'twin' was used no more, but was most fortunately preserved, together with Queen Adelaide's archaic one dating back to 1842. The Great Western Queen's Carriage of 1874 had its last assignment as a hearse car for the funeral of Edward VII in 1910. It was broken up in 1912, though some of its furnishings were preserved. The Great Northern royal saloons of the previous century suffered some occultation. Of the two eight-wheelers on the London and South Western, that with the clerestory but without bellows served with its more favoured, vestibuled fellow, when the King of Denmark was conveyed from Portsmouth South Railway Jetty in 1907, and continued to be officially royal until 1913. The two old Great Eastern saloons were still, at least officially, assigned to Sandringham availability in the mid-1930s, though one doubts that they were much used, for following some frightful train-fires occasioned by collision, gas lighting of carriages fell more and more – but still too slowly – into disfavour.

King Edward VII was not the sort of monarch to be disliked by his subjects, though prudes had sometimes disapproved of his private life. (Queen Alexandra understood, and sent for Mrs Keppel when he lay dying. A great lady! A *very* great lady!) Nevertheless, there remained as always the 'Fanatic Fringe'. The great twelve-wheel carriage built by Cravens for Continental royal journeys was the scene of an attempted assassination when Edward, Prince of Wales still, was passing through Brussels. The bullet passed through one of the windows and lodged in one of the handsome partitions. In that same instant, 'Bertie' kicked at his table and flung his great bulk on the sofa, having perceived a commotion and the vague figure of a young man with a gun. (He was a good gun himself!)

This splendid old man was gathered to his fathers on 6 May 1910. Quite away from all the official obituaries and commentaries and orations, Rudyard Kipling's story, 'In the Presence', told from the eyes and mouth of an Indian soldier, is after many years deeply moving.

During his reign, one remarkable change had taken place in the working of royal trains. As noticed, Victoria had travelled about twice as fast on her last journey, in the London, Brighton and South Coast company's royal funeral train, as ever she had done when living. Now the living monarch was *allowed* to do so. It was, however, with the new Prince and Princess of Wales, afterwards George V and Queen Mary, that the Great Western Railway cut a spectacular dash in July 1903, when the engine *City of Bath* took them from Paddington to Plymouth in $233\frac{1}{2}$ minutes for the $246\frac{5}{8}$ miles by the old route, including the heavy climbs up to Whiteball east of Exeter, and skirting the southern flanks of Dartmoor west of Totnes.

King Edward VII's funeral train went from Paddington to Windsor on 20 May 1910, after his death at Buckingham Palace and his lying-in-state in Westminster Hall. There were ten vehicles, including – as noted – the old funeral car which had been Victoria's, and the engine was appropriately the *King Edward*, one of the four-cylinder 4-6-0 Star class, designed by G. J. Churchward of the Great Western and then one of the most advanced and powerful express engines in the country. Various of the company's best saloon stock were used in the make-up as well as the regular royal set. Never had more crowned heads been assembled in one conveyance, for there were nine kings, including the acceding George V and his cousin the German Emperor.

Each side of the engine's smokebox were those great mountings of the Royal Arms which had accompanied the dead Queen a decade before, draped in violet. So the King was 'taken to the place of his fathers, which is at Wanidza' (Kipling's Havildar-Major).

During those years, there had been less construction, abroad, of royal rolling stock, of what the Germans called *Hofzüge*, for the simple reason that foreign kingdoms, grandduchies and principalities had been busy with such while British designers were – to put it rather brutally – awaiting the passing of the Great Queen. The Kaisers had had theirs in the 1890s. The Grand-Duke of Baden, incidentally, and as early as 1894, had a twelve-wheel carriage which in side elevation strangely anticipated those of the two English East Coast companies in 1907–8, but with single-door vestibules at the ends, and a double-doored one in the middle. Even the panels and mouldings, as well as the half-domed elliptical roof, had an East Coast look about them, to British eyes. William II, King of Württemberg (1891–1918) had a twelve-wheel saloon built for him in 1904. Its vestibule arrangements were similar to those of the Badenese carriage just mentioned.

It had the high windows with narrow ventilators above, and the depressed semi-elliptical roof, which one remembers from days and nights in other Württemberg carriages, ranging in one's own experience from Ventimiglia to Flushing. (The middle of the ceiling inside appeared quite flat.) King William, like his brother-monarch of Saxony, was an amiable character. While Saxony liked to go to the North Sea for his holidays, Württemberg favoured the French Riviera, where he had a house at Cap Martin below Roquebrune. All the same he visited the fighting fronts fourteen times, eastern and western, the last in January 1918, and brave Swabian soldiers were decorated by him, or in his name; also a devoted Belgian nurse. She was, in fact, a spy, and was caught, but they could not execute her, she having been much loved. In Brussels, another nurse like her, named Edith Cavell, was shot. *C'était la guerre! Krieg war Krieg!* But back to 1910.

It was a strange Realm to which George V succeeded. He was to see it utterly to change in a decade. At the beginning, it was still a sort of *späte Auslese* of Victorian vintage, which perhaps reached its dregs with the retreat from Mons, some years later. In internal politics, as far back as 1906 many British people had been horrified by a 'Liberal Landslide' at a General Election, with Labour coming in too, to form Government support on the Left. (A *Punch* cartoon showed Campbell-Bannerman, the new Liberal Prime Minister, going in to bat with Keir Hardie and accusing him in advance of 'running him out'. 'C.-B.' was shown in very correct cricket attire (he was immensely rich), while Keir Hardie was in Labour reach-me-downs with proletarian headgear.) Many people still had Family Prayers before breakfast, whether in the great houses or in detached or semi-detached ones at Wimbledon, Enfield, Sutton Coldfield or wherever. But militant ladies were already smashing windows, and burning things that ranged from letterboxes to Yarmouth Pier, in the cause of universal Women's Suffrage. In that Coronation Year of 1911, there was a formidable railway strike, with the Guards called out to protect railway property. An old photograph shows a squad on the Great Western, in presumed battle-order but still wearing bearskins on their heads.

The ship of Empire still proceeded on its stately course towards the typhoon which, all unsuspected, lay ahead. Here, and elsewhere, the royal trains also proceeded on their stately ways. Trains had long lives, then. Most of the world's monarchs had splendid things, good for many years. The King of Italy seems rather to have made do. A photograph of the reception of Humbert I at the Anhalter station in Berlin, 1889, shows in the background two ageing American Pullman cars, which had been prefabricated and re-erected at either Derby or Turin a decade before. Nearest are some old, probably Upper Italian, saloon carriages. Poor Umberto! He was not to die in his bed. His successor, Victor Emanuel III, was to wait for a very long time – indeed until 1929, to get a really gorgeous royal train. Alphonso XIII of Spain had a set of carriages, extremely spacious as befitted the Spanish broad gauge, but of distinctly austere style inside and out, apart from some fiddle-back chairs in the diner. Both aspect and styling rather suggested Indian first class of that period. The train's last official assignment seems to have been that of spiriting away into exile that nice, patient Queen Ena when the Popular Front took over Government in 1934.

One has seen the Swedish King's saloon used by Oscar II and later by Gustavus V

(1858–1950) and can now illustrate it (Plate 40). As a whole, it was of semi-clerestoried type. One's attention, as recently as 1937, was drawn to the beautiful English brass bedstead as well as to its crimson damask upholstery, and one privately investigated the royal water-closet which was comparable to that *Optimus* of 1871 which one has also personally sampled in one of the British Royal Palaces as well as in several haunts of one's youth. These things were of the highest importance, though long deemed unmentionable more was the pity in view of certain other things, even a horrid piss-box for the Royal Valet in one of the German trains. (These things were made and marketed for executive offices in both Great Britain and America at that time.) The Swedish carriage was very narrow, as Swedish carriages go, and probably would have gone fairly enough even in restricted British tunnels, save only on certain mentioned portions of the South Eastern, and on the North Eastern's Whitby and Pickering line. No other up-to-date Swedish carriage could have got beyond Dover, had there been train ferries there at the same time! Be it added that apart from Wagons-Lits no Continental, let alone Scandinavian, royal rolling stock has as yet penetrated the British Isles; nor is that likely since we took on us wings to fly, though Edward VIII was later to favour those same Wagons-Lits which, on the service called Night Ferry, were to ply between London and Paris; and later, Brussels.

The Wagons-Lits company, indeed, was to serve various royal personages; not only the British, but also such as the German Emperor and the King of the Belgians, ('Kaiser Bill' and 'Leopold the Damned' as other parties were to call them at one time and another). We are still – mark this – in the first quarter of the twentieth century!

In that time, the British Empire was still rising towards its zenith, and magnificent trains were being built for the King Emperor abroad. The Canadians, strictly following North American traditions over many years when it came to railway trains, were to provide some beauties down the years that were to follow. Even before the death of Victoria, one was provided for the Duke and Duchess of York (ultimately George V and Queen Mary) when they visited Canada in 1900. The style was entirely Pullman-standard of the period. One private car – the most important one – was named *Sandringham*, was provided by the Canadian Government, and was a double-ended observation car with balconies both ways. The rest of the cars were the contribution of the never-to-be-forgotten Canadian Pacific Railway, which was taking George and Mary from the Atlantic to the Pacific. All were beautifully finished in varnished mahogany, and named after the most important components of the Empire. The rear observation car was named *Cornwall*, and was 78 ft 6½ in. long, and, like the other eight cars, 10 ft 3 in. wide and 14 ft high from rail to top of clerestory. The *Sandringham* was built by the Barney Smith company. It had very ornate brass balconies which would not have disappointed even Pierpont Morgan. In the bedroom suites of the *Cornwall*, there were full-size bathrooms. Baths on trains were rare at that time. George V (then Duke of York) was to be the first to install them on an entirely insular British train, though showers had appeared already in India.

To India, therefore, we go next. Victoria had never come visiting. Not even Abdul Karim had persuaded her. But splendid trains were needed for both the comfort and the prestige of Emperor and Viceroy, and so they were provided. The distances, by Home standards, were immense, if less so by North American. The heat in the Plains was intense. Even the Maharaja of Jodhpur, who was used to it, had imported ice laid all over the floor of his carriage while he lay up on a handsome, and comfortable, leather-padded sofa. Overhead the punkahs went swinging, or, later, the great revolving fans turned. These, latterly with electric motors, could be powered by revolving cups as in a Robinson's anemometer. That arrangement was used over many years by the Wagons-Lits company for its dining cars in Europe and Siberia, not to mention China. The trouble was that when the train stopped, the fans usually stopped too.

Most magnificent of the Indian trains at that time were those designed and built for the East Indian and the Great Indian Peninsula companies, which, with the greatest respect to the others, were the Anglo-Indian seniors. The State was to get them in the end, but so it had to be!

The East Indian Railway, for the Delhi Durbar of 1911, provided an Imperial Train of ten carriages, each, apart from the terminal vans, 68 ft $2\frac{1}{2}$ in over bodies, and including practically identical King's and Queen's saloons, the only differences being in style of furnishing. Each contained a day saloon 18 ft between partitions, a 17 ft bedroom, a 12 ft bathroom flanked by side corridor, and appropriate servants' and service compartments. The bedsteads were of Cuban mahogany with rosewood mouldings and birdseye maple inlay. An appearance of sumptuosity was important in all Eastern countries then, not yet was Mr Gandhi studiedly to travel in the wooden third class, just as in China the austere virtues of Maoist cultural revolution, with beautiful things condemned and destroyed, were as yet unthinkable. In the Indian royal and viceregal trains – one led to the other in the way of obsolescence and replacement – full use was made of native and foreign timber harmoniously matched in decoration. Both the royal beds bore the Royal Arms at head and foot, set in lozenge-shaped panels. The King's trimmings were in fine green leather, and the Queen's in green silk tapestry. Fabrics were less liberally disposed than in the West; desirably so, for heavy drapes in the tropics give shelter not only to the harmless, indeed beneficial house-lizards and geckos, but also to their less desirable prey. The E.I.R. royal train, however, conceded Axminster carpet on its floors.

Contrary to usual Indian practice, this train had the roofs handsomely clerestoried throughout, the upper deck containing both the electroliers and very large electric fans on vertical axes. The royal dining car was arranged in railway-conventional – i.e. not 'dining-room' – fashion, having side tables and chairs in fours on one side and in twos on the other side of the medial passageway in a saloon compartment 50 ft long. There were twenty-four chairs, a massive sideboard in Spanish mahogany and oak, and a 'whatnot', also for service purposes, in walnut and oak. Metal fittings were plated in oxidised silver. Entrance to the main saloons from platform was by wrought-iron verandah gates. Externally the train, taring 430 tons and measuring just under 700 ft over buffers, was painted white, with the Royal Arms painted on the lower quarters of all carriages, and embossed, or cast, for the verandah gates of the King's and Queen's saloons. External mouldings were picked out in gold leaf.

This superb train served for some though not all of the Delhi Durbar journeys. The old Great Indian Peninsula Railway was not to let itself be forgotten. It was concerned with a royal journey to Kotah, and it built at its Parel works a complete train of eleven carriages including the end-brake vans. The vehicles were rather more traditionally Indian than those of the E.I.R., with plain roofs on a cambered curve, though in both trains, the then very common Indian sunshades over the upper portions of the windows were lacking, more attention being given in the way of improved ventilation as well as of dark glass and dust-excluders. This G.I.P. train contained, *inter alia*, a strong-room and a laundry. (Queen Elizabeth II was to be furnished with an ironing-room on a splendid train provided by the German Federal Railway in 1965, though it was not, as sometimes claimed, the first example of such a thing.)

Adornment of imperial locomotives in India was considerable, especially as to mounting of the Royal Arms and special livery, though with less of the flags and festooning then often provided in more southern parts of the United Kingdom. The G.I.P. allotted a fine Atlantic type locomotive to royal service in 1911. Her name, previously, had been *Lord Clyde*, after the Viceroy. Now she became *Queen Empress*. Further, this railway painted imperial and royal engines in dark blue with chocolate framing and gold lining out – a sort of glorified Caledonian – to which would be added chimney cap and dome casing of brightly polished brass. The great Bengal–Nagpur Railway, at that time, painted its best locomotives in a rich green, not quite Great Northern and not quite Great Western, and these also furnished royal haulage in 1911.

Many of the Indian Princes, immensely rich even by Eastern standards, had their own rolling stock and their own railways in their own States. They knew entirely how to be looked after, from His Exalted Highness the Nizam of Hyderabad, who, about a very considerable portion of Central India, owned and worked an admirable Guaranteed State Railway, to the Rulers of more modest principalities in other parts, who ordered, bought and used the finest that could be provided. Indian railways at that time were largely run by Anglo-Indians, who were Eurasians, and consulting engineers were usually of 'the English', who knew from long experience what was best for India, when it came to railway rolling stock and several other things at that time.

Other countries, far from British, but with British influence of one sort or another, patronised the British railway manufacturing industry, with imposing results. Of these, the very differing Argentine Republic and the Vice-Realm of Egypt immediately suggest themselves. In Argentina, British companies had long owned, and worked British-fashion, principal main-line railways from the Chubut to a high pass in the Andes. ('Narrow-gauge buffet-car train at Mendoza Junction', as caption to a photograph taken nearly 70 years ago, sounds extraordinarily familiar. That showed a train on the Argentine Transandine Railway, once managed by one's old and kind friend the late George Boag, who later went to do the same for the Great Southern of Spain Railway, whence he was forcibly ejected, with Mrs Boag but only such of their belongings as they could carry, at the beginning of the Spanish Civil War in the 1930s, by the Popular Front.)

That is, in our story, a long way ahead. But Argentina, through her railways, was one of our very best customers in the early 1900s, just as we bought much of our beef from her.

In England, and in Birmingham, the Amalgamated Railway Carriage and Wagon Com-

124

pany had completed coaching orders worth over £5 million Sterling in five years, so the company made a present to the President of the Republic of a magnificent railway carriage for his 5 ft 6 in. gauge lines, which allowed plenty of room for such. It was 74 ft 5 in. long over headstocks. It was 10 ft 6 in. wide like the best on the old Great Western broad gauge at home. It was 14 ft high from rail to roof-camber. It was mounted on two six-wheeled bogies set at 54 ft 6 in. centres. Its internal appointments included a Louis XVI day saloon, 17 ft 3 in. between partitions and containing, as in the earlier carriage already mentioned, a real working fireplace for cosiness, together with a kitchen, bedrooms and a bathroom. Furniture and decoration were distinguished. The roof had that internal mock-clerestory which was much favoured on Argentine railways. It was quite impossible to get this enormous carriage down from Saltley to the sea by railway. It was barged down to the great Severn, and then shipped out. Ere that, in England, the ageing Edward VII got wind of it and asked for a full report. Had he lived, he might have requested one like it for use in India, but that, as we have seen, was not to be. The bathroom, be it added, contained a needle-bath, a particularly Edwardian refinement in plumbing, which could have well satisfied, alike, Christian, Moslem and Hindu ideas on personal hygiene, not to mention the primeval and admirable Jewish ones. The carriage was fully described in the Carriage and Wagon Review sections of the *Locomotive Magazine* in 1910.

In the previous year, also in Birmingham, the Metropolitan Carriage and Wagon Company built for the Khedive of Egypt an extraordinarily elegant State saloon which still followed the traditions set at the end of the 1850s, for it had an open verandah section in the middle, with Khedival quarters at one end of it and Ministerial ones at the other. Though slightly narrower, it was fairly comparable with the Argentine carriage in its main dimensions. It was 65 ft $7\frac{1}{4}$ in. long and 9 ft $4\frac{3}{8}$ in. wide. It had an inside height of 9 ft $4\frac{7}{8}$ in. to the top of an unusually wide clerestory (5 ft 6 in. between inside deck-rails). Decoration was austerely elegant, which means that it might have pleased the late Mr Sheraton more than the late Mr Chippendale. The steel underframes were of unusual sort. The inverted bowstrings of the North Eastern design in England have been mentioned already. This Egyptian carriage likewise had its steel solebars – if that be indeed quite the word – depressed towards the rail in bow form, but in this case it was twice each side, over the middles of the six-wheeled bogies. The vehicle was painted all over in creamy-white, like Egyptian Wagons-Lits and, later, Pullman cars. It was beautiful to look upon, and so were the best of Egyptian express trains at that time. Oh, those lovely locomotives, were they British, or French, or some distinctly nice (though rarer) Americans!

About that time, Rudyard Kipling, sampling an Egyptian express up from the Canal, wrote that she reminded him of a South African one, and that therefore he loved her. Earlier, Mark Twain had been, as an American, less enthusiastic, suggesting that the locomotive was using unwanted mummies as fuel. Many, many years after, there was a terrible accident on an Egyptian express between Alexandria and Cairo, when the third-class coaches, marshalled right in the rear, caught fire, and nobody noticed as the train roared across the Delta. Old, sad, half-forgotten things!

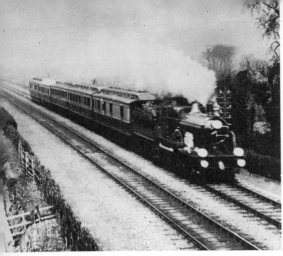

65 *above left* Near Highbridge, Great Western Railway, 3 March 1902: visit of Edward VII to the west of England, with Queen Alexandra. Queen Victoria's 1874 carriage is fourth from the 'Atbara' class locomotive.

66 *above right* Great North of Scotland Railway: London and North Western Railway royal train near Ballater, with 1903 saloons and older family saloons behind a G.N.S.R. locomotive by James Johnson, 1893.

67 North Eastern Railway: N.E.R. V-class 4-4-2 locomotive No. 1792 with the London and North Western's royal train on the High Level Bridge at Newcastle upon Tyne, 12 July 1906. Edward VII has previously opened the King Edward Bridge, just upstream.

68 London and North Western royal train at Ollerton, *en route* for Doncaster races, September 1906, Lancashire, Derbyshire and East Coast Railway engine.

69 The London, Brighton and South Coast Railway in its full, glorious pride! Edward VII and a large party going to the races, *c.* 1909, in the complete 1897 royal train with three 'Southern Belle' Pullmans added, behind engine No. 39. Photographed south of Merstham (new) Tunnel.

70 London, Brighton and South Coast Railway's train for President Poincaré, at Portsmouth South Railway Jetty, 1913.

71 The famous 'twin saloons' designed by C. A. Park and built at Wolverton by the London and North Western Railway for Edward VII and Queen Alexandra, 1903.

opposite
72 Smoking-room in the King's saloon.

below
73 The Queen's bathroom, a later addition. Observe Victorian plated-copper tub!
74 The King's buttons.

75 The Queen's bedroom: Queen Alexandra had – at least at first – favoured a tent of silk bed-curtains.

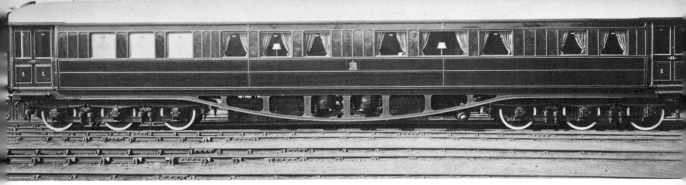

76 Great Northern Railway: King's saloon built at Doncaster, 1908, for the East Coast Route to Scotland. Observe N.E.R. style in both frames and body.

77 King's saloon,
with smoking-
room beyond.

78 Dining
saloon.

79 Netherlands Railways: Queen Wilhelmina's day saloon, 1903.

80 Van and service car, with observation platform.

81 Queen Wilhelmina's personal carriage.

82 *right* Italian State Railways: parlour in King's carriage, built by FIAT of Turin, 1929. Observe Genoa velvet.
83 *below left* Ceiling detail. Observe the emphasis of Labour and Industry, Unity and Liberty in the coving.
84 *below right* The Queen's bedroom.

Very soon, British and French were to be holding Egypt, while the Turks held Syria and Palestine, and a singularly off-beat soldier, T. E. Lawrence, was fighting a private war somewhere in between, and winning it. Nearly half a century later, the locomotives of trains he had wrecked on the Hedjaz Railway were being discovered in, and lifted out of, the Arabian sands. They had been Turkish by ownership, and of classic German construction.

In the still expanding British Empire, with colonies uniting to form Dominions which would be politically autonomous apart from formal allegiance to the Crown, the last mentioned to a great extent deputed its Constitutional authority. There were Governors-General, somewhat equivalent to Viceroys as in the Indian Empire. Special railway vehicles were built for them; several in Australia which was bedevilled with breaks-of-gauge. They served as royal saloons when the Sovereign or the Heir came visiting. Some were to last for a very long time indeed.

Under the Manchu Dynasty of China in its last days, the xenophobia of centuries naturally embraced the Western Barbarians' machines, such as steam railways, and earliest attempts to introduce them were disastrous. The old Empress Tse-si, Regent from 1898 to 1908, had greatly disapproved of them until she was at last given a ride in a train, which seems rather to have captivated the venerable lady. Nevertheless, there had been some penetration, not least assisted by European arms. The Boxer Rising at the turn of the century saw a most improbable-seeming alliance of British, French, Germans and Russians repelling and then hunting Chinamen with bloody glee and, more importantly, very sophisticated weapons of that period. The western allies then settled into their trading concessions very cosily. All four built Chinese railways, each a microcosm of its sponsors' practice at home or colonially. Thus, the Shanghai–Nanking Railway was extremely British; the Shantung Railway was very German; the Tcheng T'ai was distinctly French. So it was with various others, and even Sun-yat-sen's liberal revolution was to make very little difference. They might become Chinese State Railways, but they generally went on as before, with the same officers. The Japanese and the Russians had both been after Manchuria. Each had a substantial railway there – the Chinese Eastern (very Russian) and the South Manchurian (American/Japanese and for a while looking – in its best trains – uncommonly like the Pennsylvania west of Pittsburg).

All the same, even in the last days of the Manchus, there was not much work for an imperial train. In the last century, three French eight-wheelers were provided for Regency or Viceroyalty, and in his book, *Der rote Teppich*, Paul Dost shows one – a staff car – something like an ancient Manchester and Leeds 'gondola' (central portion alone covered) taken to its logical conclusion on bogies. He shows also, in a perspective sketch, something very like an old Pullman car prefabricated in the middle-western U.S.A. and assembled in Europe. It was of only 21 tons tare and just under 49 ft long (15 m.). It was called a 'State saloon'. That seems distinctly like an old Derby, or Turin, Pullman car, and so does the sketch. There were open platform entrances at each end. Dost's drawing shows un-American bogies without equalised suspension. Various European vehicles found their way to China, whether by sea or by the Trans-Siberian Railway. In his book *Pullman in Europe* (Ian Allan, 1962), George Behrend mentions and illustrates one which had a distinctly adventurous career, for Wagons-Lits took over old Pullmans which once had served the Indian Mail to Brindisi. One went to Russia and was put on 5 ft gauge bogies. After serving as a dormitory car for superior staff at Irkutsk, it went to China, still under Wagons-Lits sponsorship, and on the Chinese Eastern Railway which even at that time was a White Russian stronghold. Certainly it seems to have been there in 1923. A photograph from that year shows a very old Pullman car, of obvious American origin, at the tail of the Trans-Manchurian express, with a very liberal open platform at rear, certainly much more spacious and elegant than anything it had had in its previous career farther west. It has also the appearance of a deep semi-elliptical roof, with Russian-style cowls on top, which may have been a replacement, or may simply have covered the original clerestory (Egyptian-fashion in some cases). Whether the Empress-Regent rode in, and enjoyed, this carriage, one is not prepared, at present, to discuss. In 1932 it was officially recorded, by Wagons-Lits, as *voiture hors série*, and to have become a mobile Inspector's Office. Many of the better railway carriages ended thus, from the Pacific back to the Pacific. Some, as suggested, even became 'fancy-religion' churches in one place or another.

For the rest, some of the finest vehicles in the Far East were those of the foreign railway officers themselves, not only running but living on, their own lines. These parties, too, were generous in laying them on for good customers whom they also liked, though it could be hazardous if people forgot about something. The late William Adams-Oram, for many years of the Hong Kong and Shanghai Bank, was thus once doubtfully favoured on the Shanghai–Nanking Railway. Waking in the early morning, amid sumptuous bedroom surroundings, he realised that he was not in his own bed but in a railway carriage. Further, putting his head out-of-window because of the intense silence all around, he found that he was on a single-track main line, deserted and alone, as far as he could know. The saloon had been at the very end of the night train to Shanghai. Having put off some other vehicle at a wayside station, the express had gone roaring on towards the dawn, duly protected by tail-lamp carried forward in correct British fashion. Mr Adams-Oram made a fuss, and very properly too!

Such things happened at one time or another, around the world, whether to involve worthy banking men in China, as in the last case, or anxious soldiers and others on missions to foreign parts. It was no joke to be left behind in Central Asia, were it Russia or Persia, and possibly, of the two, Persia could be the more alarming when parties were alone at night upon the bare mountain.

Such things were unlikely to befall the Crowned Heads on their tours and visits, though soon there were to be awkward occasions of other sorts. In Great Britain, the Royal Family and its exalted visitors had been fortunate on the railway. There was one occasion, on the South Eastern and Chatham Railway (lampooned *ad nauseam* in the writer's boyhood) when an ordinary express was in collision on the curve approaching Tonbridge from Sevenoaks. This train was far in advance of the impending royal schedule, which, however, it threw sadly *agley*. The handsome brassy South Eastern locomotive made a sorry picture reared up with a broken bogie, and Edward VII had to be re-routed on his way to the Continent.

Although, particularly among our kings, he hated delay and was a martinet about punctuality, his first inquiry was about possible casualties. As already remarked, Edward VII was a gentleman; like most people who love life as far as they are allowed, he was considerate about other people who loved their lives.

A note or two should be made here about things apart from, but closely connected with, royal trains. They were royal waiting-rooms. The monarch was not expected to wait for anything, but the contingency had to be recognised in advance. In earlier days, indeed, there had to be some sort of a decent interval during the change from horseflesh to iron-horse (in the disgusting phraseology of the period). But even under most civilised circumstances, the royal waiting-rooms provided a sort of lobby. The Personage had sometimes to be 'received', as on those memorable occasions at Perth, which had their counterparts over most of Europe. Railway stations adjacent to the great royal houses always had such places. At Windsor, both the Great Western and the South Western had beautiful apartments of this kind: the Great Western splendid as to furniture and the South Western architecturally most meritorious. The Great Eastern at Wolferton had a delightful station. So had the Great North of Scotland such, especially at Banchory, which for some time was the rail-head for Balmoral. The station there remained quite splendid long after the line had been extended to Ballater.

At Windsor, there were at one time plans for an entirely royal station, to be served by a private branch from the London and South Western Railway near Ascot, which would have entailed a traverse of Windsor Great Park and even of the Home Park. There was even a building set up – still surviving at the time when one writes – but the line never was built. The Great Western Railway, one feels, would have been much annoyed. There was no Royal Prerogative about private stations and waiting-rooms. Various people in Great Britain had them, were they sufficiently rich. One need scarcely remark that one of these was the Ducal Family of Sutherland which, at Dunrobin, put up what in earlier days would have been called 'neat erections', comprising a station and a small shed for the private rolling stock. Amid the rocks of far-northern Scotland, the station building was in black and white half-timbered style, which might have belonged about the Welsh Marches, or in East Anglia, but not, domestically, quite in those parts!

Abroad there were many private stations, especially in Germany of the many princes, but in many other places too, and with fine ostentation at that. Yet one of the most elegant came from Republican France, in 1873. Napoleon III had died in England at Chislehurst, in exile, in January of that year, having abdicated in 1870 after the Battle of Sedan. But Ranelagh Station was built in the Bois de Boulogne, Paris, for State arrivals and departures, and continued thereafter to serve for these. It was served by a short branch from the Western Railway of France at Auteuil, and there, somewhat rebuilt, it survives, latterly called Bois de Boulogne: a neat pavilion in French-Empire style. The name Ranelagh is ancient. It is Pidgin-Latin for 'Frog-pond' which doubtless explains why both the Gauls and the Gaels perpetuated it. Paul Dost calls it 'Old French'. England got it from Ireland, and, like France, made it quite exclusive-sounding for a while.

Fully royal was the Laeken Royal Station in Belgium, outside Brussels. Connection to the main line entailed more work than from Auteuil in Paris. It was built in 1908 (last years of Leopold II) right inside the palace precincts, with heavy gradients, severe curvature, and a tunnel under the royal foundations themselves. These brought the cost up to six million Belgian francs, and what the more Radical elements in Belgium thought of that cannot be recorded. Ah, well! Belgium had the oldest State-owned national railway system in the world, a very individual one at that, and in the Low Countries there was nothing new about railways being built by Royal Command. King William I of the Netherlands had commanded the building of the first portion of the Dutch Rhenish Railway, completed from Amsterdam to Utrecht in 1843 although the Dutch Parliament had thrown out the Bill. In this case it was certainly Royal Decree as opposed to Royal Assent. Quaint, since the great House of Orange had risen through bloody toil with the Dutch Republic! But there, republics, like Royalty, are curious things. So are Political Bureaux, People's Chairmanships or whatever.

These things are secondary to this essay, though they have much to do with it, and our immediately present business is that of private railway stations. About Europe, as suggested, there have been many of these down the years. Rather surprisingly, one of the best known, though little used, is of comparatively recent origin. We have noticed already the period put to short-lived Papal journeys up to 1871. (Pio Nono expressed pontifical approval of his rarely used train.) In that year he made himself a voluntary prisoner in the Vatican as a protest against secular occupation of the Holy City, and solemnly enjoined that on his successors. He died, as even Popes must.

Not until 1929 – with Benito Mussolini sitting on the back of the ageing King Victor Emanuel III – did that finely intellectual Pontiff Pius XI (his baptismal name was Achille) break, through the Lateran Treaty, with this preposterous custom of pontifical immolation.

Then a short branch line was built from the Italian State Railways' Roma S. Pietro to within the massive walls of the Vatican. There was set a very little terminus, Città del Vaticano; Vatican City, perhaps the last of the City-States invented by the Greeks several centuries B.C. In Rome, heavy rolling doors were mounted as a sort of portcullis across the breach in the Vatican walls, against profane traffic. They were usually closed. Now and then an old Italian State 2-8-0 steam locomotive, with wagons, would be admitted, and, in due course, given her manumission, for the station was normally used only as a goods depot. While Pius XI and Pius XII permitted themselves a country seat at Castel Gandolfo, their transit was by motor. The Holy City-State went through the Hitler War in holy neutrality. That war ended at last. Pius XII survived it for some years, then was succeeded by the venerable and gentle John XXIII. Old John, sometime peasant-priest of a poor parish, was no stranger to the train, though in his young days even the hard timber-slats of the old Italian third-class carriages, and the transport they afforded, had been expensive to his kind. As he rose in the Hierarchy, he came to know, now and then, the more reasonable striped moquette of the Italian second class. At length he became a Cardinal, and then, to some people's surprise, Pope, to reign briefly but remarkably effectively from 1958 to 1963. He was the first of the Popes since Pius IX to use a train after his election. He went to Loreto, and to Assisi, which last, on its bare mountainside, seems to one without creed to be more of a holy city than some much larger places. An

Italian gentleman later told your author, beside the big station-bar in Florence during post-official conviviality, that His Holiness had said how pleasant it was to ride once more in a train, and in such an excellent one. He felt himself too old for aeroplanes, though motors were all right.

One seems to have leapt the frog, historically, for in this account the most amiable Pope John should have been a long way ahead, beyond many dreadful things. But as Vatican City Station may be numbered among the royal stations, spiritually though not temporally for many people, so let it be!

6

THE SUNDERING FLOOD

So it was to be, in that brilliant summer of 1914, though few realised it; realised how great a flood, or how sundering! William Morris (from whom the present title is borrowed) would have welcomed the idea of crowns toppling, expecting a glorious Brotherhood of Man to follow in a Socialist Paradise, living entirely on native industry, and art of the Folk, wherein a starry-eyed commune rejected the acquisition of a steam engine because they could do the work with their own shoulders and hands. It was easy enough to imagine from the Red House, Bexley, or from the idyllic Kelmscott Manor beside the upper Thames, especially with the appalling slums of post-Industrial-Revolution Britain, and its comparably appalling wealthy Philistinia, in mind. If Morris, and others, including one's own grandfather who published him and sold his books from Bond Street in London, could have seen the reality to come, they would have died of broken hearts. As it was, they died peacefully, some years earlier.

There had been more than enough domestic troubles among the great Habsburgs. Now Austrian Crown Prince Francis Ferdinand had morganatically married, to the wrath and dismay of the old Emperor. However, she was a nice and rather lovely girl, and was socially if not dynastically accepted. (Even the German Emperor kissed her hand on receiving her!) At that time, Serbia was a rather suspect neighbour of Austria. Bosnia, wrested from the Turks some time before, was a firework of an acquisition. Anarchic and nihilistic political refugees holed up in those parts: and sat there waiting. More organised communists also sat, waiting, in Switzerland.

Since the beginning of the century, trouble had been accumulating. It was trouble of the sort which all the powers of that time thought they were prepared to face, but of which they really had not a clue. Germany, with chameleon eyes (which work independently) on both France and Russia, had the most formidable army in the world. Great Britain had relied, since 1805, largely on the Royal Navy, but Germany, realising the importance of sea power at last, had acted accordingly, and very ambitiously. France was France. Russia was Russia, and her Emperor was of *All the Russias*, though there had been a most unpleasant surprise with Japan in 1904. Many people still believed, as had England's Lord Chesterfield, that war was a natural corollary to the advance of civilisation.

Then came July 1914. The Archduke Francis Ferdinand, heir to one of the world's senior empires, went on a State visit to Bosnia. With the entirely inoffensive Countess Sophie Chotek, he alighted from a narrow-gauge train, and was escorted to a waiting motor. This car, an open tourer with the hood down, subsequently took them round the city. Trouble was expected, and a *détour* was made. That was in vain. The first attempted assassination failed. Francis Ferdinand reproachfully asked the Lord Mayor whether he usually received personages with bombs. In spite of the deviation, the second attempt succeeded. Slowly, with dignity to the last, the liberal Francis Ferdinand and the gentle Sophie collapsed in their blood, side by side.

Could they have known it, all Hell was to be let loose for several millions of people, by that act and from that moment. But they could not know, wherever they had gone; let alone that an era had begun to collapse with them on the buttoned-in leather cushions of the princely motor car. Never before had Continental disaster blazed up, from the Urals to the Pyrenees, from the Golden Horn to the Hebrides, as did this one. On 4 August

1914, there was war within that area, with terrible red branches stretching far beyond.

Nobody knew quite what had been let loose, with old loyalties kept, old treaties variously kept or broken, with new and dreadful technical advance unleashed, and mud from Flanders to the Pripet Marshes in which to fight it out over bitter years. Alike in London and Berlin, people still thought that it would be over by Christmas. Perhaps the French were the realists. The great Napoleon had taught. But Napoleon was long dead.

Our present concern is not political, nor yet historical save where it involves the royal railway trains. Those, for the present, remained just as they had been; at best mobile Court conveyance, and at worst – as was quickly coming – as mobile headquarters under Government.

No sumptuous new trains were built, or were to be so for a long time. But the contending emperors and kings were to use their trains as suggested. They sometimes lived in them for many days at a stretch; that applied certainly to the Tsar, and to George V of the British and William II of the Germans, who had quite as much mutual suspicion of each other as first cousins ought to have, dynastic politics apart.

George V set a precedent, not much followed, with his London and North Western train. He had baths installed in it. Each of C. A. Park's royal saloons of 1903, made for Edward VII and Alexandra, contained a 'dressing-room'. Into these went the copper- and silver-plated bath-tubs, wooden-cased and lidded, and adequately plumbed for hot and cold water. During more than four years of war, owing to these roving commissions, the London and North Western royal train worked overtime, while relatively little use was made of the others, saving perhaps those of the Great Western and the South Eastern and Chatham. Those two railways, in the past, had often co-operated in the working of trains to and from Dover, via Reading and Redhill. At Portsmouth, not only the South Western, but the Great Western and the Brighton trains had often been seen. The last-mentioned had been cleared for the Naval branch, for all its substantial contours which had precluded it in 1901 when the old Queen died. The Great Western train was used from South Railway Jetty when the King of Portugal arrived in 1904, still including Victoria's Queen's Carriage, then 30 years old. In the following year, the Brighton train had been used for Alphonso XIII of Spain as it was, some years later, for the French President, Raymond Poincaré who in 1914, in German eyes, had succeeded Edward VII as Premier Villain; just as in British eyes the German Emperor became Vice-Beelzebub, who somehow had been patronising the South Eastern and Chatham's royal train from Port Victoria a few years before. Now all these gorgeous State visits were over, for a rather long time, and in some cases for ever.

The Kaiser, and such other German royalties as Prince Rupert of Bavaria, who took an active part in the field, were at an advantage in that they could take their special rolling stock with them to the rear of the fighting fronts. They do not seem to have included the King of Saxony, an amiable gentleman of middle age who used his train, in happier times, chiefly to take him from Dresden to the North Sea Coast, to relax on the riddle-ridden sands of his beloved Norderney (Frederick Augustus III, 1904–1918: b. 1865, d. 1932).

Though that war saw the first appearance of train ferries between England and the Continent, from both Southampton and the supposedly secret port of Richborough in

East Kent, no royal train was shipped over. At Calais there was indeed the old South Eastern twelve-wheeler in which Albert Edward had been shot at. But the train ferries took over an immense amount of other rolling stock to serve the British Expeditionary Forces in Northern France and Belgium. There were locomotives galore, at first of existing British and undelivered Dutch types requisitioned, and then 2-8-0 of Great Central and, astonishingly, New South Wales designs. Many of the British railway companies furnished, or improvised, highly sophisticated ambulance trains, in a tradition which went back at least to a beauty on 3 ft 6 in. gauge ('Princess Christian's'). This had gone to South Africa at the turn of the century. H.R.H. sponsored another, in England, in 1915 (Lancing, L.B.S.C.). From the London and North Western came a very fine mobile Headquarters Train for the British Commander-in-Chief. French High Command was served by rolling stock of the Wagons-Lits company, in a dining car whereon fateful armistices were to be signed in both 1918 and 1940. After 1918 this was kept for years at the Invalides in Paris, at first in the open air where it became rather decrepit, before being removed to a pavilion in the Forest of Compiègne, at the expense of Arthur Henry Fleming of Pasadena, Cal., U.S.A. Thence it was ripped on 22 June 1940, to stand later in front of the Brandenburg Gate in Berlin. It had seen twice the triumph and the shame of two great nations. Having hidden it away in Thuringia, the Germans blew it up in 1944, lest approaching American soldiers should recapture it. Strange history of a railway carriage!

All this has taken us a long way on from the years 1914–18, for correlation is like that. His Britannic Majesty, George V, was like no other king in Great Britain in a very long time. For one thing, his father had been very fond of him, which was scarcely the way of the first three Georges. He had not expected to become King; perhaps the untimely death of his elder brother the Duke of Clarence had been a good thing in some ways or others. Like the Emperor Napoleon, he suffered severely from indigestion, which made him irritable, as his sons knew only too well. He had an intense sense of duty. Like the German Emperor, he visited his soldiers as well as his Navy.

Without evidence, one does not know that William II ever rode around behind his front line in a 'saloon' which was in fact a sort of shed mounted on two Decauville trucks, drawn or propelled by a petrol-engined tractor. George V did so. Both the British and the French Armies made considerable use of Decauville temporary railways, sometimes the only reliable conveyance in a world of obscene mud.

This horrible war ended at last, a fight to breaking-point, which seemed to threaten one way or the other unto the end, and that came in November 1918.

Already the Crowns had begun to topple. First to go was that of the Tsar of All the Russias, Nicholas II. His abdication in 1917 seems to have been a formal one in his train, though one distrusts much information. A prisoner within a system, like so many eminent Russians, at least from the time of Peter the Great who had invented it, he was a mild but apparently rather stupid sort of man, considerably dominated by the Tsarina who had brought into the Imperial Household an abominable holy man we still remember as Rasputin, whom she believed to have some mystic power to save and preserve the sickly Tsarevich to rule All the Russias when the time came. Rasputin, shot, not by some nihilist, but by a Prince, died under the ice, still fighting after he had been flung in the river. But even such severe measures came too late to save the Romanovs.

The Russian armies broke through hunger, military bungling and bureaucratic creakings. Not least of the enormities was in the shocking breakdown of transport and communications. So Nicholas II fell. In personal aspect he resembled, most ironically, his cousins George V of Great Britain and the Kaiser's brother Prince Henry of Prussia. William II once openly envied both George and Henry because, by juniority, they had become sailors. The Kaiser loved ships, especially big battleships. One is bound to say that his royal yacht, the *Hohenzollern*, both as an example of naval architecture and by straight seaworthiness, was superior to the picturesque but sometimes erratic *Victoria and Albert*, of which Edward VII had not managed to rid himself. Nicholas II and his family, with brief though dethroned respite under the Radical-Liberal Kerensky, were to meet their ends horribly in a cellar at Ekaterinburg (Sverdlovsk under subsequent renaming).

Under the circumstances of abdication, William II of Germany was to fare better. In the West one knew during childhood, he was a nursery bogey-man. 'Boney will get you!' had threatened exasperated English Nannies in 1815. 'The Kaiser will get you!' said the Nannies of 1915, and so did worried mothers of large families on the wrong side of the railway-line, whose men were fighting in mud.

Certainly William II had the dignity of an Emperor, not least in the skill with which he managed his withered arm, whether on parade or at table. He had not a little of courage. Two fears he had; those of disease and of public humiliation. Of the first we have noted something already, as in his horror at the Berlin equivalent of a 'tube' under the city. As to that, Paul Dost has remarked that when it was a good thing to persuade him away from some expedition, it was only necessary to suggest that there was an epidemic of some sort in the region involved. But in November 1918, he knew checkmate. The year before, to destroy the Second Front (which was tottering Russia) he had got Mr and Mrs Lenin and the other revolutionary communists there, in a sealed German railway carriage from Switzerland to the Baltic. (The comment of *Punch* in London, with an appropriate cartoon of him sending off an anthropoid balloon with a revolutionary cap on, was that it was sorry work for a Hohenzollern, but that necessity knew no traditions.) Now, German officers were being turned out of doors by equally German revolutionary soldiers' councils. Field-Marshal von Hindenburg (later to become *Reichspräsident*), went home in his Staff train to face the unpleasant music. The Emperor decided that it was time to leave. There was his old friend Count Bentinck in the Netherlands. . . .

One of the more racy accounts of what happened is that of Lady Susan Townley, daughter of the seventh Earl of Albemarle, and the rather undiplomatic wife of a diplomat. She detested Germans about as cordially as Americans disliked her, she openly despising the latter. She had, they said, pooh-poohed a Senator rather tactlessly ('Lodge, of Boston – common!').

The New York *Evening Journal* somehow overheard, and seized on this, to publish some very good cartoons of her and an entirely spurious portrait. Her reminiscences were published in London by Thornton Butterworth as The *'Indiscretions' of Lady Susan*. After these many years, one can enjoy the book very well. Though undeniably beautiful, she was not, to be sure, a very agreeable lady in some respects, for one of her ideas about punishing the Germans was for the felling of all trees within a 20 mile radius of the centre of Berlin. Her account of the Kaiser's flight from his General Headquarters in Spa, Belgium, was like this (decently paraphrased):

About six o'clock in the morning of 10 November 1918, the day before the Armistice was signed, a handsome motor drew up on the Belgian side of the Dutch State Railway's station at Eijsden, near Maastricht, in which city faithful Dutchmen had fought to their own annihilation against immeasurably superior Spanish-Austrian forces in 1579.

This time, the barrier was held by but one soldier, about as stone-wallish a Dutch sentry as ever waited for trouble. A very important-looking German staff-officer leaped out, demanding instant passage.

The Dutch soldier brought his modest weapon to the ready and said: '*Geen toegang!*'

The German officer insisted that the car be passed through. He said: 'The German Emperor himself is here, and he *must* be allowed to continue his journey into Holland!'

Impasse! Or, in good Dutch:

'*Geen toegang!*' said the sentry.

A second, even more important, and certainly familiar-looking German got out of the car. From youth he had esteemed himself competent to know how to deal with soldiers. He said peremptorily (though in what language, Lady Susan did not record): 'I wish to pass at once. You surely recognise me. *I am the German Emperor.*'

Politely but firmly the Dutch soldier replied: 'I see you are the German Emperor, but my orders are to allow none to pass.'

'Who gave you those orders?'

'My captain!'

'Where is he?'

'Over there! He is asleep at this hour.' The soldier indicated a small cottage.

'Call him instantly! Say that the German Emperor is here, and must pass through the barrier.'

The soldier cogitated. Up to 1914, at least, many Hollanders had disliked the British, who had fought and humiliated their South African cousins. They had longer memories than that, with a hatred of Spaniards going back to the sixteenth century; in which, too, a Frenchman had assassinated the national hero William the Silent. They had a German Prince Consort. But German doings in Belgium from 1914 on had filled them with anger and dismay. This Dutch soldier said: 'Very well, I will call him. But first, I must lock the gates.'

So the Kaiser was locked out, and at that stage was too prudent to flout Dutch feeling. The Captain was roused, doubtless in a mixed state of annoyance at being turned out of bed, and of excitement at the extreme importance of his exalted prospective internee, even while he contemplated his morning shave. Possibly he too was thinking about things which had been happening over four years to Dutch-speaking people in Antwerp and Brussels and other places only a little way west.

For he, too, barred the German Emperor.

He said he must first telephone to Government at The Hague. It might take hours to get through to high places.

Evidently, at length, he received some sort of licence, for he gave limited parole to the fuming Kaiser, whom he allowed to pass through to Netherlands territory on condition that he be confined to the railway platform, and sent back into Belgium if further permission were refused. Dutch railway platforms, on a November morning, can be as bleak as most others and more than some. The Dutch Stationmaster, *supremo* in his sphere as was the Captain over his Company, had conceded that, but for the present barred the station offices and waiting-rooms. Eijsden Station was bang on the frontier; news had travelled quickly, and from a nearby factory came angry Belgians, yelling and hooting.

Never in his life had the German Emperor endured such a morning! He was on the platform until noon, or a little after, with nothing to contemplate save his sad fate, the sterile tracks, and the station pilot engine. This insulted him by having been built by Beyer, Peacock and Company of Manchester (which the Dutch State Railway had long patronised).

Meanwhile, at The Hague, the Prime Minister and the Foreign Minister had got up early. So had Queen Wilhelmina. At their emergency meeting, it was decided that the exalted refugee be allowed asylum on Netherlands territory, but still only on Eijsden railway station. William II had been relying on two things; on the arrival of his train from Spa, where he had his Imperial General Headquarters in Belgium, and the hospitality of Count Godard Bentinck after he had crossed the frontier. One wonders what he was thinking as he paced that bleak platform, paved with Dutch diamond-grooved brick, and whether he thought of that sealed railway carriage wherein Lenin's party had taken turns at smoking in the lavatories, with the coldly fanatical Mrs Lenin in their midst like some demoniac stenographer.

Now the Kaiser dearly wished for a smoke, too, and some kindly respectful Dutch character offered him a cigarette, which he accepted. At that the enraged Belgians on the other side of the palings put up a terrible hullabaloo. It was as if he had sat down to table to consume roast duck and champagne in front of them.

At that stage, the Stationmaster seems to have relented about having the Emperor under cover. Then the great train itself crawled in, having completed its course from Spa. Imperial Majesty entered it, to spend the rest of the day and night aboard. Count Bentinck then cautiously offered him hospitality at his country house, at Amerongen. He went.

Already, the indefatigable Lady Susan Townley had been prepared to stalk him there. She had the grace to note that he was cool and dignified. At length he took, at Doorn near Utrecht, the manor house chiefly associated with his long exile.

One recalls visiting Doorn in 1928, by characteristic Dutch roadside tramway. Suddenly the jolly conductor said in English: 'The Kaiser lives there!' So we looked at the scenery. It seemed a nice house, and though the barbed-wire fence was high – not to keep him in but to keep other parties out – the grounds behind were spacious in a sandy pine heath sort of way.

Rigid palace protocol was said to be maintained inside, just as a bitter-faced ex-policeman type lurked visibly under the pines without. The tram stopped, and there were many picture post-cards of the former Imperial Bogey-man in the village shop. Later, the ex-Emperor was allowed to go to the seaside at Zandvoort. Now with a whitening little beard

145

below his once ferocious-looking moustache, he was getting old, and to people who once hated him and feared all he stood for, he really did not matter any more.

In 1940, though detesting Chancellor Hitler as a demagogue, he was glad at the triumph of German Arms over most of Europe. He was allowed to see his sometime Empire again. Goodness knows what he thought of what he saw. He died without having to see what followed, which perhaps was mercifully just as well.

Looking back over what have become many years, one is glad that Francis Joseph of the Austrian Empire, King of Hungary, Imperial, Royal and Apostolic Majesty, was not ultimately humiliated by political history. His personal life had been sad, frustrated, and even appalling in tragedy. Born in 1830, some months before the opening of the Liverpool and Manchester Railway in England, he had succeeded in the Revolution year of 1848. His son and heir Rudolf; his brother, briefly and absurdly Emperor of Mexico; his embittered Empress Elizabeth; his nephew and succeeding heir Francis Ferdinand, all met with violently shocking ends. Rigidly self-disciplined, he believed in nothing but God and the House of Habsburg, and had he known it, in his last years he was watching the last slide of that House. Nevertheless, he had reigned sixty-eight years, longer even than Victoria of the British. Towards the end he was senile, or certainly vague in his memories. Many years ago one was told that when an Austrian victory was announced from Lemberg (now Lwow) he traced a smile through his white whiskers and said to his rejoicing Minister: 'There, my boy! I told you we'd soon trounce those damned Prussians!'

Prussians? Russians? 1866? 1916? It was only half a century! On 21 November of the latter year, he went to join his ancestors, leaving to his grand-nephew Charles a sadly tottering Empire which once had embraced a very large part of Europe. Already, Austria had tried to back out of this war somehow. In embittered England and Wales, losing the flower of their manhood as well as Scotland's and Ireland's, and far from least, Canada's, *Punch* in London published a fairly dignified cartoon of the two Kaisers, Austrian and German, outside a closing door, through which the skirts of Peace were hurriedly disappearing with an anxious, olive-bearing dove at heel. Wilhelm was saying: 'Franz! Franz! I'm surprised and shocked!' Main caption read: 'An interrupted flirtation', and poor old Franz certainly wore an expression like that of a sixth-form boy caught-out with the pretty housemaid.

By mid-October 1918 the Empire was breaking up: Austria from Hungary, where Bela Kun was busy; from Bohemia, Moravia and from dominated portions of Poland. Italy and the mangled Serbia were both waiting in the South, the one acquisitive and the other bitter.

Germany was on the brink of collapse. Save in the Balkans, the atmosphere was republican. The new Emperor Charles stayed in Austria until long after the Armistice, perhaps even as a sort of hostage. A British adviser, Colonel Edward Strutt, moved in as a tactful envoy between the last of the reigning Habsburgs and the new, famine-stricken Austrian Federal Republic. When the crunch came, the ex-Emperor Charles was in his shooting-lodge at Eckartsau, where he could live off the land whatever was happening in his cities.

According to the ex-Empress Zita, Colonel Strutt managed to get the imperial train standing by and steaming up. The nearest railway station was at Kopfstetten. There the train stood, and thither the sorrowful Imperial Pair were motored. The motor itself was a Mercedes, flying a prominent Union Jack. The Emperor Charles had normally used a Graff & Stifft car. Back in 1908, at Bad Ischl (the 'White Horse Inn' town) the visiting Edward VII had persuaded old Francis Joseph to try motoring, himself having been, as noted, a pioneer. (*Cf.* letter in the *Daily Telegraph* of 4 February 1974, from Gordon Brook-Shepherd, to whom grateful acknowledgment!) The Graff & Stifft car, indeed, was taken aboard the great and beauteous train, waiting there to make its last official journey, to enter Switzerland by way of Buchs. Ultimately both reached Lausanne. The date was 24 March 1919. The motor was put up for auction by Christie's in London in 1974.

As yet, one has not discovered any details as to haulage of this last Austrian Imperial train. In the old Emperor's time, there had been a special imperial engine, a very elegant Gölsdorf 4-4-0 express with its bun-shaped dome cased in beautiful polished brass. (Bygone Austrian children truly thought that the engine wore a golden crown!) This locomotive seems to have lasted even into the 1930s. She was lovely to look upon, but she was scarcely the sort of engine for imperial passage over the Arlberg. Probably, on that sad journey, there were two more stodgily powerful specimens, fore and aft. One imagines – no more – a 2-10-0 in front and either 0-10-0 or 2-8-0 in rear, on the big climb to the tunnel. The line was not electrified until the early 1920s.

One of the present illustrations (Plate 59) shows the Emperor Charles stepping down from the Hungarian royal saloon. One end of its Austrian counterpart is visible on the left. Protocol appears to have been extremely ragged. The token strip of red carpet is wrong for the carriage steps. The soldiers on the left are displaying singular lack of respect. The overprinted caption to the photograph states simply: 'Emperor Charles I quits the Court Train.' One asks oneself: 'Was this indeed the last time? Was this scene in Austria or in Switzerland?' Somehow, thus, passed into exile the last of the Imperial Habsburgs.

So, too, passed the Western World of its time, with broken and impoverished Defeated on one side; with rather frightened, and certainly exhausted, Victors on the other, where Europe was involved. Only America and Japan rose smiling, and not all of America at that! As to England, one may record that after the scarcely creditable South African War, decorated locomotives had come steaming up from Southampton; but from that which was then just past one recalls a solitary Class D 1 0-4-2 tank engine of the London, Brighton and South Coast Railway at Clapham Junction on the day of a Victory March in 1919. (Battersea and New Cross Sheds on the L.B.S.C. had always loved to 'dress' locomotives, whether for royalty, visiting presidents or staff outings.) On that day, the soldiers of several allied nations could march in review order through both the patrician and the slum areas of south-western London. But in the World, had we known it, many of our little worlds were ended.

Even the train itself was about to be challenged!

For while the kings and the rich had discovered the delights of the private motor car some years before, the British Realm and its allies had 'floated to victory on a sea of oil', to use Lord Curzon's expression. People were again beginning to talk in starry-eyed enthusiasm, about aircraft, as indeed they had been doing before the war. But now there were many thousands of potentially commercial motor vehicles, surplus to Government service, going a-begging at knock-down prices to everyone who sized up his war-service gratuity and contemplated going into what would be an immensely expanded road-haulage business. Clever Corporal Crapper, slick Sergeant Snelgrass and douce Driver Doughless were quick to get one, paint each his name on the side, as well as did more respectable persons. An old ambulance could make quite a good motor bus for a village which never before had had anything better than a horse-drawn carrier's cart, and was very glad of such a thing which could cover some six miles to the railway station with a teenage boy as conductor and an acetylene bicycle-lamp inside.

Few of the greater railwaymen had an inkling of what was going on, save for exceptions such as Sir George Gibb, successively head of the North Eastern Railway, the District Railway and (under Government) of the Roads Board, and of lesser ex-railwaymen on the commercial side whose experience excellently fitted what was an invisible revolution.

It was a revolution quite apart from emperors, kings and abdications signed in, on, at or against railway trains.

7
AFTERMATH

Away passed the sundering flood.

Some of the Crowns stayed, including those of the neutral nations; the Netherlands, Spain, Sweden, Denmark and Norway; also that of Romania. That of Greece was fated to topple, and be restored and to topple again at one time and another. Even that of Bulgaria survived, though Ferdinand was pushed out. Nominally that of Hungary survived, with Admiral Horthy to act as Regent for many, many years, for the Habsburgs themselves were not to return. Horthy, in the full uniform of an Admiral of the vanished Imperial Fleet, was wont to give the accolade of deserved knighthood at one time and another. The Sultan of Turkey, Mohammed V, was packed off and told to behave, while his some-time Viceroy of Egypt had already been kicked out by the British, to be succeeded, with the title of Sultan of Egypt, by his uncle Husen Kamil and then by his other uncle who became King Fuad I (1917–36) and begat the rather noisome Farouk I (1936–52).

But back in Europe, the House of Savoy still rather shakily dominated the Realm of Italy, which was threatened and coveted by Communists on the one side, and on the other a new, strange, militant party of young men calling themselves *Fascisti* and headed by the sometime acute revolutionary Benito Mussolini. The last-named marched on Rome to turn out the Communists, and then offered a polite ultimatum to King Victor Emanuel III, who could keep his throne provided that he played ball with the new Dictator, without interfering. The King accepted the kind offer. Mussolini could have the Palazzo Venezia in Rome while Victor Emanuel kept the Quirinal, and thither, a little later, Victor invited King George V and Queen Mary on a State visit from London. Light grey Homburg hats became immediately fashionable in Rome. It was a happy social exchange, and many other people were happy, save for South Tyrolean Austrians who now found themselves in Italy and in for a distinctly bad time from the new Fascist guards. Worse things were happening in Russia.

Now Victor Emanuel is presently important. Italian capitalists were much relieved at the way things had turned out. In Turin, the mighty FIAT company, better known to most people as a great firm of motor manufacturers, built three most beautiful royal railway carriages for the ageing King and Queen. They were among the last things of the kind ever built, furnished and decorated in the full gorgeous exuberance of Italian Renaissance as it could be applied to railway carriages. They appeared in 1929, and deserve rather extended description.

Outwardly, the vehicles were of more-than-Cromwellian severity. They were steel-panelled with end vestibules, rather like new Italian coaches for ordinary express trains save that one, the dining car, had a clerestory over part of its length – that portion which one could only call the banqueting hall – and that the King's and Queen's carriages had prominent external water-tanks mounted in the same position over parts of the roofs and to much the same contour. They were painted dark blue, like the much less remarkable Spanish royal train, not to mention the Dutch and the Swedish.

The Italian style blossomed in a railway train; in this one of 1929. Parenthetically, be it remarked that the Renaissance in Italy also gave to the world late in this millennium the classical music and the painting that we have loved. Sculpture had remained constant since the Greeks, though slowed down. It is fairly indestructible stuff. Literature had been kept alive by the great monasteries, for perhaps holy men alone were left undisturbed in those days, whatever happened before or since then.

Now, at last, we had the Renaissance Train!

Each of the three vehicles was 64 ft 7½ in. long (19·7 m.). The King's and the Queen's carriages, as on other lines in other countries ere this, were almost identical, containing an arrangement of vestibules, parlour, State bedrooms, lavatories, and compartments for the ladies and gentlemen of the Royal Suite and for the personal servants, all arranged in very civilised fashion and appointments. Electrical equipment, heating and plumbing were of the highest orders known at the time. In braking, the vehicles were triple-fitted, for automatic air as in Italy, Germany and the Low Countries, for the Austrian vacuum brake, and for the dually workable French systems. On the carriage solebars were those mystical letters R.I.C. (*reglamente internationale carozza*) which meant that they could go on any standard-gauge line in Europe. Subject to watching the lower vestibule steps, in relation to English close platforms, they could ultimately have come to London on the train ferry from Dunkirk to Dover, though in fact they never did.

The business of decorating and furnishing the carriages was put out to open competition. The winner was Professor Giulio Casanova. FIAT, and the Italian State Railways, gave Casanova his head and let him gallop. He did.

The King of Italy had married Helen of Montenegro long ago. So a persistent feature of the decorative scheme was a juxtaposition of the White Cross of Savoy and the Eagle of Montenegro. The mouldings and panels were splendidly rich and gorgeously gilded; not even a Medici would have grumbled. Style was kept pure, and thus all this ornateness was far better executed than some things – possibly even more vastly costly – on the other side of the Atlantic. Rather telling is a remark in the official FIAT brochure:

> Prof. Casanova has made lavish use of gold, silks, brocades, enamels, bronze, tapestries, carpets and precious woods, yet although using such a wealth of materials, his artistic skill and ingenuity have employed them to the best advantage, avoiding any effect of stolidness or gaudiness.

Remarkable is a passage about the royal dining saloon: 'Here is an austere magnificence, a riot of colour and symbols, a triumph in red and gold, a superb exaltation of the sublime and the useful in national values.' Just where the 'austere' part came in one wonders. 'Rich' was the word! To be sure, English puritans had been rich, and often had done themselves very well in the way of their domestic appointments, though John Bunyan's enforced lodging in a bridge-house was doubtless 'austere'. King Victor Emanuel's diner had not the remotest resemblance to a railway carriage such as, minus its wheels, sometimes provided a place of worship for Primitive Methodists in Cornwall, Wales or wherever. It was not gaudy, but certainly it was gorgeous. The banqueting hall plan, used by the British Kings, the last German Emperor, and others, was perpetuated, with a long table down the middle and handsome chairs on either hand as well as at head and foot.

Fabrics and hides were of the finest. There were tooled and gilded leathers; there was real Genoa velvet, which is a thing not often seen in vehicles or even in Grand Hotels. This fabric, made in Venice as well as in Genoa, could not be woven at the rate of more than six inches in a day. So it went with the carpets, which were woven by the exiled Armenians of Bari:

> a miracle of patience, there being no less than 38,000 knots in every square foot of the dining saloon carpet. The decorated leather work in the corridors is from Tollentino.
>
> Everything in the three coaches is of Italian manufacture, so that this royal train will run over the railways of Italy and of Europe, not only as a travelling royal palace, but also as a symbolical example of Italian arts and crafts. It will show the foreign Sovereigns, Princes, Ministers and Diplomats who may be received in it as guests of the King of Italy, how the ancient artistic genius of the Italians is able to co-operate with the most modern of industrial products. In this train can be seen the close collaboration of engineer and artist, steel and gold, pencil and pneumatic hammer, art gallery and workshop.

So Victor Emanuel III had his beautiful train, beyond the dreams of previous Italian kings. He died in 1946, having outlived his Dictator, and to be briefly succeeded by King Humbert II. One is glad that it was so, whether as a lover of Italy or as a student of history.

He had waited a long time for his train, which Italian State Railways still preserve, and there was little to compare with it, in advance. His war had produced for him, in loot, several Pullman-style observation cars from Austria, which had been owned by the Canadian Pacific Railway, though built by Ringhoffer and Nesselsdorf to reduced North American contours. Originally there had been eight of them, variously named in Pullman fashion: *Canada*, *Europa*, *America*, *Austria*, *Africa*, *Britannia*, *Australia* and *Asia*. In their brief prime, they had been in trains on the most spectacular of the Austrian mountain lines, and had even precipitated a preposterous Press row on the grounds that the C.P.R. had put them into Europe in order to encourage gullible Austrians to emigrate via Trieste to such a land of promise as Canada. Goodness knows whether the Canadian Pacific ever got its money back on this venture, or even on the price of the cars! There is a beautiful model of one in the Vienna Railway Museum. Italy got them in the end, and they were used there for certain special journeys. By photographic evidence, one of these Canadian cars seems to have served as a hearse car for Margherita of Saxony, widow of Humbert I and thus the Italian Queen-Mother. As suggested, the House of Savoy had already found old North American Pullman-type cars useful at one time and another.

Poor old Vittorio Emanuele!

That sounds rather like the 'Poor Uncle Claudius!' which, according to Robert Graves's transcriptions, was addressed to one of the more creditable Roman Emperors by his frightful nephew and niece, Gaius Caligula and Drusilla, many centuries before. (Claudius fortunately outlived them, by several hairbreadths.) Here it is meant kindly as well as respectfully. King Victor, once again, was one of those who had become prisoner of a system. We have seen already how the second of his name had ridden to power as a liberal constitutional monarch backed by what might seem to have been a very curious coalition. This, the third of the Victor Emanuels, had come to terms with Mussolini, and had so kept his throne. In the mid-1930s, somebody managed to ask him for his views on the Abyssinian Adventure, and somehow it leaked out that he had said: 'If Mussolini wins this, *I* shall be Emperor of Abyssinia. If he doesn't, I shall be King of Italy.'

It did not work out entirely so.

But he stands in railway history as the King who had the last truly gorgeous royal train.

There were not many such prospects in the rest of the world in those anxious 1920s which were to end with a world depression in trade, as well as a slump in royalties. Victor Emanuel stayed at home, and died full of years, leaving a brief period of sad kingship to his son Humbert.

What royalties were left? There were the Scandinavian and Dutch ones. There was the British. There were the Coburgs in Belgium.

There was Victor Emanuel's son-in-law Boris of Bulgaria, who like 'Foxy Ferdie' loved to drive locomotives. Many wished to do so. Ultimately the mass-produced motor car initiated by the late Henry Ford (whose delight in locomotion – he recorded – was originated by an agricultural traction engine on an American country road) made possible what was at least a sort of engine-driving for millions.

By the joint agency of the British battle-cruiser, H.M.S. *Renown*, and of numerous trains in many parts of the world, Edward Prince of Wales was sent on a world-wide tour of his father's Empire, very soon after the war. Already he had been sent to France and Flanders during the fighting, and had made his guardians' hair stand on end by his habit of wandering off alone to see what was really going on, and to hear what soldiers were saying, even in their baths and in other places (cf. Robert Graves, *Goodbye to All That*, London, Jonathan Cape, 1929).

One believes that for the first time in his life he enjoyed himself immensely. His upbringing had been harsh, for King George V and Queen Mary seem not to have been the easiest of parents. Further, there had been a very large tutor with buffalo-horn moustachios, whose qualities seem to have combined those of the less amiable school-masters in Rudyard Kipling's *Stalky* stories; say, those of Mr King the draconian classical-crammer, Mr Macrea who believed that in games and games alone was salvation, and that fortunately temporary Mr Brownell who was obsessed with the original sin of the *Animal Boy*. Under this alarming man – who certainly did not help his younger brother's stutter – the Prince of Wales created, it would seem, an inner life of his own, which later was to upset the Constitutional apple-cart when he first fell in love, and then became King in 1936.

But now the Prince of Wales was being sent about the Empire. From that tour, among other things, emerged a happy photograph of him, high in the cab of an enormous loco-motive of the Canadian Pacific Railway (Plate 95). *He had escaped*, for a while, just as his grandfather Albert Edward had escaped when he went to Canada and the U.S.A. in the 1860s. He was happy. He 'went down well' in Australia too, whence come pictures of singularly English-looking locomotives of New South Wales and Victoria, decorated with the Three Feathers.

It may have been with sobering thoughts that, at the end of that long tour, on the South Railway Jetty at Portsmouth, he boarded his grandfather's beautiful, but now ageing train of 1897, auspiciously headed by the London, Brighton and South Coast company's Class B4 engine *Prince of Wales*, and was borne away to Victoria Station in Buckingham Palace Road, London.

In 1936, George V died at Sandringham, slowly but peacefully as a tired old man; the first king, incidentally, to have had periodic wireless bulletins broadcast from his death-bed to the nation.

There had been no alterations of his railway rolling stock and arrangements generally since his accession, apart from the baths and save that the ancient Continental twelve-wheeler, kept at Calais, had been scrapped at last. Now there was rapid and earnest activity on the parts of both the London and North Eastern, and the Great Western, companies in the matter of the Royal Funeral Train. The L.N.E.R. provided the vehicles, those dating back to 1907–8. One of the 'semi-royal' carriages was hurried to the old Great Eastern works at Stratford, in the East End of London, where all its furniture was removed, a catafalque prepared, the windows blacked out and the inside draped in austere funebral splendour. Outside, its varnished-teak panels were painted all over in matt black, with a white roof as before, and purple mouldings. On one panel each side were painted hatchments of the King's Arms, lozengewise, a remarkable achievement in both senses of the term.

George V had died about midnight of 20–21 January, and in the afternoon of the latter day, the saloon, No. 46 which already had served as a hearse-car for old Queen Alexandra, had arrived at Stratford. Among other operations, its middle partition was removed. On Thursday, 23 January, the dead King was put aboard at Wolferton, and the train went, in and out of King's Lynn, to London; not to Liverpool Street but to King's Cross via Cambridge–Hitchin, arriving at 2.45 p.m. To Lynn, one of the old Great Eastern royal engines had been used, L.N.E.R. No. 8520; then the train reversed, and went to London behind Sir Nigel Gresley's three-cylinder 4-6-0 No. 2847, *Helmingham Hall*, of the Sandringham class. (The original *Sandringham* was not available, and the L.N.E.R. did not swap engine names with the facility of the Great Western, whether before or later.)

George V lay in state in Westminster Hall, like his father.

The London and North Eastern carriages were worked round to Paddington, and so were many others for ancillary trains to the official one. There was, one recalls, a complete London Midland and Scottish set for soldiers and others, including some old Midland clerestoried stock. (The solitary Midland royal saloon, a very nice carriage built in 1912 under David Bain at Derby, had been used last for the marriage journey of the Duke and Duchess of Gloucester in 1935.)

From Paddington, the last train of George V left for Windsor at 12.33½ p.m., played out by massed pipers of the Cameron Highlanders, the Black Watch and the Scots and Irish Guards. The locomotive was C. B. Collett's No. 4082, *Windsor Castle*, driven by the veteran driver W. H. Sparrow, who was soon to retire. George V had driven that engine himself, briefly from Swindon Works to Swindon Station on 28 April 1924, and plates on each side of the cab recorded that event. There had been eight on the footplate, including Queen Mary, herself given an exceptionally clean piece of cotton waste to protect her gloves from all she handled. Now, *Windsor Castle* carried, each side of the smokebox, two of these great and glorious mountings of the Royal Arms which had been made for Queen Victoria's Diamond Jubilee. This time they were purple-draped, as they had been for the funerals of both his grandmother and his father.

85 *left* British Royal Visit to Paris, 1938: S.N.C.F., Reg. Nord, Pacific locomotive
No. 3.1280.
86 *right* Netherlands Railways royal vehicles, 1948: Queen's study in ex-Wagons-Lits car.

87 Right, Queen's saloon (ex-Wagons-Lits), left, service carriage rebuilt from German
passenger-brake.

88 Hot Indian dawn: East Indian Railway royal train, with two North Western locomotives, near Jamrud, in or before 1911.

89 East Indian Railway: royal train and guard of honour, Delhi Durbar, 1911.

90 East Indian Railway royal
saloon, winter 1905–6.

91 Bedroom of Prince of
Wales.

92 Prince of Wales's
bathroom.

93 Canadian Pacific Railway, 1901: royal observation car.

94 *left* Ante-room.

95 *above* Edward, Prince of Wales, later King
Edward VIII, handles a Canadian Pacific Locomotive.

96 New South Wales Government Railway train for the Prince of Wales's tour, 1919, with two class C 35 locomotives. The third and fourth carriages from the engine normally served the Governor-General.

97 Victorian Government Railways class A 2 locomotive, decorated for the Prince of Wales's tour, 1919–20.

98 London, Midland and Scottish Railway Queen's saloon, No. 799, built at Wolverton, 1941.

below

99 L.M.S.R. royal train passing Berkhampstead on the evening of 7 August 1946. The new carriages are fourth and fifth from the locomotive, *King George VI*.

100 The new White Train in the Metropolitan-Cammell works paint-shop, Birmingham, before delivery in 1947. From right, King's car, Queen's car, Princesses' car and royal staff car.

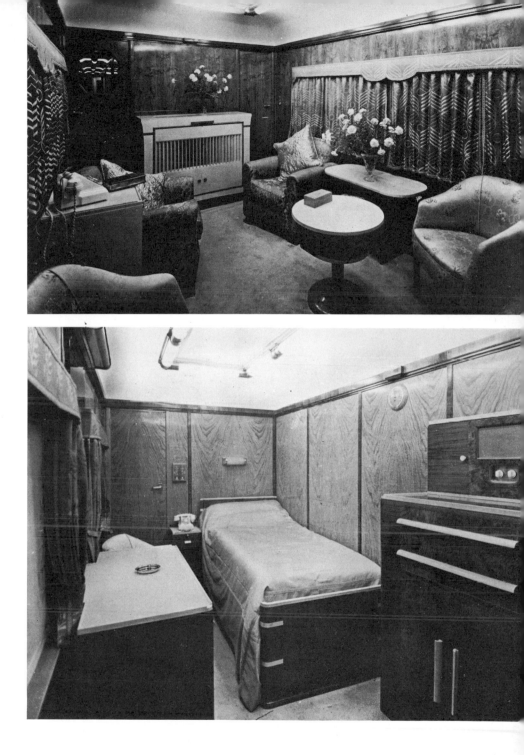

101 Royal visit to South Africa, 1947: full-width drawing-room in the new
White Train. Observe tubular lighting in 'modified-monitor' roof.
102 George VI's bedroom.

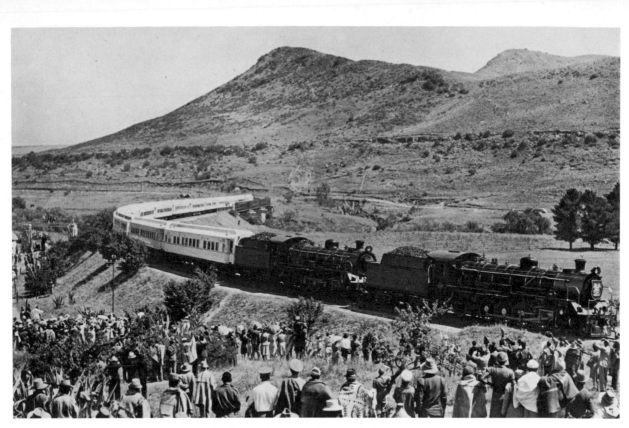

103 The White Train at the Basutoland border, headed by two 4-8-2 locomotives.

104 Beyer-Garratt locomotive banking the pilot-train up Montague Pass, Cape Province.
105 South Africa, 1947: Princess Elizabeth, later Queen, sounds the whistle on a Beyer-Garratt locomotive; left, Princess Margaret, right, the Hon. F. C. Sturrock, South African Minister of Transport.

The funeral proceeded without trouble. During that time at Windsor, whither your author had betaken himself with his womenkind, the engines were turned and the black-painted hearse carriage was hurried away An hour later, the G.W.R. Windsor branch being temporarily closed, a bus took us to Slough, just in time to see that beautiful train coming back behind *Windsor Castle*. Leopold III, King of the Belgians, looked blessedly relaxed just inside a green-curtained window. So did many other people, especially the soldiers, for such occasions are no holiday for anybody.

For almost as long as we could remember, *Old George* had been The King, and something went with him. Now it was Edward VIII, whom we had thought of as The Prince. In one's own case one thought of a fine, new, Radical King. He went into distressed Welsh Valleys, and returned himself distressed. He intensely disliked his grandfather's legacy in the way of royal trains, but he had to make long journeys at one time and another, especially on the London Midland and Scottish Railway. So the President of the Executive (L.M.S.) who was Sir Josiah Stamp (to be created Baron Stamp of Shortlands in 1938) being understanding, told the new King that his official saloon – business car would have been the American description – would always be made available on reasonable notice being given in advance.

The vehicle was a handsome one though of old-fashioned sort with a wooden body. It was simply an apartment on wheels, including kitchen and bath. It suited Edward VIII down to the ground – or to the rails, if you like – and he used it several times in his short reign. That was to end within the same year. It was a choice between the Realm and the Lady (already married). He chose the Lady. He abdicated the Realm, to be succeeded by Albert, Duke of York, who became King George VI. (Victoria had put some sort of a ban on there ever being a King Albert, there having been only one Albert for her.)

Already the great royal trains were in decline. The vehicles built by the London and North Western, the North Eastern and the Great Northern were to endure for a long time yet. But those of the old Southern companies were gradually dispersed and so departed. So did the last of the Great Western's Diamond Jubilee carriages. In the South, Pullman cars – certain of which were in some sort of reserve – or ordinarily decent side-corridor coaches, suitably fresh out of shops, were assigned to the shorter journeys, as between London and Dover or Portsmouth. Edward VIII, ex-King, settled in France as the Duke of Windsor, with his wife who had been Mrs Wallis Simpson as Duchess. Sometimes he came and went, incognito, to see old friends and relations, and when that happened he eschewed the aeroplane but gladly used the Wagons-Lits between London and Paris which had been operating by train ferry since 1935. Subject to weather in the Channel it remains the most comfortable means of travel between either Paris or Brussels, and London, between dinner and breakfast.

In Continental Europe, apart from the Low Countries, Denmark and Italy, royal trains were in some decay. The last assignment of the Spanish one had been to convey Queen Ena, sad-looking in a very English sort of dark coat and skirt, away from Madrid, in 1935. King Alphonso had been hurried out by other means while the ill-omened, if democratically elected, Popular Front took over government.

In the North, the Scandinavian, Dutch and Belgian monarchs, all democratically constitutional by now, began more and more to use their trains as mobile private hotels when they went holiday-making; even, in very recent times, having the train sent on to destination and then flying after it. In the 1930s, Norway, Sweden and Denmark all built new royal saloons of modern steel sort, and sophisticated, if rather dull-looking, appointments. Ornate show, indeed, had become unfashionable. Only in republican America did aspiring Messrs Presidents hire the finest rolling stock available for whistle-stop electioneering. Franklin D. Roosevelt – thrice President – was wise to these things. He bespoke the best possible cars; and being physically paralysed below the hips, as well as one of the most politically powerful men in the world, he needed such. He also required that the Presidential Train should not travel faster than any civilised train needed to go. That meant about 45 miles an hour, which would have suited Queen Victoria, and which enabled him to survey his great Federal Republic and its People as he went around.

As suggested already, when royal personages visited Canada – and that had begun with Albert Edward in the 1860s – the best sort of conventional North American rolling stock was provided, with, latterly, the two great undertakings of the Canadian Pacific Railway and of Canadian National Railways trying to outdo each other in magnificence. The C.P.R. was the aristocrat of Canadian railways, with the blood of the venerable Hudson's Bay Company in its steely veins. Canadian National was a State-inspired consolidation of other railways which had been on evil days, including even the splendid Grand Trunk and, by inheritance, the Great Western which once had run with green locomotives on broad gauge, as had a rather memorable railway in Great Britain. C.P.R. and C.N.R. still are there, as they ought to be. Then there was the co-operation of such respectable parties as the New York Central, the Pennsylvania and the sometimes lampooned Boston and Maine Railroads, not to mention the modestly admirable Quebec Central, and some steamships and motors where there were gaps. It was a distinctly imposing Royal Progress, and that at a time when inoffensive American ladies of riper years still prickled up in gooseflesh at the sight of a red coat on a *Mountie* across the river, feeling they were about to be massacred, while the more conservative Canadians who called each other, pejoratively, 'Ontario Scotch' and 'Quebec French', nevertheless cordially concurred in disliking and distrusting those whom they called 'Yankees'. That meant anyone living south of the 49th Parallel or north of the Rio Grande del Norte, where *Hombres* began. Europe had been like that, since some centuries before.

As North America is, was, and ought to be, a generally civilised sub-continent, the lunatic fringe remained suitably submerged about the edges of the vast pond. George and Elizabeth made one of the most extensive royal railway tours in history. In England, *Punch* published a handsome cartoon of the substantial shades of George Washington and George III; the one exclaiming 'Well, well, well!' and the other croaking: 'What, what, what?' Quaint, seeing that the one was by descent an Englishman and the other a German!

On this tour, the Canadian Pacific started off from Quebec, taking the royal train thence by Three Rivers to Montreal, and on to Ottawa, whence the Canadian National took it on to Kingston and Toronto. So far, respective mileages had been 289·7, and 374·4. Now the C.P.R., wherein your author admits a certain affectionate proprietary interest, owning about enough of it to keep him modestly for three days, took over the royal train to steam it round that splendid piece of line north of Lake Superior, which had nearly beggared the company in the early stages of its existence. From Toronto to Port Arthur was a matter of 808·6 miles, just over twice the distance between London and Edinburgh. At Port Arthur the King and Queen left the train, which was due for servicing, and were driven the short run to Fort William, where they picked it up again, swept and garnished. All the way to the Pacific Coast it was to be in the hands of the Canadian Pacific Railway, which took it by way of Winnipeg (419·1 miles), Regina (365·5 miles), Moose Jaw (41·6 miles), Medicine Hat (257·8 miles), Calgary (175·8 miles), Banff – pure Buchan-Scots in Alpine country – (81·9 miles), through the great Rockies to Kamloops (309·2 miles), and to Vancouver (250·4 miles).

How splendid are those old Canadian names! They would have excited Robert Louis Stevenson, in their mixture of Red Indian, and Gaelic, and French, and Victorian English. Rudyard Kipling, to be sure, was disappointed in Medicine Hat, but that great lover of names and of his own language was somewhat put off by the appearance of the town itself, still rather tatty when he passed through. From Toronto to Vancouver, George VI and his Scots Queen had travelled just under 2,701 miles on the Canadian Pacific Railway in a lovely train through scenery ranging from Lake Superior coastwise, through vast prairie corn, the Rockies and the Selkirks, to the splendid Pacific Coast of British Columbia (which Queen Victoria had quite possibly lost to the U.S.A. but for the Canadian Pacific company itself. It is, however, idle to consider history that never happened!)

From Vancouver, and back from Victoria on Vancouver Island, there was one of those beautiful steamships which were to continue serving such grand waters. Return from Vancouver was by Canadian National Railways, which briefly followed the Frazer River with the C.P.R. and then crossed to northward to reach Jasper in the great mountains of Alberta (534·9 miles from Vancouver), Edmonton (235·8 miles from Jasper), Saskatoon (331·1 miles) before a tremendous hop of 1,415·5 miles thence to Sudbury Junction in eastern Ontario. (Winnipeg had already received its royal visit on the outward journey, though of course the C.N.R. looked in from the south side, having crossed the C.P.R. twice in order to do so.)

This time, Sudbury itself deserved a visit, which was made by motor from its C.N.R. junction. Thence the Canadian National train resumed progress to Guelph, 340·3 miles via North Bay and so to the close-packed cities of Kitchener, Stratford, London, and Hamilton to Niagara Falls, covering on a hair-pin course north of Lake Erie, the old route by which American citizens of New York State once had been obliged to use in order to reach the Middle West. Distance from Guelph to Niagara Falls amounted to 196·1 miles, very modest by the normally vast Canadian standards, for the longest stretch had been from London to Hamilton, 80·5 miles.

Now came the great leap south east, to Washington D.C., Federal Capital of the U.S.A., under the joint auspices of the Canadian National, the New York Central and the Pennsylvania companies and covering 363·1 miles. From Washington to New York the Pennsylvania Railroad (being civilised) went on with electric traction over 224·7 miles, and thence, as guests of President Roosevelt, King and Queen were motored to Hyde

Park, N.Y. Thereafter, the train made its way back to Canada by way of the New York Central, the Boston and Maine, the Canadian Pacific and the Quebec Central, 387·2 miles to Sherbrooke, Canada, where the Canadian National once more took over for the last time, to complete the round tour of rather more than 8,376 miles by way of Levis, Rivière du Loup, and Newcastle, N.S., whence there was one more motor portage to St John and an ultimately broken railway journey to Halifax by way of Cap Tormentine and New Glasgow.

This final negotiation of Nova Scotia in some ways recalled those of the Scottish Highlands in the days when Queen Victoria first had discovered them, though there had been no mention of ponies.

First honours went to the two great Canadian railways, which between them provided the mobile equipment, including the motive power over their own sections of the route. Westbound, the Canadian Pacific used but one locomotive, all the way: 4-6-4 No. 2850, which gave the name Royal Hudson to her class. 'Hudson', be it added, meant a 4-6-4 express engine in North America, more reasonably than did the term 'Baltic' in Europe where there were indeed two specimens on the Northern Railway of France – nowhere near the chilly tideless sea – and numerous tank engines of the same wheel arrangement, many of which, to be quite fair, belonged to Prussia which had much Baltic coastline. The C.P.R.'s engine, judged by photographs alone, was a beauty, in neither pure-European nor pure-American styles, for Canada, through several generations, has been *different* in several respects. The Americans, the British, and even a most distinguished French general and ruler, all have discovered that, whether more, or less, painfully.

Canadian National Railways, for the journey which was principally eastbound, furnished four royal engines; a Pacific, two 6000 class 4-8-2 (a design dating from 1923), and one of the new and splendiferous 4-8-4 of the 6400 class. It was indeed the original one. Her sister, No. 6401 was to furnish, rather more than a decade later, probably the last Canadian royal service, by steam. The 4-8-4 type had been named the *Northern*, which was appropriate – more appropriate than that idiotic 'Baltic' – and in Canada was to achieve splendid finality through such refinements as highly improved front-end design, bearings and stokers. The 6400 class had received somewhat advanced air-smoothing contours (streamlining is *not* the word!) which involved a smoke-lifting arrangement seeming to equate David Jones's forward-mounted louvres with a sort of false clerestory all along the top of the boiler. C.N.R. itself and the Canadian National Research Council had somehow worked it out between them, rather like, in Great Britain, the L.M.S. company and the National Physical Laboratory, about the same time.

This, however, is not, by a long way, a chronicle of mechanical engineering technology! The engine of 1939, the original 6400, having done her Canadian stint, was shown at the New York World's Fair, as was a Pacific of the London Midland and Scottish (alleged *Coronation* but in fact *Duchess of Hamilton*, which ultimately returned to Great Britain through submarine-haunted Western Approaches).

Canadian cars on the 1939 jaunt were of the best types and designs of their period – North American traditional – and of massive construction. Some aspects had changed. Air-conditioning of railway vehicles in North America had been widely applied during the

1930s. In conversion for such equipment the new ducts were often laid along the external roof-angles each side of the clerestory, which still could be apparent inside while the external roof now formed a semi-ellipse, as in this royal train. Older Pullman cars in the U.S.A. sometimes appeared to have developed lateral blisters; not prepossessing but adequate for the 'damned compact majority' which never bothered about the outer aspect of its trains.

The Canadian royal train looked finely symmetrical. Painting was in royal blue with white or cream along the window quarters. The twelve cars were marshalled thus: baggage, composite baggage and staff sleeping car, business car, dining car, three compartment-type sleeping cars, two *chambrette* sleeping cars, private car for the Prime Minister (Mackenzie King at that time) and two cars for the King and Queen. These last had been assigned under normal circumstances to the Governor General. The train was preceded throughout by a pilot train, also of twelve cars, and containing arrangements for railway officers and officials, journalists and press photographers, and a special travelling post office. All vehicles were of Pullman Standard equivalent, which meant that they were very large and very heavy indeed, massively built of steel with never a whiff of the timber-built antiquities inherited from Edward VII on the Home Railways, nor of nonsense about light alloys and construction akin to that of passenger aircraft.

There had been a rather charmingly modest anticipation of all this in England. The King and Queen left London for Portsmouth on 6 May 1939, in a train composed of four ordinary Pullman cars: *Lady Dalziel*, built in 1925; *Cecilia*, 1927; *Marjorie* by Metropolitan-Cammell, 1924; and *Montana*, a veteran by the Birmingham Carriage and Wagon Company, 1923. One luggage-brake made up the rake, and the locomotive to Portsmouth was ex-London and South Western 4 4 0 No. 718. She was of Dugald Drummond's Class T 9, built by Dübs of Glasgow in 1899 and, like all her class, was to survive being taken over by the supposedly State enterprise of British Railways in 1948.

In 1939, the Southern Railway's old Royal Train, its legacy from the South Eastern and Chatham, was considered *vieux jeu*. More sumptuous things, as from the also ageing stock of the East and West Coast companies, were too big for the Admiralty's branch down to the South Railway Jetty in Portsmouth, and an ancient T 9's axle-loading was about as much as it was allowed to bear. A T 9 and some Pullman cars would do. So they did.

A few more notes on those Pullmans. *Montana* was almost a South Eastern and Chatham car. When new she had been painted dark red, more or less to match vehicles then existing on the Dover and Folkestone trains, hitherto 'Wellington brown'; *Lady Dalziel* had started her eventful life (the car, one means, not the real lady) from Birmingham Carriage and Wagon Company as *Minerva* but almost immediately became Wagons-Lits No. 60, based in Italy, where your astonished author saw her, and some other English Pullmans, early in 1927. She came back to England next year, and became a lady. Her initial career as a goddess had been brief, for the Italians in Milan had promptly wiped off the name of Minerva.

In 1939, we were on the eve of another blood-bath. But on that eve, George VI and Queen Elizabeth had made one of the longer and more memorable of Royal journeys, and in the process, as shown, had – first briefly and then lengthily – made use of the oldest and the most recently sophisticated equipment likely to be found on royal trains at that time (whatever 'sophisticated' may be intended to mean in our own). One could do all sorts of things with the ordinary British Pullman car, less than half the weight of a North American one, but most beautifully built and with all furniture moveable apart from the plumbing fixtures. As for the old T 9 locomotives, they had gone through one massive rebuilding programme, which had made them good for many a man's lifetime.

But there, your author was born on the London and South Western Railway! While the Great Western played to the stalls and the boxes – and sometimes to the gallery – the South Western was a very fine railway indeed, judged by good bourgeois values. While the railways themselves had long disliked and distrusted one another in the way of business – at Exeter, no South Western train could possibly be allowed through St David's Station without stopping there; at Winchester the Great Western was merely the tenant of an undesirable neighbour, the Didcot Newbury and Southampton – no intellectual aesthete with the slightest regard for lovely trains could fail to enjoy them both! One is not prepared, here, to explore rival Canadian loyalties.

8

'A LARGE AND LUXURIOUS TRAIN'

Shortly before beginning this chapter in 1974, one heard that two new saloon carriages were to be built for Queen Elizabeth II who, like her forebears, knows something about moving a royal household about a realm measuring several – but several – hundreds of miles from south to north. For the middle of the 1970s, it was cheering news. There was a limit to the ebb! Just at that time, electric trains had begun to top Shap in Cumbria and that rather higher summit in Scotland between Beattock and Elvanfoot, so that – subject to water-gaps partially spanned by train ferries, with 'the Tunnel' not yet in existence – one might travel in electric trains between the Clyde and the Sicilian coasts. One is a great believer in electric trains. The electric train is a *lady*. Though often plain, she does not smell.

But we must turn back to the 1930s. A new and fearsome flood had been piling up, first in the Far East, where Japan moved on a disintegrating China from the mid-1920s onwards, then during the 1930s into Europe where it broke bloodily in Spain while a previously disappointed Italy sought an empire in Abyssinia. In 1939 the European balloon went up and burst. What future was there for such things as royal trains? There were no longer many such, in any case, any more than there were reigning monarchs. There was a complete royal train – the old London and North Western one – in Great Britain. There was another in the Netherlands, and the gorgeous FIAT set on the Italian State Railways. Elsewhere there were various royal carriages, such as those of the Kings of Sweden, Denmark and Norway (closely akin in design) and of King Boris of Bulgaria; also the decidedly Wagons-Lits-style vehicles of Belgium. Back to Great Britain, there were the two majestic twelve-wheelers built by the Great Northern and the North Eastern Railway, which, with 'semi-royals', continued to serve for a long time yet, they being very useful where the royal country house of Sandringham was involved.

Once again, as in previous war, the London and North Western train became a mobile palace. It was little changed, though the ancient bed-curtains had long vanished and, as noted, the royal dressing-rooms had received proper baths; metal ones under George V, and pottery ones under George VI. Was that entirely an improvement? From the first quarter of this century, your author recalls the comfort of iron and even leaden baths, when suitably supplied with hot water, and also the cold-bottom comfort of the pottery kind. George VI, Spartanly brought up, like his brothers, under their father George V, seems not to have minded. In the previous war, George V, at the instance of his Prime Minister David Lloyd George, had declared the Royal Palaces 'dry' in terms of alcoholic refreshment, as an act of pure duty, for he hated it. In this war, fuel was scarce and consequently hot water. The sixth George did something about the bath-water. Five inches were deemed sufficient, and in his royal railway carriages a sort of red Plimsoll-line was painted inside each tub, as in the other royal baths. While on the subject of domestic sanitation, be it remarked that the rather archaic water-closets remained unchanged, but that since the royal train, making many journeys with long stops at night on remote sidings, might have caused nuisance on the latter, it was arranged that good big cans be placed under the outfalls wherever the King's caravan would rest. Something like the Greek letter *phi* (ϕ) was painted on the nearest solebar, to indicate where these should be put. Further, and importantly as to security, there was the business of making the royal train inconspicuous.

George V had requested maintenance of the London and North Western style in painting its outside, which meant a lot of white and gold, alluring to any airborne enemy worth his his salt. Now the train was painted in the rather maroonish L.M.S. red which had succeeded the gorgeous crimson of the Midland Railway, with the roof decks in lead-grey. Thus it looked merely like a rather old-fashioned L.M.S. train, which is what Security intended. Trains were subject to dive-bombing and attack by machine-gun from the air. To have had one as identifiable as the South African White Train streaking through early-morning light (a favourite time for 'train-busting') would have been inviting assassination.

Still, the old royal saloons were fragile things, built most beautifully of the best timber available in the year 1903. Very soon indeed something more substantial was on the way. There were to be, and soon were, three carriages very heavy by British standards. L.M.S. coaching stock, though very nice to ride in, had been remarkably light, even by Southern Railway standards, which allowed 32 tons for an ordinary coach. The two new royal saloons, apart from their service car, weighed 57 tons each, tare. The power car tared 52 tons. All three were twelve-wheelers, and the weight of these massive steel vehicles brought them well into the heavier Continental standards, though not of American cars. It was very much a matter of overall dimensions when it came to building really sub-stantial steel vehicles and, of course, so it remains. Further, these new L.M.S. royal carriages were at least basically armoured, with splinter-proof shutters to their windows. As already suggested, to every pilot of a fighter-bomber aircraft, irrespective of the side he was fighting on, a moving train was a captivating target, in a new form of blood-sport.

The two main royal saloons furnished by the L.M.S. company were each 69 ft long, of clipper shape and 9 ft wide over the tumblehome, which made them nearly as big as the largest carriages of the Great Western Railway at that time. (Certain routes on the Great Western still benefited from contours originally complementary to I. K. Brunel's broad gauge, though when that vanished, no more British carriages were built to the generous overall width of 10 ft 6 in., as some very admirable ones had been in the 1870s.) The new *royals*, on which construction was begun in the dark year of 1941, naturally were not proclaimed through the L.M.S. Publicity Department; nothing at all was published about them at the time. Those of us who happened to see the royal train at once observed marshalled therein vehicles that were new, and strange, and we very properly held our peace. Winston Churchill, as Prime Minister, also had a complete train for moving around, solidly L.M.S. in composition and containing one of the old 'semi-royals' for both his private office and for his living arrangements. Being of ancient vintage, it was easily distinguishable from the rest of that train by having a clerestory roof, which may or may not have reminded the great Prime Minister in this war, of the train in which, many years earlier, he had been conveyed as a prisoner of war to Pretoria after the future General Botha had arrested him. (Afterwards, they became considerably friendly on meeting again and realising, for the first time, who had arrested whom.) At the time – one goes by an old Boer photograph published years later in the French magazine *La Vie du Rail* – the South African rolling stock was of its time admirable, and obviously of Natal instead of Transvaal ownership in better times. Churchill's back view appears with a knickerbocker suit and a peaked cap, befitting a presumably harmless war-correspondent. Escaping through a prison-camp jakes, he managed to get out to Mozambique partly on foot and partly in less comfortable vehicles.

To return to the new L.M.S. royal carriages built soon after what that same man called our 'finest hour'. Substantial they were, and adequate, and remarkably comfortable, as they needed to be on those long tours about the beleaguered island. 'Elegant', one cannot say. Someone under Government had coined the term 'austerity'. That meant that furniture was made to serve but not to look beauteous; that decoration was *out*, whether with artistic or purely expensive Philistine treatment; that even ladies' coats and skirts had a minimum of cloth and two buttons instead of four where such were needed, while even full generals wore battle-dress in restaurants, where nobody was supposed to spend more than five shillings on eating. The royal carriages were furnished in plain hotel-style; adequate and indeed comfortable, with excellent plumbing, but far from beautiful.

Later (one judges from an excellent film made under B.B.C. auspices) the furniture had been considerably improved since Queen Elizabeth II had succeeded. The service carriage or power car was a vehicle of many parts. As well as its heating, lighting and ventilation equipment (the rake was ventilated under pressure though not fully air-conditioned) it contained three four-berth sleeping compartments and a shorter one with two berths, upper and lower, two lavatories, and a 25-line automatic telephone exchange. There were brake and luggage compartments. Dual heating, be it added, was furnished, by both steam and electricity. On the King's and Queen's saloons, there were also servants' compartments. As in their predecessors, there were slightly recessed vestibules with double doors, an old and admirable arrangement. The bodies were of steel, of course, double-skinned with asbestos packing between, and fully welded as to the joints. The forced ventilation, served by steam and electricity like the heating, was arranged for six temperatures, with wet ice for very hot weather.

If not beautiful, the train certainly would do.

There were several other trains and vehicles furnished for important personages. After America had entered the war by way of Pearl Harbor, the London and North Eastern Railway provided a fine travelling headquarters for General Eisenhower, remembered on this side of the Atlantic more kindly than are most allied Commanders-in-Chief, subject to so much jealousy. This train became a General Headquarters for the Allied Military Staff, and before the invasion of Europe (D-day) it was in a tunnel of the now abandoned Meon Valley line of the sometime London and South Western Railway, deep in the heart of Hampshire, containing many of the people the enemy wished most to destroy.

There was one sad casualty among Europe's royal trains, which by then were so few; that of brave old Queen Wilhelmina of the Netherlands, scarcely an international favourite, and as stodgy in her way as Queen Victoria had been in Great Britain. One must go back a little, and for that one is obliged to one's old and distinguished friend Marie-Anne Asselberghs of the Railway Museum in Utrecht. Queen Wilhelmina was married to Prince Henry of Mecklenburg-Schwerin on 7 February 1901. The two largest railways in the close kingdom of the Netherlands, the Dutch State Railways Company's and that of the Holland Iron Railway Company, between them working a very considerable traffic rather like that of southern England, combined to give them a wedding present, in the form of a sumptuous train. There were initially four carriages. There was a van (which was No. 1 jointly of both the State and the Holland companies), a balcony-portion of which is preserved now at Utrecht; there were the Queen's and the Prince-Consort's saloon carriages (joint Nos 2 and 3). Furniture and decoration of these were by the Royal Furniture Factory of Mutters and Sons in The Hague. Then there was a kitchen car with the joint number 4, which was exchanged in 1906 with that of a new saloon carriage for members of the Royal Household, the kitchen car then becoming State/Holland No. 5. After the working agreement and ultimate amalgamation of the two undertakings into the Netherlands Railways, there was no need to alter the numbering.

The five carriages were comfortable and indeed elegant, but not gaudy as – it must be confessed – was that of the Emperor William II of Germany, even unto the time when it was steamed into Eijsden station following the arrival of the imperial motor cars from Spa in Belgium. Let the photographs serve! There were real baths (albeit somewhat short) such as few European trains or even American ones had at that time. It furnished a very useful mobile lodging, as such trains have done in many lands over many years, and this Dutch one was long to serve.

In 1940, National-Socialist Germany invaded the Low Countries. The Dutch Army put up a doughty fight, taken without warning beyond suspicion. Very soon, France herself was over-run, and the British people were beleaguered. The royal-blue Dutch royal train went into a sort of hibernation during the time when Hermann Göring is reported to have told Adolf Hitler that when it came to England, he would like to have Knole, which he was carefully not bombing, and that the Royal Pavilion at Brighton would be amusing. War swayed and surged. Counter-invasion by way of the Normandy coast came in 1944. About the time of the Battle of Arnhem, the Netherlands royal train was sequestrated, with much more, to Germany. Too optimistically – for Arnhem was an initial disaster – the Netherlands railwaymen had declared a general strike, and the German retort had been to seize all the available rolling stock including every locomotive that would go, as well as lifting track and pulling down overhead wires on the numerous electric lines. The five Dutch royal vehicles, now in Germany, were pillaged of their furniture and otherwise severely damaged. With the war at last over, they were returned in 1947, but so much the worse for wear that they had to be written off as a royal train. They were indeed over 40 years old by then, but it was a sore and sad end for a noble train!

Dutch post-script: 7 June 1948, saw the offer of what Marie-Anne Asselberghs has called 'a new train'. The quotes are hers. A German vehicle was converted into a royal van by J. J. Beynes, and became Netherlands Railways No. 6. It contained, as rebuilt, a fully adequate kitchen, and was 19·66 m. long. Then there was a comfortable saloon carriage – Netherlands Railways No. 7, improvised from a Wagons-Lits vehicle built in 1926, by Allan of Rotterdam. There was some irony attached to its history. Built in 1926 and requisitioned in 1939, it had become the official saloon carriage of the German (Air-Force) General Christiansen, who in May, 1940, was appointed Military Governor in the Netherlands. Its length over buffers came to 22·84 m. After its strange vicissitudes, this carriage was scrapped in 1959. Old Queen Wilhelmina (born in 1880, died late in 1962) had abdicated in favour of Juliana in 1948 after a reign of 50 years, so the 'new train' was perhaps an accession present to the latter, shop-soiled though it may have been in the meantime. It is outside our limit of period, but be it added that to these two there came a diner, a sleeper and a third saloon carriage for the royal suite, appearing from 1953 onwards. But thereafter a complete Dutch royal train was to be a rare bird in what might be called the 'railway sky'. Bernhard, the Prince Consort of Queen Juliana, already had the reputation of preferring the real sky when it came to moving around, and in Holland they have known something about skies since Hobbema and others, blending science with art, started to paint them. The Italians had long before done the same thing with anatomy and art. But painting is another story, so why drag in Englishmen like Turner? ('Why drag in Velázquez?' said some unusually liberal Spaniard.)

Many of the Empires had fallen. Others were dying. The Dutch and the French were fighting rearguard actions in what we once called Dutch East Indies and Cochin-China, later to be known as Indonesia and Vietnam. The British Empire was styling itself a Commonwealth, because. . . . Nevertheless, as soon as the war with the Germans was over, King George VI went to South Africa on what was to be his last great State visit. The predominant Dutch there, as well as the English of Natal and the Cape, not to mention the Rhodesias, had been doughty fighters for him. In London, the figure of General Smuts, old enemy and twice an ally, strutted jauntily as a green-bronze soldier in Parliament Square, Westminster.

Out went King George with his Queen Elizabeth and his two daughters. For years, the White Train had been the conveyance of the Governors-General. It had followed entirely the South African convention, having very elegant carriages, timber-built with splendid clerestories, and in its own case painted creamy-white all over. Now there came a new White Train, with some borrowings from the old one.

For very many years, the Metropolitan Carriage and Wagon Company had been building superior vehicles. Acquired kinship with another great firm, that of Cammell Laird which built both vessels and vehicles, had produced the title Metropolitan-Cammell. From some earlier years one recalls the title Metropolitan Railway Carriage, Wagon and Finance Company, and in connection with the construction of bodies for motor buses, Metropolitan-Cammell-Weymann. Metropolitan-Cammell built the new, and last, South African royal train.

It was entirely in the South African tradition, as far as what might be called vehicular architecture was concerned. But it was a more advanced train than any of the very elegantly traditional South African ones had been. The time was 1946, when there was an order for twelve superior vehicles to South African Railways and Harbours, placed late in March, eight to be expedited for delivery at the end of the year, to be added to existing South African Blue Train vehicles including vans and diners. (The South African Blue Train, of course, is not to be confused with the French one under Wagons-Lits auspices between the Channel and the Mediterranean!) After the royal tour, the vehicles involved were to be added to the South African White Train stock, to be used by the Governor-General.

All carriages were built of steel apart from furniture and certain internal decorative features, with rubber cushioning of bodies and bogies. They followed the traditional clerestory contour of South African Railways (long faithful to this when it was fast vanishing from the rest of the world) but the upper deck now contained the air-conditioning ducts instead of being what caravanners by road called the 'mollycroft', with its deck-lights. Stone's air-conditioning system was employed, giving internal air-changes at the rate of fifteen per hour. Standard dimensions involved a length of 65 ft, a width of 9 ft 3 in., and height from rail to the top of the 'modified-monitor' roof, 12 ft 7½ in., which made the vehicles equal in size to the largest British vehicles apart from a few on the Great Western, in spite of the 3 ft 6 in. rail gauge. (The latter, by the way, is called 'broad gauge' in South Africa, to distinguish it from the 2 ft gauge of certain remoter lines.) The train had a complete internal telephone, like its variously older counterpart in Great Britain, and also a loudspeaker announcement system. The all-steel bodies and frames were partly rivetted and partly welded, and had flooring of slab cork (with rubber in the bathrooms – with full-length baths – and in the lavatories). Each vehicle was mounted on a pair of standard South African Railways compensated bogies having helical springs to the outside equalising bars and quadruple elliptical springs to the transverse bolsters; in short, an advanced form of the classic American 'truck', known in England and used, though not universally since the Midland company had imported Pullman cars in 1874. Timken roller bearings and axleboxes were incorporated.

The King's saloon, taring 46 tons, comprised compartments for a study, a state-room and a bathroom, a valet's room and an ironing-room, and bedrooms for equerry and travelling physician. George VI had never been physically a strong man. We all knew it, and he was to face his coming, fatal, decline with fortitude. The doctor was always around. Few talked about it.

Reverting to the carriage; panelling was in chestnut with walnut mouldings, while moveable furniture was in walnut and sycamore. Other compartments in this vehicle were decorated in West African betula and cherry mahogany. The Queen's saloon was comparable, but, as might have been expected, lighter as to decoration and fabrics. Looking back, one recalls the train as being much more agreeable to look at, inside or out, than the vehicles built by the L.M.S. company during the war, but stringencies and necessities as to that last have been noted already.

Then there were the two princesses: Elizabeth who rather soon was to be Queen, and Margaret, who, during a conversational exchange, was overheard to advise her elder sister to 'mind her own Empire'. They were allotted a third royal saloon between them, with the state-room and bath for each, bedrooms for each lady-in-waiting, and one for their ladies' maid.

On 19 November 1946, the King, the Queen and the Princesses all went to look at the train in the works before it was shipped. At that time, F. C. Sturrock was South African Minister of Transport. The name itself was an honoured one in railway lore, and had been so since Archibald Sturrock had been Locomotive and Carriage Superintendent of the Great Northern Railway about a century before; a Scot from Angus who sought and found his fortune in England.

The Royal Party set off by sea, on H.M.S. *Vanguard* – last of the great British battleships – and the tour lasted from 21 February 1947, to 20 April. Throughout the land trip by railway, the royal train was preceded by a pilot train (the older White Train) and the two were in continual contact by VHF radio. The Princesses had a ride on the engine – which girls as well as boys sometimes longed for – and there is cinematograph evidence that both had a go at the whistle, under the benevolent eye of Mr Sturrock. The route from Cape Town, with few breaks by other transport, was necessarily somewhat circuitous as well as extensive. It may be followed in detail on a map published with a series of articles by the *Railway Gazette* in London, for the issues in the first part of 1947. It went to Worcester, Cape Province, then by Mossel Bay, Gref Reinet, Port Elizabeth, East London, and thence northward through Basutoland to Bloemfontein, Kronstad and Bethlehem. It covered the entire electrified Y of Harrismith, Durban and Vryheid. It went northward to the old line of Winston Churchill's adventures – Komati Poort and Pretoria – though motors were requisitioned for a stage in these parts. The last lap was from Bulawayo in Rhodesia to Capetown. H.M.S. *Vanguard* took the Royal Family home.

It was, perhaps, the last of many great imperial railway journeys, and there is quaint irony in the fact that it spanned country which had known bitter anger and war, whose people whether 'Dutch' or 'English' or King's African Rifles, had won two great campaigns in the name of that same British Empire, against Germans and Italians. Soon we were to quarrel again, but one hopes that that most courageous man, George VI, died reasonably happy, as he did, quietly and without to-do, in his own bed at Sandringham in 1952.

Back in 1936, the Prince of Wales had been summoned home to be told that he was King Edward VIII. In 1952, a Queen was flown back from East Africa. Many of us remembered her as an infant, then as a still little girl, whose small sister was already being dressed in hat of identical style and coat of identical cut, though reduced in size. She was suddenly A Very Exalted Personage.

The Russian Empire had ended in a large and luxurious train. The German Empire had ended in a large and luxurious train. In both cases, the circumstances were adverse, to say the least. It is a more happy thing to note in conclusion that the British Empire, disintegrated by its particular sort of democracy and under some pressure from the two new great Empires, those of Republican America and Soviet Russia, had one of its final flings not in, but with, *a large and luxurious train*!

APPENDIX A
'THE ROYAL ROADS'

It was Sir Sam Fay (as he became) who first used this term for the London and South Western Railway, of which he became Superintendent. He even wrote a slim book about it, under the title of *A Royal Road*. That was modest of him, as well as elegant, for he was an elegant man. Many years later, the Great Western Railway suddenly styled itself with the full, splendid title of *The Royal Road*, clearly with the accent on the definite article. Both companies (which generally disliked each other as next door neighbours sometimes do) had some reasonable claims, as the foregoing story has shown.

But there was no Royal Railway Company in Great Britain, and all our undertakings apart from military railways, and that sad line between Peterhead Prison and the Breakwater, belonged to private joint-stock companies until the end of 1947. Two Queens and four Kings always paid their fares, and those of their *entourage*, and the splendid vehicles provided for them, remained company's property. They were not gifts to the Ruler, as were many foreign examples.

Nor was there any such thing in the Americas, though Canada be a kingdom, and Brazil and Mexico briefly empires. But elsewhere abroad there were indeed several royal and princely railways, the potentates having heavily invested in them and even promoted them, like William I of the Netherlands. The ever-remarkable Japanese railways were 'Imperial'. Central Europe had several royally sponsored lines, whose names proclaimed such exalted interest. To the end of the reigning Habsburgs, the Austrian State Railways carried the prefix Imperial and Royal (rendered *K.k.*) and for many years there had been, as well as the Royal Hungarian State Railways, the Empress Elizabeth's Railway. Poor lady! Long before she fell to some lunatic assassin in Switzerland, she needed consolation. Her railway supported the Orient Express over some distance east of Salzburg. From earlier years we recall the *Kaiser Ferdinands Nordbahn* (the title is too good to be translated!)

Germany – i.e. Deutschland – abounded in imperial, royal and princely titles of one sort and another, and not least when it came to the advancing railways. The very first German railway, between Nuremberg and Fürth in Franconia, opened in 1835, was called the Ludwigsbahn, though to be sure the first King Ludwig of Bavaria was very cautious about railways, since he was favouring the idea of a Main–Danube ship canal which might be thereby harmed, but which, on the other hand, might do just as well if not better.

But there were other *Ludwigsbahnen*. There were plenty of Lewises in either the German-speaking countries or in France. Harking back to the Austrian Empire; in the then Austrian-Imperial portions of Poland there had been the *Galizische Carl-Ludwigsbahn* which, like the London, Brighton and South Coast company in England, used 0-4-2 locomotives for allegedly fast passenger traffic. But in Bismarck's empire, there was for long the *Hessische Ludwigsbahn*. There were two 'Hesses' in Germany. There was Hesse-Kassel (Kur-Hessen). There was Hesse-Darmstadt, which had a succession of Archduke Ludwigs, three of them from 1830 to 1892, or four if one includes Ernst-Ludwig who lasted as such until 1918. For the first of these (Ludwig II of Hesse) was built, it is believed, the first German six-wheeled carriage – a very elegant one with four compartments – in 1847. Though small, the railway had a very marked individuality. It worked international expresses for some way west of Frankfurt-on-Main. With the very much larger Eastern Railway of France, it was one of the very last companies to employ usefully on express trains the patent locomotives of T. R. Crampton, which had been long rejected in England. One was named *Mathilde*. Most if not all of the company's engines had good, sometimes glorious, names. Of the last category there was *Beethoven*.

Many of the monarchs and princes were extremely rich. Queen Victoria's private fortune in England was a mystery which disturbed some of her more Radical subjects, though really it was none of their business. One of the richer German families, quite apart from the Hohenzollerns and some others, was that of the little principality of Schaumburg-Lippe. The Prince seems to have put up most of the money for the very important Cologne-Minden Railway, and to have furthered its very rapid linking of the Rhine with Hanover (1846) (cf. Paul Dost). With the rise of Bismarck, the railway was sold to the Prussian Government, and thus became a major component of what was to become the Imperial Prussian Railway Union, alias the Prussian-Hessian State Railways, alias K.P.E.V.

In one's own youth in Munich, in the mid-1920s when the German State Railway had been created under the Dawes Plan for war-reparations, some engines and many more vehicles still bore the initials K.Bay.St.B. with the K blocked out by a lick of black or green paint – (Royal) Bavarian State Railways. The ghost of Ludwig died hard!

One can draw dozens of other examples of this kind. One of the most grandly ornate titles of a railway undertaking came from old India – His Exalted Highness the Nizam's Guaranteed State Railway. Then, more easterly by a long way, there were the Royal State Railways of Siam. Now one glances at the *Universal Directory* and notes, with a faint shudder 'State Railways of Siam (Thailand)'. Even State Railways, which are predominant in the world to-day, have rather prudishly dropped their adjective in many places. Our own were too delicate even to assume it in 1948, and had to be austerely entitled British Railways, with 'Regions', like the French, presumably lest vociferous anti-railway lobbyists (ever with us) should smell Government Monopoly all bolstered-up against Progress. Some brave party suggested 'Royal British Railways'. The rest was silence!

APPENDIX B
THE PIRATES

Goodness knows what happened to the royal trains in some of the ex-realms. Here and there, particularly in Central Europe, the vehicles survived as precious pieces of vehicular design. Portugal, as noted, treasures the ancient vehicle of Maria Pia, while the last one heard of the Spanish rake was that it was indeed preserved, but looked somewhat decrepit. The beautiful Italian train survives, and so it ought, as does the much older Bavarian one.

There were, however, persons who travelled by rail in quasi-royal style, long after Emperors and Kings had departed. An author, being an Englishman partly tutored under the Weimar Republic, may perhaps be permitted a retrospective dislike for the German National-Socialist Government, and in its prime this *did itself proud*. Chancellor Adolf Hitler, though he allowed himself to be photographed on railway platforms and leaning out of carriage windows, seems not to have liked travelling by train. But the Mitropa company obliged considerably. One of its clients was Robert Ley, Hitler's Labour Minister, a gross man whose overnight journeys began with a colossal binge among his official cronies. These things one has heard: Mitropa bitterly complained to Julius Dorpmuller, General Director of the German State Railway (the old Reichsbahn) of the disgusting conditions left by one and another of Ley's peregrinating orgies. Dr Dorpmuller was a gentleman, and not a Nazi, yet fearless and sufficiently able and important to have the ear of highest government without much risk of dismissal. He complained, and survived. Ley seems to have been reprimanded. Ultimately he was to hang himself on a w.c. chain; a fitting end. Did not the Emperor Heliogabalus, in the year 222, quit this life in a similar situation? The Roman apparatus, however, was differently arranged: so, back to Nazi Germany.

Field-Marshal Hermann Göring had, indeed, something of the Roman magnifico about him. He was stout, courageous, clever, gluttonous, show-loving, cruel, and by many accounts a princely host. He loved trains, as well as aeroplanes and big motors. From Paul Dost we learn that he had provided for him in and after 1939, when war broke out, two living and staff trains. The first, named *Asien* ('Asia', perhaps out of esteem and respect for the Emperor of Japan) comprised fourteen vehicles, whereof the leading one and the last mounted anti-aircraft guns, each with a gun-crew of twenty men. They included, as well as sumptuous living quarters and offices, a radio car attended by eight railway policemen, and Göring's personal living carriage, which was newly built for this train. Further, and a little later, came a train of eight vehicles, of more modest sort; say, a sort of railway-runabout by Göring's standards. It had two saloon carriages sequestrated from French National Railways and three ordinary composite coaches. One of the two vans carried his motor cars. The train was named *Robinson*.

One may guess at the choice of that name. Long ago, Defoe's *Robinson Crusoe* had captivated German readers as well as those in many other lands, and had been plagiarised and bowdlerised in forms which German *literateurs* called *Robinsonaden*, whereof the unconsciously comic *Swiss Family Robinson* is remembered. Is it possible that the Reichsmarshal considered the possibility of being marooned in it, some time later? May be! He was much more of a realist than most of the Nazi Hierarchy. One other train of Göring may be remembered, though it looked like a perfectly ordinary French goods train, and was indeed commandeered from S.N.C.F. to convey to Germany as many as possible of French art treasures before Paris fell in the counter-invasion. A very fine French film, some years ago, reconstructed its misadventures, which caused it to be diverted back into France and there wrecked as gently as possible, in view of the need not to damage its priceless freight. Göring was more than something of a connoisseur, and, like many such, quite unscrupulously acquisitive. Your author recalls not only watching the film, enthralled, but feeling quite sad at the destructive impact of two veteran French locomotives, a 4-6-0 and a Bourbonnais, both off the old *Ouest*, such as he had known in boyhood.

Some ignorant purists objected to these, seeing that the noble piece of sabotage was well to eastward. But railway equipment was all over the place at that time. There were many French engines in Germany, and other things too. *Inter alia* a Great Western goods engine was found in Upper Franconia, when ultimately recaptured, and an ordinary carriage of the L.M.S. was discovered near Hamburg, to home ultimately on the Longmoor Military Railway in Hampshire, where one had a ride in it after its long wanderings from Derby. The sad story of Queen Wilhelmina's royal train has been noted already.

INDEX

Great Eastern Railway: Prince of Wales's saloon, 1864. A remarkably
sophisticated design for its time, it was later converted to run on two four-
wheeled equalised bogies, very close together. Note the water-closet disguised as a corner chair. (From the *Illustrated London News*, 28 May 1864.)